REVITALIZE YOUR CORPORATE CULTURE

Cashman Dudley
An imprint of Gulf Publishing Company
Houston, Texas

REVITALIZE

YOUR

CORPORATE

CULTURE

POWERFUL

WAYS TO

TRANSFORM

YOUR COMPANY

INTO A

HIGH-PERFORMANCE

ORGANIZATION

FRANKLIN C. ASHBY

> *To Rita and Danny—*
> *with all my love*

REVITALIZE YOUR CORPORATE CULTURE

Cashman Dudley
An imprint of Gulf Publishing Company
Book Division
P.O. Box 2608 ☐ Houston, Texas 77252-2608

10 9 8 7 6 5 4 3 2 1

Library of Congress Cataloging-in-Publication Data

Ashby, Franklin C.
　　Revitalize your corporate culture : powerful ways to transform your company into a high-performance organization / Franklin C. Ashby.
　　　　p.　cm.
　　Includes index.
　　ISBN 0-88415-279-0 (alk. paper)
　　1. Corporate culture.　2. Organizational effectiveness. I. Title.　II. Title: Effective ways to transform your company into a high-performance organization.
HD58.7.A797　　1999
658.4′063—dc21　　　　　　　　　　　　99–15329
　　　　　　　　　　　　　　　　　　　　　　　　CIP

Printed in the United States of America.
Printed on acid-free paper (∞).

Contents

Acknowledgments

I'm very grateful to the many people who have contributed to the development of this manuscript, particularly **Dr. Paul J. Mackey,** for the countless lessons he's taught me over the years; **Dr. Arthur R. Pell,** for his guidance and superb research assistance; **Dr. Jack J. Phillips,** for the opportunities and education he's provided; and **Ms. Debbie Markley,** for her terrific suggestions and attention to detail.

I also want to thank my parents, Janet and Frank Ashby; my brother, Doug Ashby; and those terrific friends and colleagues who have enhanced my understanding of this subject through their example: the late Pete Ackles, Dieter Alten, Dr. Bob Atwell, Pat Babitz, Ben Babitz, George Bajalia, Richard Bradley, Sherm Brown, Gene Cook, Bob Cook, Ollie Crom, Steve DeMorro, the late Hon. Frank Devoy, Derek Dewan, Dan Donovan, Debbie Drucker, Hon. Dave O'Flaherty, Kirsten Fleisher, Steve Fuschetti, Dr. Sylvia Galloway, Richard Germann, Dr. Ray Harrison, Dick Hatfield, John Hei, Greg Hock, Dr. Stan Ikenberry, Tom Kaletta, Dr. Sandra Kuhlmann, Paula Little, Dr. Tom Little, Dr. Nick Lisante, Mike Losey, Carmeane Mackey, Cathie Mackey, the late Matt Mackey, Pete Mackey, Dr. Victoria Marsick, Bob McCarty, John Millard, Norio Morisugi, Dick Morgal, Glyn Ed Newton, Ralph Nichols, Fred Noble, Mike Norman, Erica Pell, Hon. Mike Pizzi, Ann Pizzo, Stefan Quist, Gregg Ratliff, the late Dorothy Carnegie-Rivkin, Jo Ann Robinson, Susan Robinson, Dave Salls, Barbara Sanborn, Jim Schwab, Judy von Seldeneck, John Shand, Molly Shepard, Wendy Slater, Pete Spero, Dr. Henry Spille, Ron Stone, the late Dr. Al Swinerton, Dr. Edward Verlander, Linda Wescott, Fred White, and Jerry Wilson.

Foreword

As a result of observing all types of organizations for over 20 years, I am convinced that most companies are mired in corporate cultures that tend to stifle people and inhibit creative, dynamic performance. If your organization seems to be falling behind and your employees are just marginally productive or worse, then there is an urgent need for improvement. There is a direct relationship between organizational culture and profitability, and this book will provide the tools to evaluate and improve both.

You may need to modify or radically change the internal environment of your company to reach your goals and to obtain the optimum performances from managers and staff. Whether you are a senior executive or a middle-level manager, this book will help you understand your company's current culture. It will also enable you to apply techniques that will build up the confidence of your staff and motivate them to take the dramatic steps often needed to effect change.

To change cultures, organizations must look at themselves from a new perspective. Most related troubles, contrary to popular views, stem from management, not employees. No matter how deeply ingrained an unhealthy culture might be, it can always be changed.

Revitalize Your Corporate Culture is a guide that will take you through all the steps necessary to increase productivity and efficiency, and help you transform your organization into a more dynamic, innovative, and collaborative company. This book also provides actual and composite case histories as models to help you plan your own culture-change program. If you are committed to helping your company face the challenges of the 21st century, this book is a must-read.

James K. Schwab
President and CEO
Manchester, Inc.

Preface

During my 20 years in the consulting and training industry, I've had the privilege of observing and helping to improve the cultures of many organizations. During this time, I feel fortunate to have witnessed many of the marvelous rewards enjoyed by companies, large and small, that have incorporated positive organizational cultures as an enlightened way of doing business.

Senior-level executives contact my firm because they want their employees to be trained in the "soft skills," which include leadership development, communications, interpersonal skills, and customer relations. These executives are often shocked when our needs analyses confirm that the problems that impelled them to come to us were caused by themselves. The organizational culture they have either established or perpetuated has resulted in a lack of cooperation, poor morale, and lower productivity.

The fact is it takes more than a training program to correct these internal problems. It requires a complete change in the organizational attitude and mood. To accomplish this requires a thorough analysis of the current culture and a systematic approach to making the necessary changes. The days of the tyrannical, fear-based managers are truly ending, and new, more cooperative and collaborative approaches to building and managing positive organizational cultures continue to take root.

In this book, I've focused not on the latest management fads or theoretical concepts, but on the strategies that I know work and make for lasting change. I describe how a program of this type can be designed and installed, and the steps necessary to assure the right results. I've drawn heavily on my own experiences with some wonderful and some not so wonderful people and companies and, to protect their privacy, I have changed many of their names and descriptions.

Good organizational cultures, like all good relationships, are created and sustained by people with the right skills and the right motivations. All it takes is that simple commitment by the right person determined not to let something important become just another failed initiative—a simple resolve to making things better. Be that person—it really is all within your power and your grasp.

Best wishes.

Franklin C. Ashby, Ph.D.

CHAPTER 1

The Nature of Organizational Cultures

There's no doubt that the world is changing at a rate never before experienced or even imagined. Whole industries are born and extinguished—seemingly overnight. Those who lead, anticipate, and benefit from these rapid changes have in many cases become tremendously successful. Those who were unprepared, surprised, or overwhelmed, however, found themselves falling behind their competitors. Many of these organizations have sustained major losses or have completely gone out of business.

One reason companies fail to meet this challenge is complacency with the long-established systems and procedures in which they have always worked. They've become slaves to the culture—the organizational way of life—in which they are comfortable. To survive, managers must look at the thought processes that their organizations follow with a sense of constructive discontent. They must determine whether the practices they are using are bringing the desired results. If they're not, they must be prepared to make whatever changes are needed to guide the organization to improvement and success.

In addition, because many organizations are restructuring, downsizing, and outsourcing, employee morale has often fallen to new depths. The unconditional loyalty and dedication of employees who looked upon their jobs as careers and their employment as relatively secure has been replaced in many companies with uncertainty and skepticism. A new organizational culture must be developed to overcome this and renew in the staff an attitude of commitment and cooperation.

As technology advances, practices and methods that have been successful in the past may no longer serve current needs. However, change is not driven solely by technology. Over the past several years, new concepts of people management have come into being that have increased productivity, enriched the workplace, and stimulated creativity and innovation. It is much easier to recognize and accept technical change than it is for managers to change the way they deal with people.

QUOTES AND QUIPS

"There is nothing permanent except change."
Heraclitus, ca. 500 B.C.
Greek philosopher

MANAGEMENT STYLE

Twenty years ago, it was rare to see a computer on an executive's desk. Computer use was limited to specialists who provided printouts to managers for their use. Today the computer is an essential tool on the desks of almost every executive. Instead of depending on reports from specialists, real-time information is at his or her fingertips. Computerized design and drafting, computer-aided manufacturing, robotics, and continually changing technologies have become part of most progressive organizations. These changes have compelled organizations to reexamine and restructure those aspects of their cultures that involve technology.

On the other hand, the management styles practiced in many organizations have not changed at all. They are still patterned on customs and procedures that were dominant in the 1970s and before. This concept was reinforced in my mind when the CEO of a well-known housewares distributing company retained my firm to analyze the company's training needs. He complained: "I have invested a fortune in computers and automation in my warehouses, but the productivity of my people has not increased proportionately. How can we improve their performance?"

From our analysis we learned that the staff was well trained in the technical aspects of using the new equipment, but was not sold on its benefits to them. Some workers looked upon it as a threat to their security. They were concerned that the computers might replace them. Others felt that it dehumanized them—that judgments usually made by them would now be made by the computer. Still others felt that computers stifled their creativity. They complained that the work became so routine that it was no longer a challenge.

The CEO could not understand this. He believed that the new equipment should help the staff. Much of the routine drudgery would now be done by the equipment. The employees could use their time to do creative things. He failed to realize that elimination of drudgery alone is not enough to foster creativity.

Too often, the perceptions of the CEO and higher levels of management are much different from that of the men and women who do the day-to-day work of the organization. In this case, a complete rethinking had to be made of the interrelationships from the top layers to the bottom levels of the company.

QUOTES AND QUIPS

"Adapt or perish, now as ever, is nature's inexorable imperative."
H. G. Wells, 1866–1946
English author

CULTURAL CHANGE TRANSCENDS ORGANIZATIONAL LEVELS

Everybody in an organization must be involved in recognizing the need for culture change and be committed to taking the necessary action to make changes. Although the full commitment of the CEO and others in top management is essential, they must enlist the full cooperation of *all* employees to achieve real success. A climate must be created in which managers and workers alike are encouraged to challenge current practices without fear of reprisal. This should be enhanced by establishing an environment in which people are stimulated to think about, develop, and implement new ideas.

Complacency should no longer be tolerated. Employees at all levels must have the desire to improve their performance. The traditional industrial cultures have stifled creativity in people. Deviations from the norms, variations from standard operating procedures, and disagreements with the powers-that-be often have been punished in traditional cultures and have led to uncritical acceptance of the status quo.

Giving people who work on a job the opportunity to unleash their creative energies will generate new ideas, more efficient methods, closer cooperation, and interaction among staff members and between departments. This will lead to a new dynamic, exciting, productive culture that will enable organizations to survive and thrive.

It is not easy for most managers to look at their organization's culture objectively because it has been an integral part of their lives for many years. It is natural to resist change. Although some organizations can make this commitment to change and put it into effect on their own, it is sometimes desirable to bring in an outside consultant to help analyze the organizational culture and suggest and implement appropriate changes. Whether a company uses its own resources or outside experts, everybody concerned must be aware of and committed to the process.

TACTICAL TIPS

Success in changing an organizational culture requires not only the full commitment of top management, but the cooperation of all the people at all levels of the organization. A climate must be created that stimulates people to challenge current practices and to develop and implement new ideas.

WHAT IS A CORPORATE OR ORGANIZATIONAL CULTURE?

The *American Heritage Dictionary* defines "culture" as behavior patterns, beliefs, institutions, and all other products of human work characteristic of a community or population. I simplify this definition by calling it the *way of life* of a group—in this case, the group being the company or organization.

Management Decisions, the British management journal, comments that an organizational culture is made up of a blend of the following four components:

1. Innovation
2. Action
3. Control
4. Harmony

Most organizations reflect a combination of some or all of these components. The best cultures have a well-balanced combination. If any one of the components is overly dominant, the culture becomes distorted and this creates problems.

The overly creative and innovative organization may expend its energies in research and exploration of new concepts to the neglect of action. The action-oriented company, in its desire to see immediate results, may forego investment in developing its people. The control-dominated corporation is so involved in bureaucratic compliance with rules and regulations that it fears to change even when change is necessary. Harmony-oriented organizations are more concerned with keeping people happy than achieving results. What makes a culture truly great is combining the best of these traits into a coordinated, synergistic philosophy of management.

THE DEVELOPMENT OF AN ORGANIZATION'S CULTURE

How does an organizational culture develop? In many cases, the organizational culture evolves from a set of goals and principles promulgated by the founders or managers and encompassed in a mission statement. Employees are trained to use these principles as the touchstone upon which all of their actions will be based. The mission statement may be a simple statement such as the one used by Nordstrom, the Seattle-based department store chain:

> Our number one goal is to provide outstanding customer satisfaction.
>
> Nordstrom Rules:
>
> 1. Use your good judgment in all situations. There will be no additional rules.

Or it may consist of a detailed manual of instruction as to behavior expected of employees under a variety of circumstances. These instructions may vary from the presentation of ethical concepts to specific behavior such as dress codes and telephone etiquette.

Formal mission statements in many organizations are idealistic and are given lip service by both management and employees, but not really followed. The actual organizational culture may be quite different from the formal statement.

The Unofficial Organizational Culture

Organizational culture is not limited to what is written in a formal statement. Much of what becomes culture develops slowly and imperceptibly over time and becomes ingrained in the behavior of everybody in the organization. Company executives may have idealistic concepts about the culture of their organizations, but what actually exists may be quite different.

The actual culture often stems from the *informal organization*—the acts, thoughts, and perceptions of the rank and file workers that have evolved from a variety of sources. Let's look at some of them:

Customs

Industry, company, and even community customs contribute to the culture of an organization. In some industries, certain practices have developed over the years that may have outlived their original purposes but are still in use. For example, tipping as a form of compensation in restaurants and other service-type industries was originally intended to provide an incentive for better service. Today, in most cases, it has become an expected additional fee no matter how good or bad the service may have been. Indeed, some restaurants automatically add a 15-percent "gratuity" charge to the bill.

KEY POINT

The organizational culture is the *way of life* followed consciously or subconsciously in the day-to-day activities of the organization.

Often companies evolve their own customs. For example, until a few years ago, the Bluebird Beverage Company paid its employees in cash. On payday, the employees lined up at the cashier's window and were handed their envelopes by the paymaster, who was protected by an armed guard. To allow for the time it took to obtain the pay envelopes, lunch break was extended for fifteen minutes. When the company shifted to payment by check, the paymaster went to each department and distributed the checks. Although there was no longer the need to line up at the window, the workers expected to continue to get a longer lunch break on payday. They considered it an entitlement and it has remained a custom of that company.

Another example of companies creating their own customs is the Franklin Finance Co. A company rule requires that employees play only music on personal radios in their cubicles; however, this rule has been waived during the baseball world series. A few years ago a new supervisor, upset by the loss of productivity in her department at that time, tried to change the rule. You can guess how negatively that was received.

Dominant Personalities

Often an organizational culture is created by a dominant person such as a founder or a top manager. His or her personality sets the organizational culture for good or bad. In some companies, every decision—important or trivial—must be made by the senior executive. This custom may have started when the company was small and the CEO could keep close tabs on everything, but years later, when this practice became no longer practical, it still persisted, making the organization less flexible than it should be to deal with routine matters.

The experience of White Plastics exemplifies this. When Larry White started this business, he made all the decisions and knew what was happening in all aspects of the operation. As the business expanded, he began to lose touch with some of the activities. So he could keep informed, he required that copies of all correspondence be sent to him every day.

Today, 40 years later, his current successor still gets a file copy of every letter, fax, and memo. He rarely has time to even glance at them, yet the practice continues. When this was brought to his attention, he refused to change the practice. He commented: "It helped my predecessor and it may come in handy sometime."

Frequently these patterns have been instituted by a dogmatic executive, who must have everything done "my way" and no deviations are tolerated. Charles R., the founder of a large dress manufacturing firm, was such a person. No subordinate manager could make a decision, even on minor matters, without passing it up to Mr. R.—and it worked! His dynamism and expertise in the marketing of dresses brought his company to the pinnacle of the fashion industry.

His company, however, was actually a one-man organization. Creative people were milked for their ideas and then fired; innovators were discouraged to implement any projects unless they were approved by Mr. R. Managers tended to be yes-men. People with high potential were frustrated and left the company.

When Mr. R. died, there was no line of succession. The company's culture had discouraged creativity. It discouraged anybody but Mr. R. to engage in decision making. As a result, there was no competent manager within the organization to replace him. The company went downhill. Only after new ownership and an entirely new organizational culture was developed did the firm begin to move upward again.

Some dynamic leaders, however, set organizational cultures that are more positive. For example, early in his management of IBM, Thomas Watson established a culture that led to the immense growth of the organization. Sam Walton, the founder of Wal-Mart, set the tone for his firm's organizational culture, which is still followed today—many years after his death.

The real power centers in the organization

In some organizations, customs are inaugurated and perpetuated by informal leaders—men or women who do not have formal authority, but exert influence. Organizational charts are supposed to indicate the chain of command and enable one to see immediately who has the authority in the organization to make decisions. But this is not always so.

Often the real power is not indicated. There are often people whose position on the chart places them at levels well below their true position of influence. They carry significantly more weight than the chart indicates. One has to study the interactions among the management group to really understand the power structure. Here are two examples of how such people have extraordinary influence.

Diane Fiore, administrative assistant to the marketing manager, is shown well down in the hierarchy on her firm's organization chart, but she is a major power figure in the company. Over the years she has built her position into a clearinghouse for all activities related to marketing. Even her boss is afraid to contradict her. To obtain action, one has to first convince Diane.

José Fernandez, a bilingual clerk, is not even listed on his company's organizational chart. Early in his career, José took upon himself the role of translator and interpreter for Spanish speaking workers. He became the intermediary between them and others in the company. Because of his success in this role, other employees in the department, regardless of their ethnic background, would go to José when they had to deal with management. He became the informal spokesperson for all the workers.

In cases of this sort, the culture will most likely change when the individual leaves the company, but so long as this person wields that power, it cannot be overlooked.

TACTICAL TIPS

Don't rely solely on the organizational chart to determine where the power lies in that organization. Listen to what goes on in the lunchroom and the hallways. Observe the interactions of people to uncover the real power structure.

Unions

When a company has a labor union, much of the organizational culture is dictated by the union contract and the on-going relationship with the union. Unless union cooperation is obtained, little can be done to change the culture of the organization. Unions often resist change to protect the interests of their members.

One of the strongest unions in the U.S. is the United Automobile Workers. Over the years and through many negotiations, they have established work rules that workers and companies must follow. These are now an integral part of the organizational culture of the Big Three automobile makers. When competition from Japanese car makers cost the Big Three a significant loss of market share, the organizational culture of American auto manufacturers had to be changed. This could be accomplished only by tough negotiation with the unions.

Although some labor leaders oppose any change they feel will weaken the union's position, more and more enlightened labor union leaders are moving from an adversarial to a more cooperative philosophy. Among these leaders is Irving Bluestone, retired vice-president of the United Automobile Workers. He proposes a new type of working relationship between management and labor, which he calls the *enterprise compact* consisting of seven provisions:[1]

1. The union and management agree to pursue mutually established productivity growth targets.
2. Wage and compensation goals are set to be consistent with productivity growth in order to maintain global competitiveness.
3. Price setting in the company is subject to joint action by union and management.
4. To assure that products and services meet or exceed international standards, quality is a "strikeable" issue. Bluestone admits that using the word "strike" will impress both sides that survival depends on quality. He believes that this one issue can unite management and labor at every level.
5. Employment security is guaranteed for the workforce. This is likely to be resisted by management who demand flexibility to respond to shrinking market share by cutting jobs. In response, Bluestone points out as an example the Saturn plant in Tennessee that provides secure employment to 80 percent of its workforce, unless catastrophic economic events dictate otherwise as agreed by the union and management.

6. Extra financial rewards are provided through profit and gain sharing throughout the enterprise. Management shares profits in good times with the workers.

7. The union and management agree to joint decision making throughout the company, including labor representation on the board of directors. This provision would abolish the last remnants of the management rights clauses that assign all matters not directly covered by the contract to management's discretion and have been part of most collective bargaining agreements. This would give unions a voice in decisions such as pricing, marketing, quality, and everything else that traditionally had been exclusive to management.

Bluestone and others argue that the concept of enterprise compacts will not be readily accepted by either management or labor because both must give up cherished rights, but if we are to meet the challenges of the 21st century, all parties must reexamine their thinking and be prepared to make compromises that will work for the benefit of both management and labor.

Pragmatism

Much of what is defined as an organizational culture develops over time and emanates from practices and customs that have worked in the past and become part of the company's way of life. This is exemplified in the commonly heard expressions: "If it ain't broken, don't fix it" and "Don't tamper with success." On the surface this is true. Why change something that doesn't need changing?

If after several trials, we learn from our errors and the result is a viable process or practice, why not stick with it? Quite often we should. Change for the sake of change does not make any more sense than continuing practices just because "we always did it that way."

The longer a company has been in business, the more likely there will be patterns of behavior that are universally practiced. Taking advantage of past experience in dealing with day-to-day matters often gives established companies a competitive edge. *The danger comes from failing to recognize when what has worked well in the past may not be the best approach for the present or the future.* The challenge managers in older companies face is to identify patterns of behavior that have become obsolete and make necessary changes.

TACTICAL TIPS

Do not assume that what has worked well in the past is the best approach for the present or the future—or that just because an approach isn't new, it is out-of-date or useless.

The Image of the Organization

The way an organization wishes to be perceived by its owners, its customers, its employees, and the community often influences the developing of the culture. Image is not a superficial matter. It is more than just a public relations gimmick. It can set the stage for everything a company does.

Sometimes this image is dictated by a vision determined by the founder. George Merck, founder of the pharmaceutical company that bears his name, projected the image he wanted for his new firm: the company is committed to the ideals of advancing medical science and being of service to humanity. This mission, which has been adhered to by several generations of management, is taken very seriously and has kept the company and its employees focused on this prime goal.

The Community

The community in which a company is located often influences its organizational culture. This was demonstrated in the early 1970s, when the Official Airline Guide, then a division of Dun & Bradstreet, was having difficulty obtaining personnel for its expanding operations in a Chicago suburb. To attract the young mothers, who were the main source of clerical workers, OAG developed an organizational culture that would appeal to this market. They were among the first organizations to create a flexible time schedule, to arrange for shared work, and to open their own day-care center. As expected, OAG became known as *the* place to work in the area, which resulted in their attracting a high quality workforce and a low rate of absenteeism and turnover.

Companies that open facilities in areas that have different customs and work practices from those at the home base have to accommodate local customs. When the North Atlantic Constructors, a joint venture of four midwestern construction companies, opened its New York City office, they established a workday schedule that started at 8 a.m., the usual starting time in their home areas. They were shocked to learn that virtually all New York City offices opened at 9 a.m. In order to compete for good workers in the city, they had to adjust their working hours to the usual local hours of 9 to 5.

In communities dominated by certain ethnic groups, an organizational culture often is influenced by the customs and practices of that group. Many managers assigned to supervise newly arrived immigrants from Latin America or Asia were unsuccessful in obtaining full commitment and effort from them until they recognized their cultural differences and modified their practices to accommodate what the workers would accept.

American firms opening branches in other countries have had to adapt to the customs of that country rather than attempting to follow the same organizational culture practiced in the United States. For example, companies with facilities in Pakistan, Indonesia, and the Arab countries had to allow for prayer breaks for their devout Moslem employees.

Local customs often are incorporated into organizational culture. For example, in New Orleans, most businesses cease work at Mardi Gras even though it is not a formal holiday. In New York City, in companies whose windows face the ticker-tape parade route, the parades take precedence over work.

QUOTES AND QUIPS

"Why not go out on a limb—Isn't that where all the fruit is."
Frank Scully
Former CEO, Apple Computers, Inc.

Government

Many aspects of an organizational culture are superimposed on a company by federal and local governments. There is no choice but to comply. Laws and regulations dictate how companies can conduct their businesses, deal with employees, design and utilize equipment, handle their finances, and act and react in many aspects of their activities.

Some of these laws existed for so long they are accepted with little thought. Sure, we may be unhappy about maintaining certain records for the IRS or other government agency, but this activity has become an established aspect of a company's way of life.

New laws and rules often require companies to radically change long-established practices. Unfortunately, over the years, many companies accepted the premise that certain jobs were limited to men and others to women. Although there were some exceptions, it just wasn't the "correct" thing to hire a woman as a mechanic or a man as a telephone operator or secretary; a woman supervising men was unheard of. In many industrial companies, only male college graduates were hired as management trainees or sales people. As many business contacts were made over golf or dinner at the all-male country club, it was not considered prudent to promote women to management jobs. This was the organizational culture that permeated many companies until civil rights laws and regulations forced companies to change their cultures.

Special Situations

Long before Congress and the state legislatures passed laws requiring accommodation in the workplace for the handicapped, Henry Viscardi created a company with a culture based primarily on helping disabled people. Viscardi, who walks on two prosthetic legs, founded a company, Abilities, Inc., that only hires people with physical and/or mental disabilities, trains them, and puts them to work in productive jobs. By obtaining subcontracts for manufacturing components for other firms, Abilities, Inc. has become a successful operation.

How Organizational Culture Affects Conduct

The way employees perceive organizational culture dominates their actions and how they think about their jobs, perform their duties, and plan for the future. If employees are convinced that the company is truly concerned about quality, they will make every effort to produce quality work. But, if employees believe that the management's talk about quality is just lip service, the "quality" program will be ignored or even ridiculed.

For example, when the Metal Fabrication Company introduced its "quality" program, managers gave the employees lectures on the importance of quality and posted this motto on the office and factory bulletin boards: *We Aim for Perfection*. But, they made no substantive changes in their methods and paid no attention to quality improvement suggestions from employees. It didn't take long for the workers to become skeptical about the "quality" program, and some anonymous worker added this sentence to the motto: *But We Usually Miss*. On the other hand, Ford Motor Company's motto, *Quality is Number One*, is taken seriously by workers and managers alike. All employees are imbued with the company culture that truly puts a high priority on quality.

TACTICAL TIPS

Actions speak louder than words. Unless mission statements or mottoes are truly followed by management, employees will not take them seriously.

Organizational Culture Affects Creativity

I've observed that in the companies that devise creative ideas, innovative techniques, new products or services, their organizational culture fosters creativity. New ideas are encouraged, seriously considered, and frequently accepted. Unfortunately, too many companies stifle creativity. The organizational culture is one of complacency: Don't rock the boat.

High-Tech Industries, a pioneering manufacturer of computer components, provides an illustration of how such complacency can almost destroy an organization. High-Tech led its segment of the industry for many years. Its original products were innovative and they made the company a major player in the field. Engineers and technicians were proud to be part of this organization, and a strong sense of pride in the organization was ingrained as part of the organizational culture. Management continuously reminded the staff that their loyalty was appreciated.

On the other hand, any criticism of company products, services, or practices was considered disloyal. Any dissension, even suggestions for changing current practices, was viewed almost as treason. Innovative ideas by creative engineers were scoffed at if they varied from accepted company practices. Some people left in frustration. Others were either complacent with the status quo and believed that because they had always been the best, they would always lead the field.

Even if they felt things could be changed, employees were reluctant to do or say anything that would make them appear disloyal. As the industry changed and competitors introduced new concepts, products and technologies, High Tech began to lose market share. This resulted in the loss of hundreds of jobs and millions of dollars in revenue.

Creativity is fostered by a culture of trust and respect. Gary L., a long-time human resources manager, proved this when he left the corporate scene to open his own outplacement service. Gary resolved to practice what he had preached in his HR career. His first steps were to carefully select a highly competent staff and train them thoroughly. Staff members were encouraged to develop their own approaches to solving problems, but had easy access to the expertise of all of the other members of the staff and to Gary. All employees, whether they were on the professional staff or in the support group, could come to Gary's office and discuss any problem with him.

To supplement this open-door policy, Gary ran periodic meetings in the lunchroom, where over coffee, open discussions were held about any matters that were brought up. No question or comment was considered too serious or too trivial to be introduced. The respect given to all participants by management and by other participants led to an openness that fostered constructive critiques of practices, the introduction of innovative ideas, and a spirit of collaboration that helped Gary's firm become one of the leaders in the outplacement field.

QUOTES AND QUIPS

"Love is a given. Trust and respect have to be earned"
Earl Woods
to his son, golfer Tiger Woods

SUM AND SUBSTANCE

- To survive and thrive in this dynamic world, organizations must not only keep up with the technological changes in their fields, but must adapt their organizational cultures to meet the needs of their staffs, their customers, and their community.
- Managers cannot make a culture change alone. Everybody at all levels of the organization must take part in the process.
- Organizational culture is defined as "the way of life" of the company or the organization.
- The informal organization plays the major role in establishing and perpetuating the organizational culture.
- Employees' perceptions of the organizational culture dominate their actions in the way they think about and perform their jobs.
- Creativity is fostered by a culture of trust and respect.

Ten Precepts for Transforming an Organizational Culture

1. The opinions of the employees are much more important than the opinion of management.
2. One bad apple in a dominant position can destroy the whole barrel.
3. There is a more direct relationship between organizational culture and profitability than most people realize.
4. There is a greater gap between the perceptions of management and that of workers than most people realize.
5. The true organizational culture can be diagnosed by using appropriate tools.
6. The influence of the informal organization is greater than that of the formal organization in establishing organizational culture.
7. The concept of continuous improvement is not enough to significantly change organizational culture.
8. Organizational cultures, no matter how deeply ingrained, can be improved.
9. Most problems related to a culture arise from management, not employees.
10. Perception is reality in the mind of the perceiver.

POINTS TO PONDER

1. How would you rate the existing culture in your organization *right now?*

    _____ Extremely good
    _____ Good
    _____ Fair
    _____ Poor
    _____ Extremely poor

    Why? _____

    _____

    _____

2. What do you believe are the key factors that contribute to the culture existing in your organization today?

    _____

    _____

    _____

    _____

3. To what extent do you think the "informal organization" contributes to or detracts from the levels or enthusiasm and productivity? Why?

    _____

    _____

    _____

    _____

4. In what areas do you believe improvement can be made in your organization's culture?

REFERENCE

[1]U.S. Dept. of Labor, *State of the Art Symposium*, BLMR 124, 1989.

CHAPTER 2

Diagnosing the As-Is Condition

Before an organizational culture can be changed, it must be analyzed and assessed. It's necessary to understand the current culture and determine what problems exist and how seriously they affect productivity, quality of product or service, the morale of the workers, and the overall efficacy of the organization.

Too often, managers deceive themselves about the true condition of their organization. Of course, they know the figures: sales volume, market share, production, payroll, and all the tangible statistics. But they delude themselves on such vital information as employee attitudes and morale, the currency of the skills of their people, the willingness of their people to cooperate and extend themselves, the commitment of staff at all levels to company goals.

QUOTES AND QUIPS

"The manager who comes up with the right solution to the wrong problem is more dangerous than the manager who comes up with the wrong solution to the right problem."
Peter Drucker
Management consultant and author

Perception is Reality in the Mind of the Perceiver

It's human nature for people to see what they want to see, to hear what they want to hear, and to believe what they want to believe. People tend to overlook or totally fail to even note matters that do not agree with their perceptions. Most of us do not like to be shaken out of our comfort zones. There is a strong tendency to believe whatever is consistent with what we already believe than to accept new information that is inconsistent with our established beliefs.

Each of us tends to accept as truthful information that which is compatible with our own perceptions. To us, it is reality. However, in the minds of others, whether they are superiors, peers, or subordinates, the same information may be perceived totally differently.

Most consultants have witnessed instance after instance in which senior executives truly believed that they were respected, even loved, by their people and were literally stunned by the results of employee surveys suggesting that they were very much disliked and considered mean-spirited and even incompetent. The void between one set of perceptions and the other could not have been wider.

Why should this be? The answer is often surprisingly simple. It is difficult, if not impossible, to be totally objective about oneself. People tend to be defensive about their beliefs and perceive their actions as being the best possible course to take. They attribute negative reactions to others' lack of understanding or even the incompetence of others. It does not take long for subordinates to recognize that often the perceptions of the boss are different from theirs, but because a boss has power over them, they keep their reservations and feelings to themselves, festering inside and perhaps leading to discontent and reluctant obedience.

Often, managers misinterpret the employees' compliance, not recognizing its true cause—fear of contradicting the boss—and perceive the employees' attitude as total agreement with the manager's concepts, actions, and attitudes. To these managers, this "agreement" is the reality. On the other hand, the men and women who must live with this situation see a different reality. What to the boss is white, to them is black or perhaps a shade of gray. It's a totally different reality.

If culture change is to take place, the first step the organization must take is to identify what the perceptions of employees truly are and how they got that way. To accomplish this, the organization must undertake a comprehensive examination similar to the periodic examinations people take to assess their medical condition.

THE ORGANIZATIONAL MRI

Physicians use a variety of techniques to evaluate the health of a patient. Companies must do the same. Just as the doctor takes blood pressure, EKGs, X-rays, temperature, and blood tests to obtain basic vital statistics, so the company uses financial, production, sales, and other figures to diagnose many aspects of the business. However, just as in our bodies, many critical problems may not show up in these routine medical tests, subtle and incipient conditions exist in an organization that may not be uncovered by traditional business analyses.

In recent times, sophisticated diagnostic techniques and equipment have been developed to help uncover these hidden symptoms in our bodies. One of the most useful of these is the MRI, Magnetic Resonance Imaging, which enables the physician to look deep into the body and focus in detail on problem areas from various angles.

To enable managers to look deep into their businesses, to learn about the perceptions of employees, determine how such perceptions affect performance, analyze subtle details, and observe actions, reactions, attitudes, and viewpoints perhaps not ever explored or even considered, I have designed the Organizational MRI.

By using variations of established evaluative tools and innovative techniques, the Organizational MRI (O-MRI) becomes an instrument that can specifically uncover culture-related problems and challenges.

The Holistic Approach

In order to make an accurate diagnosis of an organization, we cannot rely on only one or two dimensional tools. The O-MRI provides a multidimensional view that not only examines a specific aspect of the organization, but demonstrates how it relates to other phases.

Key Point

Just as a medical MRI uncovers problems in the human body not easily accessible by traditional techniques, the O-MRI pinpoints organizational problems that may elude standard measuring techniques.

Let's take a look at how this was applied at an aircraft parts factory in Wichita, Kansas, where the number of industrial accidents had increased significantly. Although these injuries were not life threatening or serious, they caused increases in downtime, lengthy workers compensation hearings, and other time-consuming and annoying distractions. The safety specialists, who were retained to study the problem, corrected some mechanic defects and initiated a safety training program. This helped for a time, but within a few months, the accident rate began to creep up again.

When consulted about this, I suggested that an O-MRI be conducted. Instead of concentrating primarily on the accident rate, the entire organization was examined. Using the diagnostic tools described later in this chapter, it was found that there was a pattern of discontent and even rebellion in the company. Certain actions on the part of management had destroyed morale, leading to a loss of enthusiasm for any actions of management—even a safety program that was designed to keep workers from being injured. Only by initiating a holistic diagnosis were the real reasons for the safety problems identified and steps suggested to overcome them.

Delve for Root Causes

The O-MRI seeks the reason for the existence of a problem, not just the overt cause. Its goal is to peel layer after layer off the situation until the underlying reasons are bared.

The ultimate objective of the O-MRI system is to answer one question: Why?

In many ways, problems are like icebergs. The ostensible cause of potential problems is not the part of the iceberg that is above the water line. The real cause of concern lies well *below* the water line.

By continuing to ask "Why?" after each response, the true cause will emerge. This can be illustrated by a conversation that took place between Andy, a member of the consultant's staff, and Peter, a machine operator at the aircraft parts company:

Andy: Why did that machine break down?
Peter: The rotor wore out.
Andy: Why did the rotor wear out?
Peter: It wasn't properly lubricated.
Andy: Why wasn't it properly lubricated?
Peter: The oil is too light.
Andy: Why do you use light oil?
Peter: The boss ordered it.
Andy: Why didn't you tell him it was too light?
Peter: He never listens to anything I say.

The continuing questioning finally brings out the real problem. If workers perceive that their boss is not interested in what they have to say about the work, it leads to a variety of troubles.

TACTICAL TIPS

Ask "Why?"
Ask "Why?" again
Ask "Why? once more
Continue to ask "Why?" until the root causes are unveiled.

Earning Trust

It's normal for employees to be reluctant to provide meaningful information if they feel that their comments will be reported back to the managers, who, of course, have power over their jobs. Fear that anything they say will be held against them keeps people from telling the whole story.

Even though the O-MRI is usually conducted by an outside consultant, lower level managers and rank and file workers often look upon consultants as tools of top management. "The bosses are paying them, so they probably blab everything we say back to them" is a commonly heard remark.

The O-MRI consultant has to win the confidence of all employees before the process even begins. To do this takes time. Trust cannot be dictated or mandated. It must be earned. One cannot go into a company, announce that a survey is being taken on employee morale and expect cooperation and candor. The consultant must earn people's trust by being consistently trustworthy. This can be accomplished by using proven techniques to facilitate the process.

One approach that works well is to start with a nonthreatening series of workshops in areas that are of some value to the people involved. Some of the workshops that have been used to break the ice are:

- For first-line supervisors and middle management, a workshop on improving supervisory techniques.
- For employees at all levels, a workshop on improving communication skills, getting along with others, and building self-confidence.

These programs are given in one- or two-hour sessions once or twice a week for three or four weeks. During these sessions, the consultant gets to know many of the workers as individuals and establishes rapport with enough of them to gain their confidence and remove the stigma that the consultant is solely on the side of management. One of the most important things that the consultant should do when conducting these classes is to identify the informal leaders and make an effort to cultivate them. They are the best source of establishing credibility among the employees.

Once these informal leaders have been identified, either through the classes or other means, a rapport must be developed with them and other staff members. In short, get to know them as individuals. Get them to talk not only about the job but about their personal interests. Get to know them as they really are—as multi-dimensional human beings.

KEY POINT

Identify and cultivate the informal leaders in the organization. They can be a major source of information and a significant aid in implementing change.

Six Terrific Techniques to Obtain Reliable Information

Over the years through my own trial-and-error approaches and research on the effective methods used by consultants, I have pinpointed six techniques that help encourage candor and provide for a free flow of significant and accurate information from employees. These are briefly noted in the following paragraphs. Details as to how they are used will be discussed later in this chapter.

Get 'em away from the company environment. When people are relaxed, they are much more likely to share ideas, complaints, and true feelings. As we know, executives and sales people often make their best deals on the golf course or over a relaxing meal. Why limit this informality to big deals? Participate in some extracurricular activity with those from whom you need helpful information. Find out about their interests. Join them at the bowling alley, attend a soft ball tournament, or go to lunch or dinner with an informal leader.

Rita Sable, a successful human resources consultant, found that the women employed by her client were reluctant to express their feelings about their attitudes, observations, and thoughts about the company. She tried to find some way to overcome this resistance. Rita noted that at lunch or dinner in social situations, women often would leave the table together to freshen up, and in that most informal environment, talk about matters dear to their hearts. She decided to use this approach with these women employees. She joined them at the breaks and became a participant in their chitchats. This opened up a channel that enabled her to learn a good deal about how they really felt about the bosses, the company, and specific situations.

Quotes and Quips

"To improve your listening skills, challenge yourself to say nothing for the first half-hour next time you have a meal with a group."
Jeffrey Gitomer
Sales consultant and author

Organize focus groups. The concept of focus groups was developed by market researchers to learn about the reaction of typical consumers to a company's product or service. Many consumer product manufacturers have potential customers try out a product and then conduct a focus group to obtain the opinions of its members. Service organizations use focus groups to evaluate the service they provide.

Over the past few years, human resources consultants have used this approach to reveal the true attitudes of employees about their company, their department, their managers, and specific aspects of their jobs.

Let's look in as the facilitator of a focus group begins his orientation:

As you know, I've been working with most of you for several months as part of the company's efforts to improve the quality of the workplace. I've spoken to you individually from time to time. You've been selected as a focus group to discuss one particular situation about which we're concerned—the proposed changes in the health insurance program. You were chosen as typical members of our staff. You represent several departments and range in years of employment from one to twenty-two. You've been given copies of the current plan and the proposed plan to study before this meeting. Our first step is to give you the chance to ask Linda, the benefits manager, questions about the plan. Then we'll ask for your comments and reactions. Please note that the proposed plan hasn't as yet been adopted and no decisions will be made until much further study is done, beginning with this focus group.

Note that the facilitator identified the matter to be discussed and assured participants that this was not an attempt to sell them on it, but to obtain input. This is essential for a successful focus group experience. Participants must be assured that their ideas and feelings will be considered.

Also note that the benefits manager is there to answer questions. However, she will not express her opinions or participate in the discussion in any way other than to elucidate technical aspects of the plan. The facilitator will be just that—a person who facilitates the discussion, who will keep it on keel and assure that it runs along smoothly and in a reasonable time frame.

Although focus groups are most effective when restricted to a specific area, they can also be used as means of identifying basic problems that can be explored later in other groups.

Conduct confidential employee surveys. Employee attitude surveys have been used for a long time as a means of determining employee morale and locating problem areas. In recent years, these have been refined to make them an even more sophisticated diagnostic tool. Inasmuch as such surveys should be designed to fit each company's special needs, they should be developed and conducted by organizations geared for that purpose. Getting the most from an employee survey goes beyond just obtaining information. The ways an attitude survey is used in the O-MRI will be described later in this chapter.

Conduct individual employee interviews. Unlike the informal conversations with employees discussed earlier, some consultants prefer to use more formal interviewing techniques. The same series of questions is asked of each of the respondents. In addition, the interviewer will ask follow-up questions so that the respondent can expand, explain, and elucidate when doing so helps clarify an answer.

The advantage of this technique is that it assures that all of the aspects that are being investigated will be covered in a systematic manner. A knowledgeable consultant can design very comprehensive questionnaires that will shorten the time it takes to obtain key information.

Questions are framed that will help in the diagnosis of the situation. Although the questions should be related to the organization's activities, examples of such general questions as the following often help set the stage and lead to more questions on more specific areas:

- What do you like most about working in this organization?
- What do you like least?
- In what way could the organization improve its relations with its employees?
- Describe your supervisor's style of managing?
- How do you relate to this style?
- How effectively do you feel management communicates its ideas to the staff?
- How do you believe you can be a more effective employee?

The main limitation of such a formal tool is that unless the interviewer is very skilled, such interviews tend to become stilted and only routine information is developed. Informal approaches often uncover the hidden areas that formal methods may overlook. My colleagues and I have used these formal interviews as a means of obtaining the basic information about the organization and have followed it up with informal discussions. If an area of specific concern develops from these questions, I follow up by immediately asking for more details including specific examples. If some situations are more complex, I'll arrange to explore them in more depth in later informal discussions.

Conduct 360-degree assessments of key managers. Multilevel assessments have become an increasingly popular approach to identify how a manager is viewed by his or her bosses, peers, subordinates, and even such outsiders as vendors and customers. Usually referred to as 360-degree assessments, they have been adopted by such companies as AT&T, IBM, and hundreds of other large and small organizations.

According to Tom Pawlak, a principal with the prestigious management consulting firm, Towers Perrin, the use of multisource feedback is growing rapidly. He predicts it will be the most widely used form of performance appraisal by the end of the decade.[1] How 360-degree assessments are conducted will be described later in this chapter.

People do not see themselves as others see them. We perceive our actions as rational, our ideas as solid, our decisions as meaningful. Traditionally, performance is evaluated only by one's own manager. This does give us insight into how our work is perceived by that person, but he or she is not the only person with whom we interrelate.

Even more complex is the evaluation of senior managers, who frequently are not evaluated at all. When these executives are assessed by peers and subordinates, they may learn much about their management style. Many are shocked to realize that they are perceived by others much differently than they believed and, as a result, have taken steps to change their management styles.

Despite these advantages of multisource assessments, there are also serious concerns about them. Mary N. Vinson, director of the regulatory relations group at Bell Atlantic-Virginia, is a strong advocate of these programs, but she cautions that there is a downside.

She notes that feedback can hurt, and points out that evaluators aren't always nice or positive. Some people see their role as a feedback provider as an opportunity to criticize others' behavior on the job.

Another flaw concerns conflicting opinions. Who decides who is right? Also, the feedback may not always be truthful. If the evaluator does not like the person being evaluated, the responses might be skewed negatively; if the assessee is a friend, they might be skewed positively. In addition, Ms. Vinson reported that often people rating senior executives thought it was dangerous to be completely truthful.

In order to ensure that the 360-degree feedback has a better chance of producing a change, Vinson recommends:

- The feedback must be anonymous and confidential.
- To have sufficient knowledge of the person being rated, the appraisers should have worked with the appraisee for at least six months.
- A feedback expert should interpret the feedback.
- Follow up on improvements made as a result of the assessment should be made about six months later.
- Appraisers should give written descriptions as well as numerical ratings. This enables them to be more specific and the results more meaningful.
- The feedback instrument should be statistically reliable and valid.
- To avoid "survey fatigue," the 360-degree feedback should not be used on too many employees at one time.[2]

Scheduling a multilevel retreat. Assembling people away from the workplace for training or for discussions has been used by many companies. Combined with recreation and social activities, the relaxed atmosphere lends itself to accomplishing a good deal of creative work. Usually these retreats are restricted to senior managers and the subjects covered involve long-range planning or dealing with specific situations.

Multilevel retreats involve inviting people from various levels of the organization. A theme should be chosen that will give the participants opportunity to express ideas and ask questions that will stimulate management to identify where change is desirable or even necessary for the health of the organization. The consultant charged with facilitating the retreat will draw out participants both during the formal sessions and in informal conversations. A description of the multilevel retreat in action is found in Chapter 6.

QUOTES AND QUIPS

"The difference between success and failure in problem-solving
is the amount and quality of the questions generated."
Harvey Brightman
Statistician and author

THE FOUR WORST TECHNIQUES

We all learn from our failures, and my colleagues and I clearly are
no exception. Here's a look at a handful of approaches that seem to
fail more often than they succeed.

Town Meetings

I recently attended a town meeting on Long Island, New York. Several important issues were on the agenda, but most never reached the
floor. Men and women with their own agendas dominated the meeting. They grabbed the microphones, harangued the audience, plugged
their messages until most listeners left in disgust. It was, at best, a dis-
concerting, uncomfortable, and unproductive experience.

Company "town meetings" may not get that far out of hand, but
organizations that have used them find that often they become little
more than gripe sessions. Some people with personal agendas tend to
dominate the meetings. At one such gathering I attended, a small
group of employees attempted to use the meeting as a forum on a
grievance that already had been adjudicated—but not to their satisfaction. This distracted from the objectives of the meeting and not
only wasted the time of the majority of participants but soured everybody on the concept of "town meetings."

Meetings Led by the Managers of the Attendees

When a boss conducts the meeting, employees are inhibited from
telling the whole story. They may fear that dissension from the boss'
opinions will be long remembered and may be reflected in their next
performance evaluation. This happened to Douglas T. At a meeting of

engineers from various departments of a public utility in Pennsylvania, Douglas voiced his reservations about a program his boss supported.

Douglas reported: "I had told my boss about these reservations in one-to-one discussions so he knew I had doubts about the project. But because I expressed them at an open meeting, he called me disloyal and our relationship has seriously deteriorated."

QUOTES AND QUIPS

"You cannot motivate a person—you can only provide the environment, climate, or atmosphere for motivation. One of the most challenging and thrilling experiences of life is to develop ordinary people into extraordinary people."
J. D. Batten
Business author

Poorly Designed Problem-Solving Teams

Problem-solving teams can be an effective way of identifying and seeking solutions to problems. However, such team activity must be carefully planned and participants thoroughly trained in problem-solving techniques.

Unfortunately, this often is not the case. The manager identifies a problem and appoints a "team" to study it. Often, these people come from several departments and have not worked together before. The team members are primarily concerned with how what they say or do will affect their own departments and perhaps their own careers. At the minimum, this results in wasted time and often in more conflict than resolution.

Employees Interviewed by Company Managers

In many cases the person assigned to diagnose a problem that involves relationships between a supervisor and his or her people is that very supervisor. In such cases, most people will be afraid to be truthful. Even if the investigator is another supervisor, the fear, although somewhat less, still exists. These interviews should be conducted by an outsider such as a consultant or, in a divisional or departmental situation, an executive from the home office.

Often these type interviews are conducted by representatives of the Human Resources Department. Unless employees view the HR staff as impartial and fair-minded, they will be unwilling to be fully truthful. In my experience, using outside consultants or independent survey groups bring the best results.

CONDUCTING THE O-MRI

In conducting the O-MRI, it is wise to follow a carefully planned agenda. The steps that should be taken are described next. To help implement these steps, a set of step-by-step guidelines is provided.

Secure Full Support of Top Management

Once the consultant and the client have agreed that an O-MRI is to be conducted, careful preparation must be made. It starts with gaining the full support of top management. Often, the CEO and other senior executives feel that they know all of the problems and call in a consultant to provide solutions or to impose their preconceived solutions on the lower echelons. In many cases, senior managers are reluctant to really delve too deeply into how the people they supervise perceive things for fear that it may bring out negative aspects of their own managerial styles and actions.

Often managers tell me that they know the problems facing the company and have retained a consultant to persuade others to their way of thinking. First, it must be made clear to all that senior executives are often unaware of significant issues facing an organization. People at lower levels are closer to the problems. They often may see them more clearly.

There are many examples of companies in which critical matters were either not known by top management or were perceived by them to be unimportant. It is also essential that executives truly understand how they are viewed by peers, subordinates, customers, and others with whom they relate. They must accept that if the diagnosis indicates that they are the cause of part of the problem, successful change depends on their willingness to change their behavior. Obviously, this must be done in a diplomatic manner. Top management must fully agree with the changes. If not, at the minimum, sulking and reluctant cooperation will result, or at the maximum, the entire process could be sabotaged.

Once this hurdle is overcome, senior managers should be given an overview of how the O-MRI will proceed. It must be clear that this is a diagnostic process. The objective is to obtain information, not to solve problems. This can be done only if an accurate analysis is accomplished.

The process will include conducting surveys and speaking formally and informally to lower-level managers, rank-and-file employees, and perhaps to vendors and customers. There must be clear understanding that the process is nonjudgmental and is concerned only with getting as much information as possible that will bring out facts, feelings, and perceptions about the organization.

It is advisable to assign a small team (two to four people) to act as internal coordinators. These people will assist the consultants by acting as the liaison between them and top management. They also provide the necessary links with other managers and employees with whom the consultants will interact. This team is usually made up of managers drawn from varying departments such as Production or Operations, Finance, Marketing, Research & Development, and Human Resources.

QUOTES AND QUIPS

"In all affairs it's a healthy thing now and then to hang a question mark on the things you have long taken for granted."
Bertrand Russell, 1872–1970
English philosopher

The first step is to work with this team to design the program. This cannot be done haphazardly and may take several weeks. The consultant orients the team about the process and works out the specifics of the process. A timetable is developed. Once this process is established, the program is announced to the entire organization.

The Announcement

As virtually everybody in the company will be involved to some extent in the O-MRI, it is essential that they are not only made aware of what is being done, but become part of the process from the beginning.

When the Excelsior Paper Box Company initiated their O-MRI, CEO Douglas Stewart sent a letter to each employee describing briefly why the program was being conducted and the importance of his or her participation. This was followed by brief departmental meetings in which the consultant was introduced to the various staffs. In both the letter and the meetings, the importance of each person's contribution was emphasized and the confidentiality of all matters related to the process was assured.

The first step, after the announcement, is to gain the confidence of the middle- and lower-level personnel. The consulting team identifies the informal leaders and through workshops, off-premise meetings and personal contacts, as described earlier in this chapter, begins the process of getting to know them and win their support.

The Confidential Employee Survey

Another tool that we recently used to help uncover situations that may not be easily identified is the confidential employee survey. A carefully designed survey form was prepared by a professional survey organization. They designed an instrument that was as specific as possible to the organization's culture. It also had to be easily understood, designed to yield usable data, and could be distributed in a way to ensure a significant response.

For any attitude survey to be truly meaningful, confidentiality had to be stressed. Employees had to be convinced that their interests were protected. A cover letter with the questionnaire assuring that no individual employee's answers would be identified was mailed to each employee's home. Because a computer was to be used to tabulate the results, questions were formulated so the responses would be easily codified and retrieved.

The purpose and methods to be used in the survey were explained to the participants before the questionnaire was distributed through company newsletters, bulletins, and in a letter sent by a senior executive that accompanied the questionnaire. In addition, face-to-face meetings were held to discuss the questionnaire before distribution.

Before putting the questionnaire in its final form, a small group of employees was selected to review a draft. This enabled the survey team to identify and correct ambiguous questions, and determine the ease of response to the questions.

Once the questionnaires were returned, they were evaluated immediately. A report was prepared that included:

1. The background of the survey
2. The process used to obtain the information
3. A summary of the key points that were learned
4. Recommendations for implementation

The remainder of the report included details on specific aspects of the survey. A place had been provided in the questionnaire for comments by respondents, and these comments were presented in raw form for perusal by management.

The results obtained from the survey were used as the basis for further investigation and as taking-off points for the other approaches that were used in the O-MRI.

To the delight of the survey group and management, a 67 percent response was received by the deadline, and additional questionnaires trickled in for the next few weeks. Responses were tabulated and key comments studied. The report was examined by the CEO, the O-MRI team, and by the consultants.

The survey showed four major problem areas and a variety of lesser ones. The four key areas of concern were:

1. A pervasive sense of insecurity, distrust, fear, and resentment
2. Poor internal communications
3. Inequities in compensation
4. Too much internal politics

Focus Groups

Peer-based, rather than multi-peer groups, were selected to form focus groups to explore the problem areas the survey had identified. A peer-based group consists of people at the same level in the organization, for example, all rank-and-file workers with no managers or supervisors; all first-line supervisors, but no workers or higher-level managers. Multilevel groups are drawn from all echelons.

Using peer-level grouping minimizes "us vs. them" inhibitions. Multilevel groups often are useful because of the interactions that can be observed. They have a place in the O-MRI; however, because the survey uncovered distrust of management, the use of peer groups was the preferred way to go.

TACTICAL TIPS

Focus group participants should be close to the situation being studied, knowledgeable about the subject, and willing to express their ideas.

Three of the four focus groups were drawn from rank-and-file workers: two groups from plant personnel and one group from office personnel. The fourth group consisted of first-line supervisors. It was decided not to have a middle-level management group because there were relatively few people in that category.

The eight members of each group were selected from men and women who had shown some signs of serious concerns about the company in the workshops or in early informal discussions. Each focus group was facilitated by a member of the consulting staff.

The meetings started with a brief discussion about the purpose of the group. The leader greeted the members and congratulated them on being chosen for this important work. They were assured that their individual comments, concerns, and contributions would be kept confidential. Then, the process was described in terms similar to this:

By authorizing this program, the company accepts the fact that there are challenges that are keeping all of us from giving our whole-hearted cooperation to achieving company goals. The survey all of you have participated in has given us an overview of some of these problems. In this focus group, we are going to delve deeper into the situation and identify the real problems and seek their causes. Often what is perceived to be the crux of the problem is only a symptom of something more serious.

You have been selected for this group because all of you are respected members of the employee staff. When the number of years each of you has been with the company are added up, we find we have over 120 years of tenure in Excelsior Paper represented in this room. You have observed, experienced, and were affected by what has happened in this organization over the years. Your input will be extremely important in getting started in our efforts to make working for this company a more rewarding endeavor.

Participants were then asked to express their opinions about each of the factors brought out in the survey. The objective was to keep the conversation flowing, to encourage—even urge—the participants to express disagreement, to provide added ideas, and wherever possible, give specific examples illustrating the matters under discussion. The facilitator made no comments on the content, but concentrated on keeping everyone on target, stopping digressions and making sure that the concern was on finding problems, not seeking solutions. If a participant suggested a possible solution, it was pointed out that solution finding will come later, but at this time, all energies should be devoted to seeking the roots, the real causes.

As comments, suggestions, and ideas were brought up, they were listed on a flip chart. This became the tool for the next step, which was to separate the items into categories related to their importance.

Most focus groups usually complete their business in one two-hour session, but it may be extended if needed. The information developed by the four groups was then discussed by the O-MRI team and plans were made for the next steps.

In some cases, focus groups are also drawn from customers, vendors, or other outsiders with whom the company interrelates. The format and technique are the same as with employees, but of course, the matters discussed are geared to the experience the members of the group have had with the organization.

QUOTES AND QUIPS

"Approach each new problem not with a view of finding out what you hope will be there, but to get the truth, the realities that must be grabbled with. You may not like what you will find. In that case, you are entitled to try to change it. But do not deceive yourself as to what you do find to be the facts of the situation."

Bernard M. Baruch, 1876–1965
Presidential advisor and
investment broker

Interviews with Informal Leaders

From observations made during the pre-O-MRI workshops and from discussions with supervisors, managers, and employees, several people were identified as being informal leaders. These are men and women who are respected by their peers and often have been spokespersons for them in dealings with management. Their views reflect those of their coworkers and they are usually articulate and willing to express these views to whomever will listen.

Interviews with informal leaders should be conducted by the principal consultant or a member of his or her staff. Because of the need for complete frankness, no representative of management should be present. In the Excelsior Paper O-MRI, seven informal leaders were interviewed.

In each case, the interviews were conducted away from the premises. The interview with one man, an avid golfer, was combined with a round of golf. The consultant conducted an interview with a woman while she drove to the school to pick up her daughter after band practice. Others were interviewed at lunch or dinner at a local restaurant.

The interviews started with discussions of the results of the questionnaire and what had been learned at the focus groups. As rapport with employees increased, quite often they opened up and expressed their feelings about various aspects of the job and the organization. They provided specific examples of both positive and negative practices that they had observed, either augmenting what had been learned or adding additional information. To maintain the integrity of the procedure, the confidentiality of sources was carefully preserved. These results were then discussed with the O-MRI team.

360-Degree Assessments

As a result of the information thus far obtained, the consultants inferred that one of the most significant problems was a basic distrust of management by both rank-and-file workers and lower-echelon supervisors. To verify this and to develop more specific aspects of actual perceptions of these executives, 360-degree assessments of all middle- and senior-management people were instituted.

QUOTES AND QUIPS

"It is not who is right, but what is right that is of importance."
Thomas Huxley, 1825–1875
English biologist

To start this process, a comprehensive questionnaire was designed to be completed by the four levels of personnel each manager usually interacted with:

1. **Superiors.** Except for the CEO (who was also assessed), the person to whom the manager reported and at least one other higher ranking executive with whom he or she has frequent contact.
2. **Peer group members.** Persons at or close to the same level as the assessee who interface with that person on a regular basis.
3. **Subordinates.** Personnel who report directly to the assessee. In some cases, people who report to the assessee's subordinates.
4. **Others.** This varied according to the person being assessed. In some cases, it included outside people, such as vendors or customers. In one case, where the assessee had experienced a high turnover of subordinates, some former employees were interviewed.

Written surveys were mailed to each respondent. For those who did not respond, follow-up calls were made and, when pertinent, a member of the O-MRI team personally requested the respondent to participate. Results were close to 100 percent.

The written surveys were augmented by personal interviews with many of the respondents, who pinpointed specific areas that had to be addressed if the culture change process was to succeed.

QUOTES AND QUIPS

"Listen to the whispers and you won't have to
hear the screams."
Cherokee proverb

Multilevel Retreats

The participants in a multilevel retreat come from a variety of levels within the organization. Who should these people be? Most companies select representatives from middle- and first-line management. Occasionally, informal leaders from the rank and file workers may be included.

The participants should reflect a cross-section of the entire organization and should include both long-term employees, who have intimate knowledge of the company, the department, and their people as well as relatively new employees who may look at the company with fresh views and can contribute their experiences with other organizations where they had been employed.

Why bring this group together? In order for a culture change to take place, all levels must be involved. Senior managers have a broader outlook on company matters, so their input can provide important information. However, depending only on senior executives can be short-sighted. They often do not observe significant facets or are themselves the causes of the problems.

Lower-level personnel see things in a different light and can be valuable contributors. Also, by including them in the O-MRI, they are assured that the organization is serious about changing its culture and is going about it in a smart and respectful way. This is reinforced when serious consideration is involved in designing the strategy for change.

The meeting will be coordinated by the consultant. It will start with a discussion led by the CEO or another senior executive outlining the reason for the importance of change. Opportunity should be given to participants to ask questions to clarify the information. However, discussion of the items should be deferred until after the senior manager leaves. As indicated earlier, the presence of a high-ranking executive during discussions often inhibits free expressions of thought.

TACTICAL TIPS

In order to achieve a full, frank, and open discussion among lower echelon staff members, their bosses should not be present at the meeting and they should be assured that their comments will be kept confidential.

Report of Findings

The O-MRI for Excelsior Paper identified a number of areas that were causing problems. The two most serious centered on (1) the authoritarian style of management (not surprisingly, most of the offenders assumed that such behavior was "normal") and (2) the failure of management to effectively communicate with their staff. In addition, there were a variety of lesser areas that required revised thinking before specific steps to correct them could be taken.

The O-MRI team discussed the results of these findings and, together with the consultants, wrote a detailed report to the CEO. This included recommendations for the next step: determining what changes in the culture should be made and designing the strategies to institute them.

THE O-MRI REVIEW AND REMINDER SHEET

The following is intended to help remind you of the various important elements involved in each step of your O-MRI study. Use it as a prompt to help plan your study and to assure that each step in your O-MRI process is completed properly and on time.

STEP ONE: *Securing the Full, Unwavering Support of Top Management*

- Who will be responsible for this step in the O-MRI process?
- Who will contact the members of top management?
- Will an appointment be set or a meeting planned to discuss the project? If so, when? Where? At what time?
- Who will prepare the agenda for the meeting?
- Who will conduct the meeting?
- Are any visual aids to be used? If so, who will prepare them?
- Who will assume responsibility for a successful outcome?
- How will we know whether or not management has committed its full, unwavering support?

STEP TWO: *The Announcement*

- Who will be responsible for this step in the O-MRI process?
- How will those within the organization be told about the study? Company bulletin? Staff meeting? Internal memorandum? Other?
- What specific benefits might employees expect to realize from the O-MRI study?
- What specific benefits might the organization at large expect to realize from the O-MRI study?
- How will these expected benefits be communicated?
- What, if any, resistance might you encounter?
- How do you intend to allay the fears and any apprehensions of employees about the study?
- Who will actually make or release the announcement?

STEP THREE: *The Confidential Employee Survey*

- Who will be responsible for this step in the O-MRI process?
- Who or what organization will design the survey form?
- Are any approvals necessary before the form is printed and distributed to employees?
- How will the survey forms be sent to employees? By mail to each person's home? Via the interoffice mail? Some other way?
- Will a return envelope and postage be provided?
- Will a cover letter to the respondent accompany the survey form?
- How will assurances of confidentiality be communicated to employees?
- How will we assure confidentiality?
- Will an independent, third-party agency be used to calculate results and prepare the reports for management? If so, which one?
- Is there a date by which all responses must be received?
- What is the budget for this step in the O-MRI process?
- How will the results of the survey be communicated to employees?
- Does the company expect to comment on the results of the study? If so, how will this be accomplished?
- How will the report to management be structured/organized?
- Will recommendations for improvement and/or follow-up action be included in the report?

STEP FOUR: *The Focus Groups*

- Who will be responsible for this step in the O-MRI process?
- How will those participating in focus groups be selected? By a random selection process? By some other way?
- Who will comprise each focus group? Employees, vendors, customers, others?
- Who will conduct/facilitate each meeting? Will an outside agency and/or facilitator be used?
- What will be the focus of each meeting?
- Will a formal agenda be prepared? If so, who will prepare it?

- How long will each meeting be?
- Are refreshments of any type to be provided?
- Who will be responsible for accumulating and organizing the data?
- Will the meeting be recorded or videotaped? If so, who will be responsible?
- Who will observe the meeting while it's in progress? (e.g., members of management, consultants.)
- How many participants and observers will be invited to each meeting?
- What is the budget for this step in the O-MRI process?
- What will the facilitator do to put the participants at ease and stimulate a free flow of conversation?

STEP FIVE: *The Confidential Interviews with the Leaders of the Informal Organization*

- Who will be responsible for this step in the O-MRI process?
- How will you determine who comprises the leadership of the informal organization?
- What percentage of this group will you interview? All of them? A random sample?
- How will you assure the confidentiality of whatever is learned from each person?
- How will you encourage candor?
- Who will conduct each interview?
- Where will the interviews be conducted? (Somewhere offsite is often best.)
- Who will be responsible for gathering the data generated by this step in the O-MRI?
- What is the budget for this step in the process?
- How will you notify the people invited to participate?
- How will you protect the identity of those providing sensitive or potentially troublesome insights and information?
- Will an agenda for each interview be used? If so, who will design it?
- Will the interviews be recorded? If so, how will this be explained to each participant? How will any resistance to this be overcome?

STEP SIX: *The 360-Degree Assessments*

- Who will be responsible for this step in the O-MRI process?
- How will you determine who should participate in the 360-degree study? Which levels of employees? Who from outside the organization (suppliers, customers, etc.)?
- Who will design the strategy for the 360-degree assessments? The instruments and/or questionnaires? The interview formats?
- During what period of time will this step in the process be conducted and completed?
- Who or what group of people will conduct each portion of the study?
- Who will be responsible for organizing and assembling the data?
- Who will be responsible for preparing the report(s)?
- Who will interpret the results?
- What is the budget for this step in the O-MRI process?
- What follow-up action is expected once the reports are prepared and analyzed?
- Who or what group(s) will be privy to the results?

STEP SEVEN: *The Multilevel Retreat*

- Who will be responsible for this step in the O-MRI process?
- Who will be invited to participate in the retreat?
- Where will the retreat be held?
- Will participants be asked to prepare anything in advance of the meeting(s)? If so, what?
- Will any social or recreational activities be included? If so, who will be responsible for organizing these events?
- Will a formal agenda be used?
- Who will actually conduct each meeting and/or facilitate each discussion during the retreat?
- Will some meetings involve only distinct levels of the organization? If so, which ones?
- How many joint meetings (i.e., meetings involving those from multiple levels of the organization) will be organized?
- How will participants be notified of their invitation to the retreat?

- Are any travel arrangements required? If so, who will be responsible?
- How will the meeting conductor encourage candor and stimulate an open dialogue among the participants?
- Who will be responsible for gathering and organizing the data and other information acquired during the retreat?
- Will a summary of the meeting(s) be provided? If so, to whom?
- How are people expected to dress during each meeting? (Business casual seems best in most cases.) How will this be communicated?

STEP EIGHT: *The Preparation of the Final Reports and Recommendations*

- Who will be responsible for this step in your O-MRI process?
- Who will actually do the work preparing the report?
- How will the report be structured?
- How many copies will exist?
- Who or what group will determine the recommendations to be made and included in the report?
- To whom or what group of people will the report be submitted?
- Are there any deadlines to be met?
- How will the confidentiality of certain information and the identities of those participating in all steps of the study be assured in the report?
- Will a meeting be scheduled to discuss the details of the findings? If so, who or what group of people will be responsible for making the necessary arrangements? Who will be invited to attend?
- Who will conduct this meeting?
- What results are expected from this meeting?
- What follow-up or future actions do you expect after the meeting and in an effort to maximize your benefits from your O-MRI study?

Points to Ponder

1. What do you believe are the key advantages of the O-MRI system?

   _____

   _____

   _____

   _____

2. What disadvantages or risks, if any, does conducting an O-MRI incur?

   _____

   _____

   _____

   _____

3. Has your organization ever conducted a confidential employee attitude survey? _____ If so, what was learned and how was it used to benefit the organization?

   _____

   _____

   _____

   _____

4. Has your organization ever conducted 360-degree assessments of key personnel? _____ If so, what were the results and advantages of the process? What was done to follow up on the results?

   _____

   _____

   _____

   _____

5. Have you ever participated in an organizational retreat? _____ If so, describe how this benefited the organization.

   _____

   _____

   _____

   _____

Describe any disappointments that you or your colleagues felt about the retreat and its aftermath. _____

_____

_____

_____

_____

6. In your own experience, what have you found to be the most and least effective approaches for managers to obtain truthful information about the organization's culture?
Most effective: _____

_____

_____

Least effective: _____

_____

_____

SUM AND SUBSTANCE

- Before an organizational culture can be changed, it must be analyzed and assessed. It's necessary to understand the current culture and determine what problems exist and how seriously they affect productivity, quality of product or service, morale of the workers and the overall efficacy of the organization.
- Perception is reality in the mind of the perceiver.
- The first step in changing an organization's culture is to identify the perception of the employees about their company's culture.
- Hard data—sales volume, market share, costs, profits, return on investment—serve an important purpose, but by themselves do not identify many of the subtle problems that plague an organization. To obtain a realistic evaluation we must delve deeper. The O-MRI provides the tool to accomplish this.
- For the O-MRI to be most effective, all levels of the organization from top managers to rank-and-file workers must become involved.

- The six best techniques of obtaining data for the O-MRI are:

  1. Meet with managers and employees away from the company environment.
  2. Create focus groups.
  3. Use confidential employee surveys.
  4. Interview employees at all levels.
  5. Conduct 360-degree assessments of key managers.
  6. Hold multilevel retreats.

- The culture change program should be carefully prepared. By following the O-MRI Review and Reminder Sheet, you will assure that all aspects of the preparation are covered.

REFERENCES

[1] *Newsday,* Long Island, New York, March 12, 1996.
[2] Vinson, Mary N., "The Pros and Cons of 360-Degree Feedback: Making It Work," *Training & Development,* April 1996, pp. 11–12.

CHAPTER 3

The Exponential Effect

The need to replace complacency with a desire to continually improve goes back to the early days of the modern management era. This idea has been accelerated by the Total Quality Management (TQM) movement, in which the theme of commitment to continuous improvement has dominated management thinking.

WHY CONTINUOUS IMPROVEMENT IS NOT ENOUGH

The fact is that most changes within an organization are made incrementally. People believe that it's easier and safer to move one step at a time toward better quality, higher productivity, or increased sales. And there's no question that this approach has worked. However, things are moving much more rapidly today as we enter the 21st century. We are in an age of constantly changing technological processes, innovative marketing, and management programs. Our society is dominated by the reinventing of business, government, and societal cultures. We must ask ourselves if, in this environment, incremental transformation is enough.

TACTICAL TIPS

By creating the proper climate, the right incentives and attitudes augmented by a compatible set of processes, most people—and through them, most organizations—can dramatically accelerate the rate at which change, growth, and improvement is accomplished.

THE EXPONENTIAL EFFECT

In my experience and observations during the 1980s and 1990s, the organizations that have done more than just survive through the peaks and valleys of a constantly changing economy have been those that did more than aim for slow and steady improvement. By taking dramatic, innovative jumps instead of one-step-at-a-time progressions, they have leaped to the forefront of their industries. I call this phenomenon the *Exponential Effect*.

Contrasted with the traditional incremental evolutionary practice exemplified by the notion of continuous improvement, the Exponential Effect is based on the concept that individual and organizational performance is largely a *function of expectation*. By creating the proper climate, the right incentives and attitudes augmented by a compatible set of processes, most people—and through them, most organizations—can dramatically accelerate the rate at which change, growth, and improvement is accomplished.

PERFORMANCE IS A FUNCTION OF EXPECTATION

Most of us function at a level consistent with our perception of what is normal. We establish a pace, a rhythm, and a routine that fits into this perception. We become comfortable with this routine and inasmuch as this often is the same routine followed by the people with whom we interact, we assume it is "the right way" to behave.

Our perceptions of this norm, and indeed of what is *normal,* are developed over time—partly by our own intuitive sense of the world and partly by the information and feedback we get from others. First as children and later as adults, when we do something that deviates from this norm, it is considered *abnormal* and is frowned upon by others. We are told about it, sometimes chastised, and are admonished to follow accepted behavior patterns. It is clear to us that we had better change the way we are behaving. Conformance is encouraged and valued. Nonconformance is discouraged and often punished.

We see this often in the classroom. Teachers tend to favor students who follow instructions, regurgitate what they have read and heard in class, and behave predictably. Students with original ideas, who dare to question the conventional wisdom and approach assignments innovatively are too often looked upon as troublemakers.

This attitude is often repeated in the workplace. The worker who follows orders, agrees with the boss, and does routine work is rewarded. The gadfly who may have innovative approaches is considered to be a poor team player, is stifled, and perhaps, not considered for promotion.

From this conditioning process, a mindset evolves that is dominated by the idea that to do well in this world, one is wise to model his or her behavior and thinking patterns on the thinking patterns of the majority of the group. The safe course is to concentrate on the traditional, the accepted and to be fearful of the new, the unproved, the untried, the innovative.

QUOTES AND QUIPS

"Problems are only opportunities in work clothes."
Henry J. Kaiser, 1882–1967
American industrialist

This results in a withering of the creative abilities with which we are born. We limit our thought processes to patterned routine ways. These paradigms become the basis upon which all our thinking emanates. We are comfortable with them; our friends and colleagues approve, and indeed, follow the same paradigms in their lives. To deviate makes us appear different and unaccepted.

To be competitive and to insulate against the potentially devastating effects of not innovating and not improving fast enough, organizations that operate in competitive environments must move beyond the concept of continuous improvement and adopt a more aggressive strategy that restructures old paradigms and leads to much higher levels of innovation and risk taking, which in turn, results in exponential advances for the organization.

QUANTUM LEAPERS

The Exponential Effect mandates that continuous improvement be replaced with what has been called a *quantum leap*—sometimes called a *mega-leap*. Instead of the evolutionary change of moving from Point A to Point B, giant steps are taken that jump over two or more generations of progress. In simple terms, it means jumping from Point A to Point D.

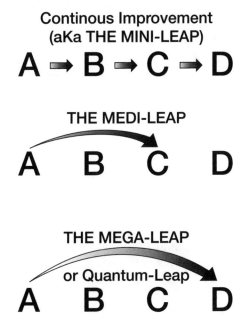

Figure 3-1. *Creating organizational breakthroughs.*

A good example of a Quantum Leaper is Syntel, an electronics manufacturer. Probably the most significant technological innovation in the computer field in recent years was the introduction of the silicon chip, that smaller-than-a-dime-sized wafer on which tremendous quantities of information are stored.

The early chips could store 4Ks of memory. Gradually this was increased to 8K, and then 16K. While the typical producers were aiming to increase that to 64K, Syntel jumped way ahead of the entire industry by working toward and producing a chip with a whopping 256K of memory. Even though their competitors quickly came up with a competitive chip, Syntel realized an immediate profit of more than $130 million and developed a new long-term customer base.

What Syntel did was take a "quantum leap." Instead of moving from Point A to Point B (16K to 64K), Syntel found a way to go far beyond the expected. They jumped directly to Point D.

But quantum leaping is not always possible. There are times when it's necessary to move more slowly at first. It may be more expedient at times to take what I call *medi-leaps* (jumping from A to C) or even be restricted to what I call the traditional *mini-leap* (moving from A to B). Exponential-thinking organizations recognize that although conditions may circumscribe how far one may jump, every effort should be made to make those mega-leaps. Only when a mega-leap is not feasible should medi-leaps or, as a last resort, mini-leaps be considered.

TACTICAL TIPS

Mini-Leaps, Medi-Leaps & Mega-Leaps

A Mini-Leap is consistent with the notion of continuous improvement. It means moving from Point A to Point B.

A Medi-Leap is more ambitious. It means skipping one iteration of progress. Moving directly from Point A to Point C.

A Mega-Leap or Quantum-Leap is the most ambitious of all. It means skipping two iterations of progress or improvement. Moving from Point A to Point D.

THE SEVEN ATTRIBUTES OF QUANTUM LEAPERS

In my work I have had the opportunity to observe hundreds of organizations in a variety of industries. Those that have demonstrated the greatest achievements in growth, market share, and profits have demonstrated quantum leaps in one form or another. From top management down the line, The Exponential Effect was realized. I have identified seven characteristics that these firms share.

1. They Institute a Climate of Innovation.

Quantum leap companies encourage employees at all levels to speak up about any and all matters concerning the organization—even in aspects outside of the areas in which they work. Sure, they may receive unworkable suggestions, but any idea is treated with respect and appreciation is expressed.

When one of my colleagues made the mistake of asking the CEO of one such company why so much time was wasted reading and discussing what appeared to her to be unproductive concepts, the CEO responded that no idea is unproductive. He added that some good suggestions often emanate from these discussions, and encouraging such suggestions also develops the feeling in all of the participants that they should observe what's going on around them and not be afraid to speak up.

The administrator of a hospital told me that some of the best ideas she has received came from nonprofessionals who saw things from a different viewpoint than the medical staff. They contributed ideas ranging from methods of making patients more comfortable to redesigning an operating room fixture that made it possible for surgeons to facilitate certain procedures.

Ye Olde Suggestion Box

To develop this innovative atmosphere, these organizations have used both formal and informal approaches. The most commonly used formal approach, the suggestion box may appear to be "old hat" because it has been used by companies for decades. Many of these programs have had poor results and the idea has been derided by some business people.

If the suggestion box program, however, is taken seriously by management, publicized adequately, and if suggestions are carefully considered with rapid feedback to the suggester, the programs not only succeed, but add to the culture of innovation. A few years ago, I revamped an archaic suggestion box program for a hosiery plant in Pennsylvania. In the year following this restructuring of the program, the number of suggestions contributed quadrupled and the number of suggestions accepted doubled over the average of the preceding three years.

QUOTES AND QUIPS

"Make suggestion systems more exciting by:
- running periodic special award contests
- conducting a lottery. (All persons who make suggestions participate in a drawing for a big prize)
- having a monthly or quarterly luncheon for all winners
- sending award winners' photos to local newspapers."

Arthur R. Pell
Consultant and author
The Complete Idiot's Guide to
Managing People

The I-Meeting

"I-Meetings" are another form of program that generates ideas and cultivates creativity. The "I" stands for *ideas*. Several days before the meeting, participants are told the subject that will be discussed and are required to bring to the meeting at least one idea related to it. At the meeting, ideas are expressed and explored. One of my clients, a specialized publishing house, has come up with some highly creative solutions to some of their problems through these meetings.

The CEO augments the excitement generated in these meetings by giving crisp ten-dollar bills to participants who bring up something he considers particularly innovative. Occasionally, when he feels the idea has merit, but needs more thought, he will tear the bill in half, give one half to the suggester with the promise he will get the other half after it has been more fully developed.

The Brainstorming Meeting

Many Quantum Leapers conduct brainstorming sessions to generate ideas. These freewheeling exercises encourage participants to express any and all ideas that pop into their heads on the subject under discussion without concern as to their validity or even whether or not they make sense.

The psychological principle on which brainstorming is based is called "triggering." Any idea, no matter how ridiculous it may sound, may trigger in the mind of another participant an idea that does have relevance. Possible solutions to a problem may be buried deep in one's subconscious. The triggering mechanism brings it to the surface.

Although formal idea-creating programs have value, probably the most effective way to set the stage for innovative thinking is to establish a climate in which creativity is considered an integral part of the company's culture. All of the companies I have identified as Quantum Leapers encourage people to informally bring up ideas, critiques, or general comments on any and all areas of their work. Not only are employees free to speak to their supervisor or other managers about production, quality, and new concepts, but many managers make it a point to ask workers their opinions.

Kevin O'Leary is one of these managers. He is an advocate of MBWA, Management by Walking Around. Unlike some executives who casually stroll through the plant, make observations, and chat with employees about their families or other matters, Kevin carefully plans his walks. He selects one large department or two smaller sections at a time for the visit. Before leaving his office, he reviews what that group is working on, any problems they are facing, and other pertinent data.

Not long ago I accompanied Kevin on one of his visits. He stopped at one workplace and asked the operator about some new soldering flux they had started to use. He wanted to know how it compared to the formerly used flux, what problems, if any, were encountered, and what ideas he had concerning the operation. He stopped at a work bench where several women were assembling units. He asked pointed questions about how the job was going and listened to and wrote down some of their comments.

When we returned to his office, Kevin told me that these periodic visits gave him real insight into what was actually transpiring on the factory floor. More often than not he came away with helpful ideas. More important, he commented, the employees know I listen to them and take what they say seriously.

QUOTES AND QUIPS

"Progress is a nice word. But change is its motivator and change has its enemies."
Robert F. Kennedy, 1925–1968
U.S. Senator

2. They Benchmark.

"If we didn't invent it here, it can't be any good." "My company is different; what works for others won't work here." I'm sure you've heard these comments over and over again. But you won't hear them from Quantum Leapers. They are the first to admit that they do not have all the answers and are anxious to learn what other companies are doing. Commonly referred to as *benchmarking,* this process involves seeking out ideas from other organizations who have faced and solved similar problems.

One of the requirements for entry into the competition for the prestigious Malcolm Baldrige National Quality Awards is that participants must share what they have done to improve quality of their product or service with others. Xerox Corporation, a Baldrige winner, has assigned a vice president to head its National Quality Award Office and willingly shares its know-how with hundreds of companies on a regular basis.

Many trade associations encourage sharing of ideas among their members. For example, Donna Tellasole is the operations manager for a distributor of ladies shoes. When she attends the monthly meetings of her industry's association, she makes a point to sit at a table with people she does not already know. Often from the table discussion before the formal meeting she has learned as much or more than from the speakers. More important, she has made new friends whom she can contact when faced with situations where their expertise and experience can be helpful. This networking has played a major role in Donna's success in her job.

QUOTES AND QUIPS

"Only one thing will train the human mind and that is the voluntary use of the mind by the person. You may aid, guide, suggest, and above all else, you may inspire him or her, but the only thing worth having is that which the person gets by his or her own exertions, and what is attained is in direct proportion to what is put into it."
A. Lawrence Lowell, 1856–1943
Former president,
Harvard University

Benchmarking is not limited to one's own industry. Quantum Leapers know that they can learn from any and all types of businesses. The Connecticut Limousine Group provides ground transportation to and from terminals located throughout Connecticut to the three major airports: LaGuardia, Kennedy, and Newark.

Like many transport services, they received countless calls and letters from customers complaining that when they telephoned for reservations, they had very long waits before the phone was answered. Then, each time they called, they had to answer a number of questions including their name, address, phone number, and destination. Not only did customers become impatient, but market surveys showed that busy business people, their major market, often preferred to get a lift from friends or colleagues rather than use the service.

Connecticut Limo's management contacted other airport transporters in various cities and found that they had the same problem. One of their executives commented that he had a similar situation with L. L. Bean, the outdoors equipment and clothing mail order firm. He said that formerly, when he placed an order, he often waited through nine or ten rings before the phone was answered and then had to give the sales clerk his name, address, phone, sizes, etc., despite the fact that he ordered merchandise several times a year.

No more, however. Now, he reported, the phone is answered on the first or second ring and all he has to do is provide his phone number, which enables the clerk to obtain all the basic information required from a computer terminal. Then all that is needed is to indicate what he wants to order at that time. The order is completed in a fraction of the time it previously had taken.

Connecticut Limo arranged for their marketing and computer managers to visit L. L. Bean, who willingly explained the system and referred them to the computer consultant who set up the system. Within a few months, Connecticut Limo installed a similar program, reducing average waiting and processing time to less than two minutes per call.

3. They Foster an Entrepreneurial Spirit.

As we know, all too often, as companies grow, they tend to become bureaucratic. More effort and energy is expended in following procedures than in accomplishing goals.

QUOTES AND QUIPS

"The old adage 'two heads are better than one' tells only part of the story. Tapping the brain power of every head in the group multiplies the results geometrically."
James K. Schwab
President, Manchester, Inc.

A few years ago, I had the opportunity to observe a specialty store chain's program to develop more employee commitment. One of the company's complaints was that the company had instituted a campaign to increase the number of store charge cards. Incentive awards were offered to sales associates who opened new accounts. Although many new accounts were opened, the program fell far short of what had been expected. The company blamed it on the lack of enthusiasm of its people and pointed out that this was only one manifestation of employee attitude.

To prepare for the program, my colleagues and I visited several stores and spoke to managers, sales associates, customer service representatives, and administrative staff. Sally, the manager of one of their outlets in a small town in Nebraska, summed up the problem:

"We're a small operation in a small town. Yet, I have to follow rules, regulations, and procedures that may be fine in Chicago or Kansas City, but just bog me down here. We tried to push the charge card program, but in order for a customer's credit to be approved, she had to fill out a long form, which was sent to the home office for processing. It took one to two weeks for approval. Many of my regular customers saw no point in going through all that red tape, and preferred to use their bank credit cards.

"This is a small community," she continued. "We know most of our customers and we also know that they come here rather than shopping at a discount or department store because we give them personal service. We have to be able to react rapidly to changing circumstances and must often make decisions without having to follow corporate red tape.

"Last month another shoe store in this mall ran a special sale on sports shoes. In order for me to meet their price, I had to get an OK from the home office. It took two days before the permission was given. I don't know how much business I lost, but I should have the authority to make those decisions on the spot. Sure, we may make some mistakes, but in the long run we'd get better results. That feeling of trust and responsibility would truly make us more committed."

Sally has the entrepreneurial spirit and she is willing to make decisions and take responsibility for them. True, delegating decision making is not always feasible, but where it can be done within established guidelines, if necessary, not only will an organization get more cooperation and commitment from its people, but it will encourage and stimulate innovation.

Entrepreneuring is not limited to small, independent-type environments. Many large organizations have encouraged internal entrepreneuring, sometimes called "intrapreneuring."

According to Gifford Pinchot III, who coined the term, an "intrapreneur" is a person "who take hands-on responsibility for creating innovation of any kind within an organization. The intrapreneur may be the creator or inventor but is always the dreamer who figures out how to turn an idea into a profitable reality."[1]

The Lockheed Company was a pioneer in the concept of intrapreneuring. When faced with a deadline to develop a prototype aircraft for the Department of Defense, a group of engineers at Lockheed complained to management that if they had to follow the usual company procedures, in which every move, every purchase, every plan must be approved by layers of management, they would not meet the deadline. Even more importantly, they would probably not come up with any innovative ideas. They suggested that an independent group be set up to pursue whatever it took to design the plane. This group would work in its own facility and be allotted a budget they could use as they saw fit.

Lockheed agreed and they went to work in an old warehouse next to a garbage dump. Because of the smells emanating from the dump, they called their facility, "the skunk works." Left alone to use their creative powers, they came up with a prototype of a top-secret plane that won a lucrative contract for Lockheed. The term, *skunk works* has been affectionately copied by other organizations, which have adopted this technique.

TACTICAL TIPS

"If it ain't broke, don't fix it." Wrong! Today's world is tough and competitive. You no longer can wait for things to break before fixing them. If you don't come up with better ideas—better ways to do things—your competitors will overwhelm you. Look at everything you are doing with constructive discontent. Keep asking yourself—and encourage other people to ask themselves—"Is there a better way?"

3M, the manufacturer of Scotch tape and many other products, has encouraged intrapreneuring long before that term was ever conceived. William McKnight, the long-term CEO of 3M promulgated this concept from the earliest days of the company's existence. His admonitions to his people are still quoted in the company:

- Listen to anyone with an original idea, no matter how absurd it might sound at first.
- Encourage; don't nitpick. Let people run with an idea.
- Hire good people and leave them alone.
- If you put fences around people, you get sheep. Give people the room they need.
- Encourage experimental doodling.
- Give it a try—and quick.[2]

4. They're Willing to Take Risks.

The turtle is safe from most harm if it stays inside its shell. If it wants to move, it has to stick its head out, opening it up to attack. The exponential company doesn't stay inside the safe shell of complacency. It's willing to take risks to move ahead. All successful companies have taken risks to get started and to climb the ladder of success, but often, once they reach a certain level, they become gun-shy and avoid new and daring challenges.

MCI took a giant risk when it chose to take on AT&T, the largest and most powerful company in the communications industry. By taking risks in new technologies, creative marketing concepts, such as the Friends and Family Program, it made a major mark in this growing market.

Dov Seidman is another example of a Quantum Leaper. *The Wall Street Journal* reported that Seidman, a 30-year-old Harvard Law School graduate gave up a high-salaried position in a prestigious law firm, and borrowed money from relatives and friends to pursue an idea. One of the most expensive costs of litigation is the research involved. Typically, law firms assign junior associates who toil repetitively on this research and develop memoranda for the senior partners. Clients are billed for this on the number of hours it takes. By some estimates, this accounts for as much as 20 percent of legal costs.

Seidman determined that this research could be done more efficiently. By assembling a network of specialized attorneys who are experts in various fields and therefore have experience in researching appropriate cases, the research can be done in much less time and with greater accuracy.

At the time of this writing, 250 lawyers have agreed to work for the network on a when-needed basis. They include partners on maternity leave, lawyers between jobs, law professors, and retired judges and attorneys. Seidman chose to pay his researchers more than the hourly rate most law firms pay, but because of their extensive knowledge in various fields, the time involved is usually much shorter. Although only in business for a short time, he has already acquired major insurance companies, large industrial firms, and even some law firms as clients.

Risk taking is not limited to entrepreneurs. It must be part of the corporate culture of all Quantum Leapers. Employees are usually reluctant to take risks. After all, the punishment for failure can be severe; yet, risk taking must be built into most situations if any progress is to be made.

When innovation is encouraged, it must be expected that mistakes will be made, and the organization must be ready to accept them as a calculated risk. An example of this occurred when Linda L. was assigned her first major project in her new managerial position. She worked very hard to assure that it would be successful. Despite all of her research and preparation, however, she made a major miscalculation that cost the company $100,000. When the situation stabilized, she was called into the boss's office. Linda was sure she was going to be fired. Instead, the boss said: "Linda, here is your next assignment." She was flabbergasted. "I thought you were going to fire me." "Fire you," he responded, "I just spent $100,000 training you."

5. They Anticipate Trends.

The computer industry is loaded with examples of people who, by anticipating trends, made quantum leaps in technology and marketing. Steve Jobs anticipated the demand for personal computers with the Apple Computer and later the Macintosh. Bill Gates saw the trend toward packaged software. The founders of Amazon.com revolutionized the book-selling business.

Such people are often called "trend setters." In most cases, the trend has already been started by market factors, and the Quantum Leaper identifies it early on, recognizes its potential, and takes action.

Although Ray Kroc, the founder of McDonalds, did not invent the fast food business, he identified the need for clean, rapid, inexpensive food service in a society where people were busy and in a rush. He saw the trend and fulfilled the need.

Trends, of course, change. The true trend anticipator has to know when a trend has ended and a new one has begun. The toy industry is an example of how trends can make or break a company. Anticipating what toys will sell is always a big risk. Producing the toy that will be the next Hula Hoop, Beanie Baby, Furbie, or Nintendo of the year can make a fortune for the manufacturer.

It is even more complex, though, to determine when the trend will end. Many toy companies have suffered major losses and have even faced bankruptcy when stuck with large inventories when the toy-of-the-year suddenly became the toy-that-was.

As reported in *Fortune*,[3] Kevin Clark is a man who capitalized on trends. Since he founded his company, Cross Country Healthcare, in 1986, he has placed health-care workers in 25,000 jobs. Clark conceived his idea when he read in John Naisbitt's *Megatrends* about two major trends: the move toward temporary employment and the growth of the health-care field as the population aged. Clark decided to combine them. He developed a special database that contains information about 1,500 hospitals and over 110,000 job applicants. Cross Country links nurses, therapists, and other health-care workers with job opportunities anywhere in the country. The business has expanded to over $70 million in its first five years and is now planning for significant expansion.

QUOTES AND QUIPS

"It is not the strongest of the species that survives, nor the most intelligent; it is the one that is most adaptable to change."
Charles Darwin, 1809–1882
English scientist

One doesn't have to be a major player to anticipate trends. After 20 years as office manager and chief accountant for a sales organization, Arlene Kaplan left to set up an office services business, working from her home. Her original intent was to use her expertise to provide small local businesses with computer and bookkeeping facilities. She converted her basement recreation room into an office, purchased a PC and appropriate software, and soon developed a small group of clients.

During the first few years, Arlene identified a trend. More and more men and women, either because of company downsizing or voluntary desire, were leaving traditional jobs and attempting to conduct businesses of their own from home. Often friends and even people she met through business or personal contacts would ask her advice on setting up an office.

With this growing trend, she thought: "Why not become a consultant to home businesses?" By networking through the chamber of commerce and service organizations, Arlene has developed a successful operation. She helps her clients start up home businesses. This involves teaching them to use the space in their homes in a most effective way, purchase and install appropriate equipment, set up filing systems and computer programs, and even develop sales and marketing campaigns.

Arlene has enabled her clients to avoid many of the mistakes and pitfalls new businesses face and helps them get underway rapidly and effectively. She continues to run her own services business, but the consulting activity is expanding and more of her time is now devoted to this new aspect of her work.

6. They're Always Thinking Two or Three Moves Ahead.

Like good chess players, the Exponential Manager plans several steps ahead before making a move. To make a quantum leap, one must be able to anticipate what the effect will be on a variety of factors on the way from A to D.

Rupert Murdoch thinks like a chess champion. When his Fox network outbid CBS for the television rights to National Football League games, everybody in the industry decried it as a foolish move for which he greatly overpaid. However, Murdoch was planning several steps ahead. His real goal soon became apparent. Within a few months, six CBS affiliate stations shifted to Fox, giving the new network major outlets in key cities. He knew that the first move—acquiring the football rights—would lose money for the network, but like a good chess player, he gave up pawns as a step toward winning the game.

Then there's the story of Max Harper. Max ran a successful executive employment service in New York City for several years and was ready to expand. He looked at a variety of ways to do this. He could open branch offices in other locations in the city. That would increase applicant traffic flow and develop new local business—a mini-leap. He thought of franchising his agency in other cities—a midi-leap. Or perhaps an entirely new venture would be feasible.

Like a good chess player, Max strategized his moves. He studied the chess board. He looked upon his assets as his chess pieces and the competition as the opponent's men. His major competitors were opening branches or franchising, making small moves one at a time toward expansion. He could follow the same plan and perhaps make a smart move and win the game or he could find a different route across the board.

Over the years, Max had often heard his clients bemoan their high turnover and their discontent with mediocre employees. He had always felt that a good part of the reason for this was poor interpersonal relations within those organizations. He pondered over this. Would a better path to expansion be the development of training programs to train people in this sensitive area? It meant moving in a different direction from the competition, and taking the risk of sacrificing income from a field in which he already was a factor.

Max made the quantum leap. He offered this new program to his employment service clientele and in a few years his training subsidiary became a significant profit center. By thinking several steps ahead, he avoided becoming just another face in the recruiting industry.

7. They Truly Believe in the Concept of Empowerment.

"Empowerment" is the buzzword of the 1990s. Everybody is talking about it. Business publications devote pages to it. CEOs of many organizations give lip service to this concept, but only a few actually embody it in their operations.

What exactly is "empowerment"? In a general sense, it's the giving of power held by a manager to those being managed. Traditionally, the higher one's position, the more power one has to make decisions concerning work. True empowerment starts with the CEO and filters down to the first-line supervisor, who in turn empowers the rank and file.

One of GM's television commercials for their Saturn cars plays up the empowerment concept at its basic level. A worker tells the audience how happy he is to work at Saturn because management has given him and his coworkers the authority to stop the line at any time they see a quality problem—a decision that in most assembly line operations is reserved to a manager. He proudly points out that one time he actually did stop the line when he saw a defective part. A small thing? Not to this worker. It reinforced his commitment to the job and to the quality standards GM expects of the Saturn.

How does empowerment work? Traditionally, when a supervisor received an assignment, he or she would determine how it should be done and then assign it to workers. In an empowered environment, the supervisor brings the workers together and says: "Here is our project, let's determine how it should be done together."

There are three major advantages to this:

1. **Ideas.** No matter how experienced the supervisor may be, no one person can come up with all possible approaches to a problem. The people who work on the job day by day often have insights into a situation that may have eluded the supervisor.
2. **Synergy.** When people work together in developing a project, an interrelationship develops among them that leads to collaborative efforts to achieve success.
3. **Ownership.** When people participate in determining how a project should be designed, they are committed to its success. "It's our idea, it has to work."

Many managers resist empowering their people. Some fear it will result in losing control of matters for which they are still responsible. Others want power for power's sake. Still others do not fully trust their subordinates to make good decisions. There also are many employees who don't want to be empowered. Some don't want to take responsibility; they just want to be told what to do. Still others feel that they are not paid to make decisions.

These are serious matters that cannot be ignored. True empowerment takes all these problems into consideration. Supervisors and workers are trained in decision making, controls are built into systems, and individual counseling is provided for those at all levels who resist the new approach. In more and more organizations, compensation is adjusted to reflect the accomplishments of empowered teams.

Quantum Leapers trust their people. They back up this trust by giving them the tools and training to make decisions and the power to implement them. Managers at all levels share their ideas with their people and encourage them to share what they think with them. True empowerment goes well beyond pronouncement and memos. It involves action—action by top management, action by middle- and first-line managers, and continuing action by rank-and-file workers— all geared to achieve company goals.

QUANTUM PEEPERS, QUANTUM WEEPERS, QUANTUM SLEEPERS

It takes a special type of management to make a company a quantum leaper. Too often, managers are so bogged down with day-to-day operations that they neither have the time nor the energy to make exponential jumps. Some will fall into the trap of complacency and will be surpassed by more dynamic competitors. Many will just hold their own —surviving but not growing. They somehow missed the boat. I have classified these companies as Quantum Peepers, Quantum Weepers, and Quantum Sleepers.

QUANTUM PEEPERS

Quantum Peepers are companies that, often intentionally, choose to let other organizations innovate and be the first to market exciting new products and advances. They are the companies that specialize in *watching* and learning from the top players in their industry. Then they respond very quickly and effectively when a particular product or service gets hot.

The minor golf club manufacturing companies are a good example of this. Many of them are notorious for watching how new models offered by the major club manufacturers sell. They identify the best sellers and manufacture and market "knock-offs" (i.e., clubs with a look and feel that's remarkably similar to the major, much more expensive brands) quickly and at dramatically lower prices.

It's a strategy that's worked many, many times. In fact, many Quantum Peepers are remarkably successful. By letting others (the industry leaders) research, design, test, develop and introduce new products and services, they avoid most of the risks of failure and most of the upfront developmental costs absorbed by the industry leaders. All they have to do is get good at responding quickly with a competitive offering. They simply watch their competitors, keep their eye on what's hot or getting hot, then rush into the marketplace with products and services that are remarkably similar and often much less expensive.

This practice is common in many industries, notably the fashion field, in which a great number of manufacturers offer "knock-off" designs of the major couturiers almost as soon as they are introduced. A recent addition to the list of companies advocating this practice is the computer industry, which has been deluged with IBM PC clones.

KEY POINT

Quantum Leapers identify the true situation, and not only tolerate, but encourage taking risks to achieve their goals. *Quantum Peepers* watch what other companies do and follow their lead when they succeed.

QUANTUM WEEPERS

Quantum Weepers, on the other hand, are those organizations that (more often than not) are comfortable letting others lead, are often aware of important developments within their industry, but for whatever reason, fail to respond quickly enough and/or well enough at critical moments in their history. Quantum Weepers are organizations in trouble and often in noticeable decline. They're at risk of being left behind by the leaders of their industry.

In many cases, organizations that find themselves defined as Quantum Weepers were once Quantum Leapers or Quantum Peepers. In fact, in many cases, a Leaper or Peeper suddenly becomes a Weeper after some devastating change in the organization—the death of the founder; a series of bad decisions by senior management; some negative, very damaging publicity; the loss of public confidence for some reason; or perhaps the sudden advent of some new, unexpected industry advance or development.

However, there's hope for Weepers. If they identify the problem and take fast action to correct whatever ails the organization, they can often rebound.

Macy's, the world's most famous department store, is an example of a Quantum Weeper. Several years ago, Macy's went into a slow decline that gradually accelerated into a major loss of market share. What happened? Discount clothing chains like Marshall's and T.J. Maxx and appliance chains like Circuit City made major inroads in the customer base on which Macy's had built its business. This forced Macy's into Chapter 11 and the company was eventually acquired by Federated Stores.

Another example of a Quantum Weeper is General Motors. Back in the late 1970s and 1980s Americans, faced with rising gasoline prices, turned to more fuel-efficient foreign cars. For a long time, GM resisted shifting to a smaller and more fuel-efficient car. The results were disastrous. The Japanese car makers invaded the formerly inviolate U.S. market. GM only recouped much of its market share by producing the kinds of cars Americans were buying.

QUANTUM SLEEPERS

While the Quantum Weeper may not be aware of the real problems or initially accept innovative solutions, with good guidance and leadership from others it has a chance to catch up. On the other hand, the Quantum Sleeper is not even conscious of changes that are taking place. In short, they're asleep at the switch.

Quantum Sleepers are consequently the biggest losers of all. They're the organizations that often literally go out of business overnight because of a failure to even sense some massive industry change or a switch in consumer buying habits. Quantum Sleepers don't have a chance to recover. They're caught totally off-guard, asleep at the switch and are, in essence, run over by their competitors.

Every day we read of businesses fading out of the picture that were household words only a few years ago. Western Union was a Quantum Sleeper. Once a major factor in the communications field, today it has declined to a purveyor of money transfers. Royal Typewriters once dominated its industry, but failed to recognize that computers would make their product almost obsolete.

One may ask how anybody in this dynamic world could sleep through the tremendous upheavals that are occurring in our work environment. Yet, it happens all the time. An example of this is the recent experience of a local hardware retailer in Bergen County, New Jersey. This once busy, successful store, had lost a significant share of its market to a major cut-rate hardware and building supply outlet that opened in a nearby town.

The owner of the local hardware store had read in the trade journals and had observed from his own experience how these major chains were taking over the market. He ignored the signs and convinced himself that his store would not be affected because of his long-term relations with the local building contractors, home owners, and others in his community. He boasted: "I can provide them with personal service. I know their needs and their problems. They won't leave me just to save a few cents at the discount store." He made no effort to make any changes to counteract the competition.

Within a few months, his business fell off by 50 percent, and he was forced to go out of business by the end of the year. Of course, he didn't take responsibility for his failure. He blamed it all on the "unfair competition" of the discounter.

Was there anything he could have done to save his business? Compare his experience with that of Robertson Hardware in Baldwin Park, Minnesota. Joe Robertson was the third-generation owner of this 75-year-old store. His grandfather and father had prospered as this suburban area grew and flourished in the 1950s and 1960s and Joe continued its success in the '80s and '90s. Although the boom times were over, business was steady and prosperous.

Joe learned, however, that one of the major hardware discount chains was planning to open an outlet a few miles from Baldwin Park. He realized he had to take some firm steps to counter the potential loss of business that would inevitably occur.

Unlike his counterpart in New Jersey, Joe was not a Quantum Sleeper, he leaped forward. He looked for alternative solutions. The result: He joined a hardware retailers co-op. This enabled him to purchase materials at lower costs and provided him with counsel on inventory control and other cost-saving techniques. It also enabled him to benefit from their national advertising and gave him the license to use their well-known trade name and logo, which he could add to his store's name.

Although Joe could not match dollar-for-dollar the prices of the discount chain, his prices were lower than they had been. In addition, the personal service he could offer his customers not only enabled him to retain most of them, but attracted others who preferred dealing with a local store rather than dealing with the hassle of a giant discounter.

KEY POINT

Quantum Weepers watch what more aggressive companies do, but do nothing or wait too long to take effective action.

Quantum Sleepers either don't see how innovation has changed their world or, even if they do see it, they are reluctant to take the necessary risks to make needed changes. In short, they do nothing.

Entire industries have become Quantum Sleepers. They either do not see how innovation has changed the world or are reluctant to take the necessary risks to make the needed changes. The three major television networks have dominated the airwaves since the introduction of television. When the cable phenomenon came into the picture, the networks looked upon it as a minor nuisance—not as a threat to their standing. It wasn't until CNN became a major factor in TV news and MTV captured the youth market that they woke up to the threat and made moves to develop their own cable outlets. They were Quantum Sleepers.

QUOTES AND QUIPS

"I am only one; but still I am one. I cannot do everything, but still I can do something. I will not refuse to do the something I can do."
Helen Keller, 1880–1968
American author and educator

INDIVIDUAL PATTERNS OF BEHAVIOR

It is important to recognize that most organizations are staffed by people with varying perspectives. In many organizations, a strong CEO may lead the organization into exponential changes. However, there are many organizations in which the CEO's concepts and ideology are nullified by staff members whose approach to work is so different that their action or lack of action can defeat the CEO's endeavors. In still other organizations, the CEO may not be the prime mover. Whoever fuels the change, whether it be the CEO or another person, he or she most likely exhibits the characteristics of one of the following behavioral types:

Quantum Heroes

True leaders are more than just people able to persuade others to follow them. They are men and women who bring out the best in their followers. I like to call the best of them Quantum Heroes. History has countless examples of evil people who were able to manipulate large numbers of people to do evil things. They were "leaders" in the Machiavellian sense, but in the long run their accomplishments were outweighed by the consequences of their acts.

True leaders are *heroes*. They have value systems that are well thought out, communicated well to others with whom they work or interrelate, and to which they adhere even when it may not be the expedient thing to do. They are not only creative people, but bring out the creativity of their subordinates. They are inspirers—not only by the words they write or say, but by the example they set. They have high standards for themselves and expect high standards from others. They learn from their own mistakes and failures and when others make mistakes, they do not condemn them, but help them learn from the experience.

Let's look at what makes a real hero. Yes, he or she must be intelligent, creative, persuasive, and have all of the other obvious traits. But it takes much more than that. The Quantum Hero must demonstrate in his or her behavior what I call the Four Vs: *vision, values, valor, and validity.*

Vision: The Quantum Hero not only knows the as-is situation, but visualizes where the organization should be going and has a clear sense of how it will get there. Recognizing that nobody can accurately anticipate all of the hurdles between concept and accomplishment, this leader prepares his or her staff to face problems and trains them to deal with them.

The Quantum Hero communicates this vision to all those who are involved in accomplishing it in a manner that engenders enthusiastic cooperation and personal commitment. As creativity and imagination are needed to reach goals, the leader establishes a climate in which the visions of all people in the group are tapped and the opportunity to be creative and contribute ideas, innovations, and suggestions is an integral part of the organization's culture.

Values: The integrity of a Quantum Hero is expressed in a set of values that is not just preached but practiced day to day. Customer service and high-quality production is the core of these values and all employees are trained to understand and apply this on the job. Concern for the best interests of all employees, not just the return on investment of the share holders, is a major factor in decision making.

Valor: The Quantum Hero is courageous. He or she is willing to take chances, try new processes and approaches, innovate ideas that may not be guaranteed to work, and persevere when problems arise. The leader's own passion to achieve goals inspires others to be courageous. Employees are not afraid to disagree with their bosses and present their arguments for or against concepts because they know they will get a fair hearing and their dissent will not be held against them.

Validity: The Quantum Hero knows that he or she doesn't know everything. The ideas, opinions, feelings, and concerns of others—employees at all levels, customers, vendors, the public—are sought out and seriously considered. Being a good listener enables the leader to validate actions before they are undertaken. Because participation in decisions are basic to the decision-making process, validity of the decision is most likely assured.

True leaders do not have to be charismatic. Indeed charisma is something possessed by evil as well as good leaders. What makes them heroes is their ability to apply the four Vs. Abraham Lincoln was such a man. He spent hours listening to people from all walks of life—not just "experts" or political insiders, but the countless "common men," as he referred to them, who came to the White House to talk to him.

In America's most trying period, he rallied the union to victory—not as a general on a white horse, brandishing a sword, but as a man of the people who had the vision to save the country, the values to do it with integrity, the valor to stand up for what he believed, and the validation earned over years and years of caring for his constituents.

Not just leaders of countries, but also leaders of industry, have exemplified the characteristics of Quantum Heroes. One such leader is Aaron Feuerstein, CEO of Malden Mills, a Lawrence, Massachusetts, textile firm. When most textile firms left New England to take advantage of non-union, low-paid labor in the South, Feuerstein determined to stay in Lawrence.

"Southern town officials made it clear that we'd be welcome if we didn't bring our liberal Northern ideas with us," he told the *New York Times.* "My grandfather came here from Hungary for political freedom, and I was not about to sell my soul for cheap labor."

To succeed in the highly competitive textile field, Feuerstein chose to concentrate on producing two specialized fabrics used in outdoor wear by upscale clothing manufacturers. Malden Mills holds patents on both the fabrics and the machines used to make them. These items now are sold in 60 countries and his workforce has tripled over the past ten years. His managerial staff share his commitment to providing good jobs to people, who in turn, produce high-quality merchandise.

But that heroic act was only a prelude to what was to be an even more magnanimous gesture. Just before Christmas in 1995, the Malden Mills plant burned to the ground. Rather than close the facility and lay off 3,000 workers, Feuerstein announced that he would keep all employees on the payroll for a month while he started rebuilding the facility. When the month was over, he extended the pay period for a second month—and then a third.

He encouraged his employees to contribute ideas to make the new facility even more effective than the destroyed one. By March most of the employees had returned to full-time work. This not only prevented a major catastrophe for his employees but also for the entire community, which depended on Malden as its major employer.

His decisions cost Feuerstein several million dollars. One of his employees commented: "Another person would have taken the insurance money and walked away, but he was not that type of person."

When Feuerstein was asked by *Parade Magazine,* what set him apart from other CEOs, he responded: "The fundamental difference is that I consider our workers an asset, not an expense. I have a responsibility to the workers, both blue-collar and white-collar. I have an equal responsibility to the community. It would have been unconscionable to put 3,000 people on the streets and deliver a death blow to the cities of Lawrence and Methuen. Maybe on paper our company is worth less on Wall Street, but I can tell you, it's worth more."[4] The heroism of men like Feuerstein provides a role model to guide business leaders as they evaluate their own management thinking.

Quantum Hi-Pos

I call young people with high potential Quantum Hi-Pos. They possess the drive, the attitude, the talent and the commitment to become Quantum Heroes, but lack the necessary experience, seasoning, and maturity. They are the seedlings that must be cultivated by current leadership so they will grow and develop into men and women who will lead the organization in the future.

Identifying these hi-pos is not easy. They could be anywhere in the organization. True, many will come from colleges and graduate schools, having acquired academic credentials, but education by itself is not an adequate criterion. Limiting the search to only MBAs or people with similar education can often be very shortsighted. Hi-pos can be found among the rank and file, team leaders who came up from the ranks and others within the organization who display the characteristics of leadership.

Quantum Hi-Pos demonstrate the four Vs early in their careers. They show they have vision by the goals they have set for themselves and the farsightedness of their ideas. Their values show up in the integrity with which they pursue their work and the manner in which they treat others. Their valor is displayed in the energy and perseverance they put into their work even when it involves personal sacrifice or difference of opinion with the powers-that-be. They validate their performance by their ability to collaborate with others, exceed performance standards, and their commitment to learn, improve, and change when change is needed.

Later in this book we will explore some of the approaches successful companies have used in developing the talents of these high-potential people and thereby ensuring that there will be a built-in reserve of future Quantum Heroes.

QUOTES AND QUIPS

"Change comes about when followers themselves desire it and seek it. Hence the role of the leader is to enlist the participation of others as leaders of the effort. That is the sum and essence not only of leading change, but of good management in general."
James O'Toole[5]
Professor
University of Southern California

Quantum Dodos

Quantum Dodos are people who live in the past, who are happy with the status quo, and hesitate to make any changes that will shake up their comfort zones. They resist efforts to institute any and all changes.

Even when a company may have leaders who are Quantum Heroes, these Quantum Dodos put hurdles in the way of changes that are proposed. They moan, "It'll never work!," "Why tamper with success," "We never did it that way." Unfortunately, in many organizations, these negative people can influence the decisions that are made and forestall needed changes.

Changes are perceived as threats to their jobs. They perpetuate inefficiency and it takes a traumatic experience for them to even accept the need for change. They are not bad enough to fire, but not good enough for optimum performance.

Often these are people who should never have been placed in the jobs they now have. Jerry T. is a good example of how dodos get where they are. Jerry was hired by a bank as a messenger and he performed his job adequately, running errands, getting coffee for the bosses, and doing other simple jobs. After a few years on the job, he was promoted to mail clerk.

Because Jerry was a "nice guy" and had a three-year record in his messenger job of no absences or latenesses, the manager felt he had earned the promotion. However, the new job required quite different skills, and Jerry was slow in learning them. Even after several months on the job, he misdirected letters, made occasional blunders, and caused delays in other people's work. His manager felt he would overcome this, but Jerry just didn't have the basic aptitude for the work.

Like many other "Jerrys" he was tolerated and became another of the many dodos that bog down organizations. With proper training, their performance may be improved, but it is unlikely they will ever become top producers.

Quantum Dodos are not found only in lower-level jobs. Often people in important positions demonstrate the same traits. One may wonder how a dodo could even reach a high position. Here are two examples:

Rhoda K. was always a dodo, but she was the big boss' favorite niece. A sweet and pleasant young woman, Rhoda was liked by everybody, but she just didn't have what it takes to be a business success. Her supervisor spent hours teaching her job fundamentals and once she did learn them, she was barely able to keep up with the pace required. When it became apparent that the department was being pulled down by her work, she was transferred to another department—and, of course, similar problems arose.

Bill B. was not always a Quantum Dodo. Early in his career he had been a go-go, and rapidly moved up the corporate ladder. But as Dr. Lawrence Peter pointed out years ago, there comes a time when a person may be promoted to a position above his or her level of competency. Bill met the "Peter Principle" when he was promoted from managing a department, where his technical knowledge was key to its success, to a higher position in which administrative and interpersonal skills were more important.

Bill did not feel comfortable in this area. Rather than risk making mistakes, he concentrated his efforts on the technical aspects of the job and procrastinated on making decisions in the administrative areas. This slowed down the entire department. Fortunately, his manager recognized this and, together with Bill, drew up a program to train him in the areas in which he was weak. If this had not succeeded, the best course of action would be to return Bill to a technical-type assignment. Keeping Quantum Dodos in positions in which they cannot effectively function is neither fair to the organization nor to the person involved.

Quantum Dodos are often fixated on costs. They are the type of manager who always gives the order to the lowest bidder—with little consideration of quality or innovation. Yes, it is important to consider the costs involved in making decisions, but other factors may be equally or more important in the long run.

For example, the purchasing agent of a direct mail firm chose not to buy a new paper folding machine because it was much more expensive than the model they were now using. Some months later his boss learned that he was losing customers to another direct mail house, which had purchased the new machine. Due to its increased speed, quality, and productivity, it enabled the competitor to do a better job at lower cost.

Unfortunately, too many firms are held back by the dodos in their ranks. In order for the organizational culture to be changed, Quantum Dodos must be weeded out or placed in positions that will not impede the transformation.

SUM AND SUBSTANCE

- To make real progress in changing an organizational culture, commitment to continuous improvement is not enough.

- Companies that have taken dramatic, innovative jumps instead of progressing one step at a time have leaped to the forefront of their industries. I call this *the exponential effect.*
- Performance is a function of expectation.
- The exponential effect mandates that the concept of continuous improvement be replaced by the Quantum Leap, moving directly from Point A to Point D instead of from Point A to B to C to D.
- The seven attributes of Quantum Leapers are:

  1. The organization provides a climate in which innovation is nurtured.
  2. They benchmark, researching and applying ideas that have been successful in other organizations.
  3. They foster an entrepreneurial spirit. Entrepreneurship or intrepreneurship is inculcated as part of the corporate culture.
  4. They are willing to take risks.
  5. They anticipate trends and are prepared to act on them.
  6. They are always thinking two or three moves ahead.
  7. They truly believe in the concept of empowerment.

- Organizations may follow one of these patterns:

  1. *Quantum Leapers* identify the true situation and not only tolerate but encourage taking risks to achieve their goals.
  2. *Quantum Peepers* watch what other companies do and follow their lead when they succeed.
  3. *Quantum Weepers* watch what more aggressive companies do, but do nothing or wait too long to take effective action.
  4. *Quantum Sleepers* either do not see how innovation has changed the world or, even if they do see it, they are afraid to take the necessary risks to make needed changes. They do nothing.

- People often follow these patterns of behavior:

  1. *Quantum Heroes* are true leaders who possess the four Vs of leadership: vision, values, valor, and validity.
  2. *Quantum Hi-Pos* are young people with the drive attitude, talent, and potential for development.

3. *Quantum Dodos* are people who resist all change. They want to keep things as they always were. Often, their work is slow, sloppy, and unimaginative. If real transformation is to be accomplished, dodos must be removed from positions of influence.

REFERENCES

[1]Pinchot, Gifford III. *Intrepreneuring*. New York: Harper and Row, 1985, p. ix.
[2]Collins, J. C. and Portas, J. I. *Built to Last*. New York: Harper Business, 1994.
[3]Dumaine, Brian. "America's Smartest Entrepreneurs." *Fortune*, March 21, 1994, pp. 34–36.
[4]Ryan, Michael. "They Call Their Boss a Hero." *Parade*, September 6, 1996, pp. 4–5.
[5]O'Toole, James. *Leading Change*. San Francisco: Jossey Bass, 1995, p. 133.

CHAPTER 4

The Look and Feel of a Great Organizational Culture

Diagnosing of the current culture helps clarify and identify existing problems. The next step is to determine what type of organizational culture best suits the company, followed by taking the steps to build the kind of commitment and momentum necessary to assure success. To help us understand, let's first take a look at what I've found to be some of the characteristics of a great organizational culture.

THE TEN IDENTIFYING FEATURES OF A GREAT ORGANIZATIONAL CULTURE

1. An Almost Missionary Zeal

It is no secret that the excitement and dedication of Bill Gates and Sam Walton were enthusiastically shared by their respective management teams and this positive energy permeated their organizations. This same fervor is found in companies of all sizes and throughout all industries.

Leading the *Fortune* list of the 100 fastest growing companies in America a few years ago was Grow-Biz International, a franchiser of four separate retail chains specializing in new and used goods including PCs, children's clothing, sporting goods, and musical instruments.

Grow-Biz started as a one-store unit selling used sporting equipment. Once the founders, Ron Olson and Jeff Dahlberg, identified that this was a growing market, they began franchising stores. But, what was it that made Grow-Biz the fastest growing company despite the competition of so many other, and better known, franchisers? In short, it was the excitement and enthusiasm generated by the founders and the franchisees.

Olson and Dahlberg not only had an idea whose time had come, but they chose as franchisees men and women who were in many ways as excited and enthusiastic as they were. Many of these people were former middle-management staffers who had been downsized, reorganized, or frustrated in corporate jobs. The challenge offered by Gro-Biz to give them the chance to run their own stores in an atmosphere that generated a passion for the work was a major factor that brought this relatively new organization to the top of *FORTUNE's* list of the fastest growing companies.

Over the years, countless authors and business consultants have recognized and written about the power of enthusiasm. Author and adult trainer Dale Carnegie, in fact, called it "the little recognized secret of success." He wasn't wrong.

QUOTES AND QUIPS

"Nothing great was ever achieved without enthusiasm."
Ralph Waldo Emerson, 1803–1882
American essayist

2. A Sense of Pride, Sincerity, and Cooperation

Not just managers, but all employees of Nordstrom, the Seattle-based national retail chain, seem to radiate pride in their company and their jobs. This is projected in the demeanor shown in dealing with each other and particularly with customers. Nordstrom prizes its reputation of going out of its way to serve customers.

Countless stories of customer service in action not only circulate within the company, but have spread throughout the communities it serves. These stories are frequently commented on in business literature. Among the common practices: employees write "thank you" notes to customers, personally deliver merchandise when the customer needs it faster than the normal delivery time, and exchange merchandise with no questions asked.

Nordstrom's staff are also known to take special pains to assure that customers leave every Nordstrom store thoroughly satisfied with both their purchases and the level of professionalism and helpfulness demonstrated by each of the employees with whom he or she had contact.

Another example of an organization with a deep-seated sense of pride and a one-for-all-all-for-one spirit is Home Depot, the largest home improvement retailer in America. This special mind-set is instilled in employees right from the very start, beginning with an inspirational orientation program at hiring, to regular reinforcements on the job. Has it paid off? You bet! Home Depot has with record-breaking sales volume year after year, steady expansion, and new store openings throughout the United States and Canada.

QUOTES AND QUIPS

"A great business success was probably never attained by chasing the dollar, but is due to pride in one's work—the pride that makes business an art."
Henry L. Doherty, 1870–1939
Utility executive

3. An Attitude of Constructive Discontent

"If it ain't broke, don't fix it." This old saw has dominated the thinking of many organizations. "Why tamper with success?" is another variant of this mode of thinking. On the surface this appears to have merit, but as we all know, given the rapid advances in technology and competitive forces, few organizations can ever be complacent about what they do. To assume that a process or system that "ain't broken" still serves the organization effectively is a dangerous course to take. Complacency can lead to stagnation. In the most severe cases, it can literally destroy a company.

The following is a quick example to help demonstrate the point. Not long ago, the manager of a well-known sales organization complained to me about the high turnover among his salespeople.

"We have an excellent screening process," he claimed, "so we know we're attracting and selecting top candidates for our jobs. We also give them a solid orientation and training program. Yet, we lose over 50 percent of our people every year."

Surprising? Not really. In fact, according to some experts, a 50-percent annual turnover in sales personnel is not at all uncommon. It happens for a variety of reasons, but in the case of this company, it was a classic example of failing to keep pace with changes in the expectations of employees. Among the problems were a badly outdated compensation structure and a failure to recognize that most sales programs today emphasize the building of relationships with customers and the exceeding of expectations.

The sales manager's program was based on the "old model" of salesmanship emphasizing memorized "closing techniques" and a highly standardized, inflexible sales presentation. While this approach was excellent in its day, it now was the reason for the manager's major problem: He assumed that what once had been "state-of-the-art" was still so.

In this dynamic world, however, no organization can be content to assume that what worked in the past is still the best way. Every system, every program, every approach must be continuously reevaluated and, where appropriate, adjusted to keep it at the cutting edge of productivity.

Several techniques to foster constructive discontent will be discussed in Chapter 6.

TACTICAL TIPS

Companies with an imbedded attitude of constructive discontent never stop looking for ways to improve things. They're never entirely satisfied. They never stop asking the question: How can we make this situation, or this product, or this service, or this environment, or whatever, even better.

4. A Value-Based Mind-Set and Management Style

Emphasizing values is not a new phenomenon. As pointed out earlier, Merck & Company, a 100+-year-old organization, is dedicated to the ideals of advancement of medical science and of service to humanity. These values are never far from the minds of management. Decisions concerning new products, expansion, personnel, and every aspect of their activities are made with these values in the forefront.

When the CEO of Merck was asked why the company had decided to provide a certain drug to Third World countries at no cost and even to pay for its distribution, he responded that not to do so would demoralize Merck scientists, who view seriously Merck's commitment that they are in the business of preserving and improving human life. Indeed, that is why for years, Merck has been looked upon as one of America's most admired companies.

Changing management style is often essential to changing a lackluster organizational culture into an outstanding one. A good example of this is SurfSoft, Inc., listed in the 1998 *Inc. 500* as one of the fastest growing private companies in America.[1]

Chuck Hickey, CEO of SurfSoft, an internet software consulting company based in Capitola, California, had previously headed Microport Systems, another software firm that had gone bankrupt in the 1980s. After several years of working as a consultant, he decided to try running a business once again. He took control of a company that had two full-time employees and was generating annual revenues of about $500,000. Following the practices he had used at Microport Systems, he quickly grew the company to $1.7 million in sales. But then sales leveled off to $400,000 a month and employee turnover soared to 25 percent.

Just at this time, Hickey read *Deming Management at Work* by Mary Walton, on the works of quality guru W. Edwards Deming, and was shocked by his concept of management. It read like an indictment of the management practices that Hickey had practiced all of his life. Deming warned against sales quotas; Hickey had sworn by them. Deming stressed collaboration among employees; Hickey prodded his workers to compete. Deming favored continuing training education of workers; Hickey had spurned such benefits.

Faced with this new crisis and fearing a repeat of his Microport failure, Hickey decided to follow Deming's teachings and make a radical change in his organizational culture. He junked all sales quotas, scrapped his organizational structure, and established interdepart-mental teams to foster cooperation. Remembering Deming's emphasis on education, he required his management team to read and discuss one business book a month. This resulted in the development of a statement of the company's core values that Hickey says has helped improve morale and productivity.

In March 1997, SurfSoft's monthly sales topped $500,000. Employ-ee turnover had dropped to five percent a year. Revenues were expect-ed to reach $10 million in 1998, up nearly 50 percent from 1997.

QUOTES AND QUIPS

"It does an organization no good when its leader refuses to share the leadership function with his lieutenants. The more centers of leadership you find in a company, the stronger it will be."
David Ogilvy
Founder, Ogilvy & Mather
advertising agency

5. An Emphasis on Creativity and Innovation

The Research & Development departments of companies often have formal innovation programs and this has paid off in the intro-duction of new products and methods over the years. Truly creative organizations must budget for long-term growth, not only in R&D, but in all aspects of their activities.

One company that has proven the value of commitment to innova-tion is Motorola. Each year a significant portion of its earnings is ear-marked for future innovations. Here's one example of how this paid off: The company's Research & Development team devoted two years to developing a satellite system to connect calls anywhere in the world, even in remote locations where there is no cellular infrastruc-ture. This will make it possible to reach a person in a canoe, fishing in a remote lake in Alaska; or a medical team, working with primitive tribes in the rain forests of Brazil.

Chrysler (now Daimler Chrysler) exemplifies how creativity brought the company back to profitability from a long period of depressed sales. They encouraged their designers and engineers to make a radical change in car design. This resulted in the development of the minivan, the first significant change in the look of American cars in decades, and opened a new and growing market for Chrysler.

A climate of creativity is not limited to just encouraging employees to be innovative. It must extend to suppliers and other outside sources. When UPS wanted to improve its package tracking capabilities, it called on Motorola to design a more effective system than that used by most of its competitors. Using its cellular technology, Motorola came up with an electronic clipboard to send a signature instantly to a central station. As a result, delivery information can be provided almost instantaneously to customers around the world.

6. A Focus on Building Role Models—Not Just Leaders

Many men and women are successful leaders in government, industry, or other phases of life, but they are not role models for their employees and, indeed, for the entire world. A leader gets things done, often for good, but sometimes for evil. Stalin, Hitler, and Mussolini were leaders. They had great powers of persuasion, but their ultimate end was self-aggrandizement, which ultimately led to the destruction of their followers.

In business organizations, there are countless examples of managers who built great empires, but due to their lack of ethical or moral standards, led to the decline or failure of their companies. On the other hand, there are industrial leaders who put ethical standards first, even though it may involve making decisions that result in lower profitability.

One example of a positive leader is Aaron Feuerstein of Malden Mills, whose heroic activities were described in Chapter 3. Another role model in American industry is Robert D. Haas, chairman and chief executive of Levi Strauss, the manufacturer of the famous Levi jeans and other clothing products. Haas believes that the corporation should be an ethical creature, an organism capable not only of producing profits but making the world a better place to live.

He has done this in Levi Strauss by making all the workers, from the factory floor on up, feel they are an integral part of the entire process of making and selling the company's products. He gives them opportunity to express views on all issues, no matter how controversial. The company will not tolerate harassment of any kind, and Haas will not do business with suppliers who violate their strict standards regarding work environment and ethics. The company has issued the following set of "aspirations" that guides all major decisions.[2]

WHAT LEVI ASPIRES TO:

NEW BEHAVIORS: Management must exemplify "directness, openness to influence, commitment to the success of others, and willingness to acknowledge our own contributions to problems."

DIVERSITY: Levi "values a diverse work force (age, sex, ethnic group, etc.) at all levels of the organization. Differing points of view will be sought; diversity will be valued and honestly rewarded, not suppressed."

RECOGNITION: Levi will "provide greater recognition—both financial and psychic—for individuals and teams that contribute to our success, those who create and innovate, and those who continually support day-to-day business requirements."

ETHICAL MANAGEMENT PRACTICES: Management should epitomize "the stated standards of ethical behavior. We must provide clarity about our expectations and must enforce these standards throughout the corporation."

COMMUNICATIONS: Management must be "clear about company, unit, and individual goals and performance. People must know what is expected of them and receive timely, honest feedback. . . ."

EMPOWERMENT: Management must "increase the authority and responsibility of those closest to our products and customers. By actively pushing the responsibility, trust, and recognition into the organization, we can harness and release the capabilities of all our people."

Haas practices what he preaches. He has instituted policies in the company that have implemented the "aspirations" including more participative management, better customer service, and he has even made decisions that have cost the company significant business rather than engage in conduct considered unethical. As an example, Haas with unanimous consent of his board, pulled $40 million of Levi's business out of China to protest human rights violations there.

7. A Sense of High Expectations and Professional Standards

Hewlett-Packard has a culture in which all of its people are dedicated to excellence. This started when David Packard and William Hewlett founded the company in 1938 and it has continued to this day. Everybody is expected to do the very best, and to work at the highest level of professional competence. Nothing less is accepted. The result? A well-established history of innovating new ideas and producing superior products.

QUOTES AND QUIPS

"Excellence is an art won by training and habituation. We do not act rightly because we have virtue or excellence, but we rather have those because we have acted rightly. We are what we repeatedly do. Excellence, then, is not an act but a habit."
Aristotle, 384–322 B.C.
Greek philosopher

This concept is not limited to large and well-known organizations. I recently had the opportunity to visit Claudia Gardiner, owner of a small but profitable fabric designing firm. She is a stickler for perfection. In her company, which specializes in the design and fabrication of customized fabrics for interior designers, this attitude is instilled in all the employees—from the creative artists to the sewing machine operators.

When Gardiner screens candidates for employment, she tells them that she only hires the very best people and that working for her will be tough and demanding. Unlike many of her competitors, Gardiner insists on a thorough retraining of all new employees, no matter how experienced they may be, so they recognize and accept the high standards she demands.

In short, she gives her staff a fine reputation to live up to. This has resulted in a team of men and women who pride themselves in their work and in the work of their colleagues. Each knows that everybody in the group is committed to excellence, to each other, and, most importantly, to exceeding their customers' expectations.

8. A Fair, Commensurate Compensation and Incentive Program

Unless people feel they are being fairly compensated for their work, it is difficult to get their full cooperation. Most companies use the traditional mode of compensation: Annual raises are often automatic and based on a set percentage of increase over the previous year's salary. Under such a program, the highest-paid people in any grade are those who are the most senior—not the most productive. This is neither fair nor does it reward competence.

Although many types of incentive-pay plans have been used, they are often some variation of profit sharing. The assumption is that when a part of the workers' income is based on the profits, they will have the incentive to work to maximize those profits. Unfortunately, in many profit-sharing plans, employees have no idea about how profits are calculated and often perceive the determination of the amount of profit as an arbitrary decision of management. This may cause more ill will than benefit.

One company that has made their profit-sharing program meaningful to its employees is Wal-Mart. It has created an internal culture in which every employee knows each month how well the store, division, or plant met its profit, sales, and production goals. Any year in which the anticipated goals are exceeded, one-third of the excess goes to the hourly workers. All Wal-Mart stores give their staffs monthly updates of their profits, and this information is reflected in the employee's concern for customer satisfaction.

Bill Gates, the creator of Microsoft and one of the world's wealthiest people, strongly believes in sharing the wealth. His profit-sharing and stock-option opportunities for employees have made over 2,000 of them millionaires. Microsoft staff know that their personal wealth depends on keeping Microsoft on top, and in most cases, they aim to do their best to assure that it is.

In order for a culture change to be successful, organizations that are engaged in this process should carefully reevaluate their compensation systems and adapt them to any changes that are made.

QUOTES AND QUIPS

"When profit is unshared, it's less likely to grow greater."
Malcolm Forbes, 1919–1990
Editor and publisher

Boyett and Conn, in their book *Workplace 2000*,[3] comment that to correct the inequities in compensation systems, more companies are adopting a four-part approach:

- Slowing or stopping entirely the growth in base pay
- Relying more heavily on bonuses tied to group performance
- Linking base pay to knowledge and skill rather than position
- Providing expanded opportunities for employees to share in company profits and, in some cases, acquire ownership in the company[4]

9. A Habit of Celebrating Successes

One of the characteristics of happy organizations, of companies where morale is high and employees are excited about their work, is a practice of showing appreciation for accomplishments. This can be expressed in warm, private moments of hearty congratulations by a manager to a subordinate or by team members to each other. Or it can be a public demonstration of an achievement by rallies, parties, dinners, or just informal get-togethers.

When festivity and jubilation accompany achievements, it adds to the achievement itself. Making it possible for everybody to share in the accomplishments of associates inspires them to work toward accomplishments of their own.

10. Adhering to the Golden Rule

Perhaps all of the characteristics of a great organizational culture can be summarized in the Golden Rule:

Do unto others as you would have others do unto you.

One of the indicators of a great company is that management truly believes in this rule and carries it into the workplace.

Of course, it would be unrealistic to expect that everybody in any organization always follows this practice. Companies are made up of people, and people differ. In applying this precept we can only comment that when top management treats its employees, its suppliers, its customers, its shareholders, and the public equitably, it enhances the company's reputation as a good place to work, to deal with, and to patronize.

CULTURE CHANGE STARTS AT THE TOP

Unless top management is totally committed to making a change in the organizational culture, it is more likely than not that nothing significant will happen. Unfortunately, too many CEOs give lip service to the need for change, but resist any real efforts to shake up their traditional way of doing business. One of the most common comments I hear is, "My boss talks a big game, but when it comes to action, it's business as usual."

The complacency that so many organizations have with the status quo opens the door for wide-awake competitors to move in. The banking industry is a good example of this attitude. In the early 1980s, Morgan Guaranty virtually dominated the ADR market. ADRs or American Depository Receipts are certificates traded in the United States as proxies for foreign securities. Sponsoring banks earn fees for issuing and processing other transactions related to them. The culture of the Morgan Guaranty was common to old traditional banking organizations that depended on their reputation to attract business. Suggestions that they engage in promotion and marketing were dismissed as being beneath their dignity.

On the other hand, J. Carter Bacot, CEO of the Bank of New York, was one of the first bankers to recognize that the ADR market was a profit center just waiting to be tapped. Bacot dispatched a sales team to foreign companies to solicit their business. As reported in *Forbes,* it was two years before Morgan even realized what was going on. By that time, the Bank of New York had obtained a 20-percent market share. By 1993 more than half of all ADR business in the United States was controlled by the Bank of New York.

QUOTES AND QUIPS

"We decided to create an open and dialogue-intensive corporate culture. This generates creativity and motivation and brings out entrepreneurs at all levels. This is the true power of success of Bertlesmann."
Mark Woessner
CEO, Bertlesmann Group

CREATE A CLIMATE OF UNDERSTANDING AMONG ALL LEVELS OF THE ORGANIZATION

Employees of culture-stagnant companies bemoan the often stubborn adherence of their managements to archaic and morale-destroying methods and concepts. Middle-level managers are frustrated when their bosses veto innovative ideas. Rank-and-file workers feel that they are ignored, or worse, looked upon as expendable components instead of contributing participants.

The prevalence of such attitudes was reinforced recently when I conducted two surveys in a number of manufacturing and service companies in various parts of the United States. I queried mid-level managers regarding the major complaints they had about the people who directed their organizations. This was followed by a survey of top managers asking about their complaints about their staffs.

These surveys showed that until management fully appreciates how they appear to their subordinates and employees see how they appear to management, cultural changes cannot even begin to be effected. This knowledge paves the way for planning and implementing a program for a culture change that will be meaningful to all involved.

Let's look at the results of both of these surveys.

COMPLAINTS EMPLOYEES HAVE ABOUT THEIR MANAGERS

Gross compensation inequities. Compensation for top managers in most organizations is based on a combination of salary, bonus, stock options, and a variety of perks. Their earnings are often considerably more than other employees. Although some people may resent this disparity, it is a generally accepted practice. However, when employees' wages are frozen, bonuses curtailed, and people laid off, and senior managers continue to receive high salaries and bonuses, there will be increased dissatisfaction in the company.

In a highly publicized case a few years ago, a Fortune-500 industrial conglomerate was faced with increased costs and lower return on investment. It instituted a cost-reduction program including downsizing, wage freezes, and tightening of expenses throughout the organization. However, the board of directors voted to give the CEO a seven-figure bonus despite the fact that he was already one of the highest-paid executives in the industry. The outcry from employees, customers, and the public was so great that the CEO was shamed into declining the bonus.

In less well-known companies, particularly those that are privately held, such inequities are not publicized, but everybody within the organization is aware of them. This often leads to poor morale and the loss of talented people. In one company in my survey, the CEO brought his management staff together and told them that because of a business slow down, raises for all employees would be eliminated for that year, there would be no bonuses, and the company would cut back on their contributions to the 401K and medical plans.

Shortly after this announcement, the CEO persuaded the board to give him a substantial salary increase and buy him a new Mercedes. At the same time, he issued an order that employees who travel must select the least expensive way possible and even limited the amount these travelers could pay for hotels and meals. Additionally, he upgraded his accommodations to $900-a-night presidential suites and unlimited "entertainment" expenses. You can guess how that affected the morale of that company's employees.

A fear-based management style. Too many bosses act like "bosses"—they manage by intimidation. Why, in this so-called age of participative management and empowerment, do so many managers still revert to the "I am the boss" mentality? Just as parents who mistreat their children had most likely been mistreated by their parents, I suspect that managers who rule by fear were most likely treated that way by their early bosses. It takes a major change in thinking to overcome this attitude.

The sad part is that many of these managers do not realize that instead of developing loyalty and the desire to cooperate, the result of intimidation is anxiety, indecision, and low morale. My survey brought out some of the tactics managers use that cause or aggravate anxiety among their people:

- Intolerance of disagreement. The owner of a machine shop prided himself on his knowledge of his field, and he did have considerable expertise in the type of machining the company did. If any of his workers made suggestions for improving a method that differed from his ideas, he disparaged their concepts and made them feel stupid. Continued disagreements led to termination. He refused to accept that even experienced "experts" don't know everything about an activity. Progressive managers encourage disagreement and learn from it.
- Telling an employee you want to see him or her the next day and not explaining what it is about. Has that ever happened to you? I bet you stayed awake most of the night trying to guess what you did wrong, worried about how you could defend possible accusations or criticisms. In many cases, all the boss wanted to discuss was some routine matter. The smart manager lets the associate know the subject to be discussed. Not only will this alleviate tension and worry, but it will enable him or her to prepare information that may make the meeting go smoothly.
- Constantly looking over an employee's shoulder. Certainly, it is occasionally necessary to check a person's work, but most people are intimidated by a boss who watches every step. People, once trained, should be trusted to do the work properly. A more effective way to do this is to set control points at strategic intervals. This method is usually adequate to assure things are moving along as scheduled.
- Eavesdropping on employee's conversations with other workers, or worse, listening in on telephone calls and reading their e-mail. Not only is this an invasion of the employee's privacy, but it creates a climate of suspicion and fear.
- Assuming employees are wrong before getting all the facts. This forces people to take defensive positions on everything they do. People who have to be constantly on the defensive spend more time and energy providing protective measures than getting their work done.

QUOTES AND QUIPS

"Fear is an acid which is pumped into one's atmosphere.
It causes mental, moral, spiritual asphyxiation, and
sometimes death; death to energy and all growth."
Horace Fletcher, 1849–1913
Author and nutritionist

Lack of a clear career path. Although not all people are career-oriented, those who look upon their jobs as steps in a growing career are the hope for the future of most every organization. Of course, no company can or should guarantee employees a growth pattern in the company. Employees who see opportunities for advancement on the job, however, will likely put out the effort to earn the chance to move ahead.

Several of the companies in my survey were family-owned businesses, and it was generally accepted in those firms that many senior management spots were reserved for family members. This, obviously, limits the potential for advancement for all other employees.

In cases like this, a key question looms: How can such companies attract and retain good people? The answer depends on the approach to advancement taken by the powers-that-be. Owners who follow the "blood-is-thicker-than-water" concept and restrict most management jobs to family will probably lose their best people. However, there still can be good opportunities in many family-owned businesses. Often there are a number of high-level jobs in these organizations that family members cannot or do not want to hold. Non-family members who hold such positions often move up to significant management jobs.

Lack of opportunity is not limited to family businesses. I saw this happen when one of my friends—a bright, creative marketing specialist—was stymied in his career because the company for which he worked promoted people primarily on the basis of seniority. It would have taken him years to move up to a management position for which, based on his capabilities, he was well-qualified. He had no choice but to seek another job. By sticking to the archaic promotion policy of seniority, the company lost this high-potential employee—and probably many others like him.

To help such high-potential employees move ahead in their careers, some companies have instituted formal programs called "career pathing." These organizations use techniques such as performance evaluations, psychological testing, assessment centers, counseling sessions, and informal meetings with senior executives to evaluate the potential of their employees.

What have these programs accomplished? People who have gone through the programs report that they learned much about themselves. As a result, many of them have undertaken additional training, both within the organization and on their own, to build up their capabilities.

Other companies encourage all managers to cultivate employee's skills and build productivity by providing career counseling and training as part of their regular activities. The human resource (HR) departments of these companies provide the tools and training that managers need to accomplish this.

The HR department of Motorola, for example, provides career planning modules for both managers and associates. Chrysler Corporation's HR department has a similar program. Susan McGraw, an HR executive at corporate headquarters, explained how it works:

"During the first day of supervisory training, managers assess themselves in terms of their own careers and planning. The second day focuses on coaching and facilitation strategies. Nonsupervisory training includes a lot of exercises on self-assessment, value clarification, receiving career feedback, and developing career networks."[5]

This training is followed through with periodic discussions between the manager and the associates concerning progress made and additional steps that should now be undertaken.

Kathryn Tyler summarizes the manager's career development coaching function as follows:[6]

- Identify areas in which the employee needs professional growth.
- Communicate the direction, needs, and expectations of the organization.
- Provide information about job and career development opportunities and refer the employee to available resources.
- Guide the employee in selecting appropriate goals.

- Help the employee identify on-the-job learning opportunities and assign projects accordingly.
- Managers need to be involved in identifying development activities, situations in which employees can contribute to the department's needs and also learn.

Less formal programs are more common. Here employees who show promise are encouraged by their supervisors' practice of giving them more and more responsibilities, special assignments, and tuition-paid advanced education—all to help prepare them to take leadership roles.

Tolerance of poor performance. One of the major complaints of those who expend their energies, talents, and expertise to do superior work is to see others who just barely get the work done receive the same recognition and reward as they do.

It is important for people to know what performance standards are expected of them. Unfortunately, too many people interpret "standards" to mean acceptable production and make no effort to do better than "what is expected."

QUOTES AND QUIPS

Performance standards define the results that are expected from a person performing a job. For performance standards to be meaningful, all persons doing that job should know and accept those standards."
Arthur R. Pell
Consultant in human resources
development and author

One of the respondents in my survey reported: "In my company, the CEO favors the plodding drones, those who come to work a little early and work a little late despite the fact that all they produce is average work. When this was called to his attention, he commented that he'd rather have a 'team of average workers who consistently meet production standards than temperamental stars.' Over the past four years the company has lost several high achievers, who felt frustrated by this accent on mediocrity—and the company's business has lost market share to its more progressive competitors."

Another respondent complained that her CEO withdrew the tuition reimbursement for her MBA program because he felt she should put all of her energies into the job and that the time and effort spent in "unnecessary schooling" was distracting her from her work. When she continued the program at her own expense, he let her know that he was unhappy about it and "it would be reflected in her next performance review." You can bet that when she obtains her degree, she'll be moving to a more enlightened organization.

Broken promises. A businessman, whom I will call Paul Cullen, was the type of businessman who makes a mockery of the term "business ethics." He built his business on the Barnum principle: "There's a sucker born every minute." Making promises he had no intention of keeping was just one of his commonly used practices.

In 1994, he read in a trade journal that the patent on a well-known industrial product was to expire in 1997 and that several companies were tooling up to manufacture what had been the monopoly of the patent holder.

"Why wait three years," Cullen figured. "I'll get a head start." He approached several of the patent holder's engineers and offered them big bonuses and salaries to leave their current jobs and join him. As one of these engineers told me, "it was the kind of offer you couldn't refuse. I would get a much better starting salary than I was now making, plus a very large bonus once the product was on the market. Three of us left the old company, sold our homes, and moved 1,000 miles to his facility."

For the next nine months, they taught Cullen and his staff all they had to know to manufacture the product. Now that Cullen no longer needed their expertise, he fired them. He gave them one-month's separation pay and no bonus. This exemplified Cullen's concept of management. Achieve your goal even if it involves infringing of patents, breaking promises, or disrupting people's lives.

To a lesser degree, the world of management is strewn with broken promises. There are some companies that promise raises and benefits they have no intention of granting or they hint at company cars, country club memberships, and other perks that somehow never are realized. Never forget: Unless managers are truthful and loyal to their people, it's hard to expect loyalty in return.

Putting personal interests ahead of what's best for the company. Over the years, I have observed many situations in which decisions were made by managers who were motivated, not by what was best for the organization, but by the personal interests of the decision maker. Bob Hansen, executive vice-president and general manager of the Friendly Finance Company, is one of those managers.

A few years ago, the company outgrew its office space in downtown Atlanta and needed to move to larger quarters. Two facilities were under consideration. One was about a mile from the present office in a newly constructed high-rise building; the other was a freestanding building in a suburb close to Bob's home.

As most business is done by phone and fax, customer accessibility was not a factor. Although the downtown location was more easily reached by most of the employees, Bob chose the suburban space. Sure, it would be much easier for him to get there, but it caused a great deal of inconvenience to everybody else on the staff.

Being treated as second-class citizens. In discussing the complaints employees have about their managers, one that came up over and over again as being most annoying was lack of respect. "The boss thinks he is much better than we are and this shows up in the way he talks to us, gives us orders and condescendingly 'listens' to our ideas." A good example of this is someone I'll call Lt. Col. Carl Carlson. When he retired from the army, he was hired to head an administrative department of a large hospital. He never let anybody forget that he had been a lieutenant colonel in the army and insisted that employees call him "Colonel." He treated them as "enlisted personnel." He ran his department like a military unit.

During the first year of his tenure, the employees filed seven grievances against him with the Human Resources Department, several clerks requested transfers, and others quit. Despite counseling by his supervisors and HR staff, he could not accept that his position was not as a "superior officer" but as a team leader. As a result, he was asked to resign.

Carlson's attitude may have carried over from his military training, but such behavior is not limited to former officers. Many managers are "rank conscious" and build barriers between themselves and their staffs. Although there are times when a person needs his position of authority to make decisions, managers should not depend on their rank to run their departments. The best managers have rejected authoritarianism in favor of understanding, diplomacy, and team work.

QUOTES AND QUIPS

"Good managers recognize that the road to achievement is replacing barriers with bridges that create a spirit of collaboration and cooperation."
Dr. Paul J. Mackey
Management consultant

Lack of reward for superior work. In my survey, many respondents were unhappy with management's lack of appreciation for superior performance—work that is above the standards that have been set for that assignment. As mentioned earlier in this chapter, many managers will settle for "satisfactory" work. Inasmuch as there is no showing of appreciation, financially or otherwise, for workers who produce more than what is expected, there is no incentive for them to exceed performance standards. This is exacerbated when coworkers put pressure on peers not to exceed quotas "because it makes the rest of us look bad."

Some companies have overcome this attitude by awarding production bonuses to the entire group or team when standards are exceeded. Although financial reward is naturally welcome, even nonfinancial rewards such as team recognition, a team dinner when the project is completed, and similar signs of appreciation can be effective.

QUOTES AND QUIPS

"One way of winning the full support of your staff and assuring their enthusiasm to meet the company's goals is to reward them with more than they expected."
Robert J. McCarty
Executive coach

Feeling unappreciated. Pioneer psychologists, from William James to Abraham Maslow, have pointed out the importance to individuals of having their worth recognized and appreciated. This can range from simple feedback from one's boss to elaborate recognition awards and ceremonies.

A survey conducted by the Council of Communication Management indicated that recognition for a job well done is the top motivator for employee performance.[7] For feedback to be most effective, it should be face to face and given as soon as possible after the accomplishment. Positive feedback provides immediate acknowledgment that what the employee has accomplished is not just "doing the job," but that it has also been greatly appreciated by the boss and the organization.

This follows the principles advocated in *reinforcement theory,* which states that behavior is contingent upon reinforcement. This theory is based on the work of B. F. Skinner and advocated by most behavioralists as the most effective way to motivate and modify behavior.

There are times when criticism is needed to correct errors, to get mediocre workers to meet your standards, but even then, it should be positive and constructive rather than negative and degrading.

Managers should make it a practice of communicating with their associates all of the time, not just to criticize or compliment them. Day-to-day interaction between managers and staff members leads to a smooth flow of activity, and an ongoing commentary on both bad and good aspects of their work can be used to reinforce, to improve, and to obtain full commitment to achieving departmental and company goals.

LACK OF TRUST

All of the above complaints can be attributed in some degree to the lack of trust employee have in management. Seventy-five percent of executives who responded to a survey conducted by Manchester Consultants of 215 companies, said that trust in their workplaces had decreased during the past two years. Only 15 percent said trust had improved and the balance said trust remained about the same.

"Trust in corporate America is at a low point," said Lew Stern, Senior Vice-President with Manchester Consulting, who has studied workplace trust for two decades. "Employers feel they have had little input into major changes that have affected them, and they believe they can no longer look to their employers for job security. As a result, workplace trust has dramatically declined."

The survey also showed that organizations that downsized during the period studied received the lowest trust ratings. Tying for the next-lowest ratings were companies that restructured and those that merged with another organization. On the other hand, companies that expanded or acquired another company were rated with the highest level of trust.

The level of trust in the typical workplace was judged to be the best between front-line employees and their immediate supervisors. The level of trust considered worst was between front-line employees and top-level executives. It is easier for direct supervisors to communicate and stay connected with the employees, while senior managers must make special efforts to understand, interact and serve as examples by what they say and do.

The survey also reported that it took an average of seven months for executives to build their trust in a leader, but less than half that time (about three months) for them to lose trust in one.[8]

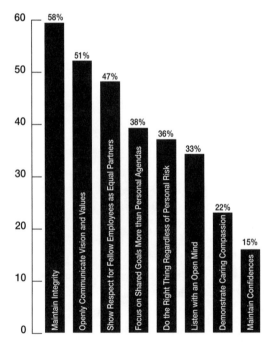

Figure 4-1. *How leaders build workplace trust.*[9]

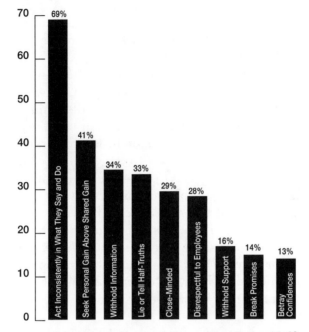

Figure 4-2. *How leaders lose workplace trust.*[10]

COMPLAINTS MANAGERS HAVE ABOUT EMPLOYEES

To obtain the other side of the picture, I also conducted interviews with a number of senior managers to elicit how they perceived employees. Most managers agreed that their people were basically satisfactory, but felt that there were many areas in which they could improve. The following were the seven most commonly mentioned complaints.

Poor work habits. Frequently heard in my interviews was the comment that the so-called "work ethic" which at one time permeated American industry has long since past. Many workers, they said, no longer consider it an obligation to give their full energies and efforts to their jobs. To paraphrase John F. Kennedy, they ask "What can this company do for me?" rather than "What can I do for this company?"

A typical complaint about rank-and-file workers is that they have no interest in their work. They watch the clock, put out just enough production to meet minimum standards and are constantly seeking ways to beat the system. One manager told me that he spends excessive time arguing about and defending himself and his management staff from unfounded gripes and grievances. "One woman filed six separate charges of sexual harassment and discrimination—all of which were found to be groundless, taking an inordinate amount of time and expense, and was looked upon by her coworkers, who knew them to be false, as a sideshow."

Another respondent, the CEO of a warehousing and distribution company, reported that her human resources department has to train new employees, most of whom are recent high school graduates, in the simple common-sense concepts of coming to work on time every day, that assigned work must be completed on schedule, and that a ten-minute break is really only ten minutes in duration.

This is not limited to hourly workers. Several CEOs complained about the work habits of some of their first-line and middle-management people.

"When I entered the work force in the 1970s," one executive commented, "my job was the most important thing to me. I worked long hours, took work home, and went anywhere the company sent me at short notice without complaint. Now, many of these young MBAs don't have this dedication. I hear things like 'Sure this work is important, but I have family obligations that are equally important.' With such an attitude, how can I expect them to put out the work that is needed for the company to grow."

These complaints about work habits and attitudes, justified or not, must be taken into consideration in managing people with different backgrounds and goals. What appears to be unreasonable to one person is an accepted principle of others. The successful manager of the early 21st century will have to be perceptive enough to recognize these differences and change what should be changed and accept and adjust to what cannot. With a changing culture in which family values are considered as important as job values, managers may have to adjust their organizational cultures to conform to the larger community culture.

They don't care enough about doing quality work. Despite the emphasis being placed on quality and the installation of Total Quality Management programs in many organizations, many managers in the survey pointed out that their employees resisted the company's efforts to help them improve the quality of their work.

An example of this was exhibited at Collins Electronics. This company manufactures precision electronic parts as a subcontractor to a manufacturer which deals primarily with the U.S. Department of Defense. In order for the payment for their work to be received reasonably fast, the paperwork must be in perfect form. One slight mistake requires redoing the work and delaying payment—sometimes for several months.

Despite careful training and reiteration of the importance of accuracy, many clerks do not take the time to check and recheck their work. Errors are found late in the process or not at all. Charles Collins, the company CEO, blames it on the schools. In his community, he says, teachers pass students even if their work is substandard. They are so accustomed to getting away with slovenly work in school, it continues in the workplace.

Companies which have become involved in the Total Quality Management (TQM) movement report that one of their first tasks is to change employee's attitudes about quality. Until they are convinced that poor quality cannot be tolerated, that "slightly off the standard" is not acceptable, the TQM program cannot even be undertaken.

Employees spend too much time socializing. "Every time I walk through the office, I see people gabbing with each other. I can't see how any work is ever done." I have heard this complaint over and over, not only in this survey, but in many other companies with which I have had dealings. Yes, the workplace is a social environment. We spend more time with the people with whom we work than with any other group other than our immediate families.

Socializing on the job is normal and should be expected. It serves a valuable purpose. It results in better communications among co-workers. Especially when people work in teams, this social interaction solidifies the team relationship. However, when non-job-related socializing interferes with accomplishing goals, managers must step in and bring it to the attention of the offenders.

Even non-business-related chatting among employees can serve a positive purpose. It can be an antidote to stress and boredom. Some people find taking a break from the tensions of the job to discuss last night's sporting events, the latest movies, or television shows gives them new energies to resume work.

This was brought home to me when I was given a tour of the assembly department at a plant, in which the workers spend their entire shifts putting together small plastic parts. I noticed that the workers seemed to be spending an inordinate amount of time talking and socializing. I commented about this to my host.

"The work is tedious and boring, the pay is low, and the turnover of new workers is exceedingly high," he responded. "However, we have found that workers who stay on the job for at least three months tend to remain with the company for years. We attribute this to the social interaction on the job. Once these workers get into the swing of things, they become part of the social group. They know about each others' families, activities, romances, troubles and triumphs. Despite the boredom of the work, they look forward to each workday—and notice that all the time they're talking, their hands are working. Productivity is really good here."

Lack of initiative. Several managers in my survey commented: "My employees depend on me to make every decision, to come up with every idea. They're good people. If I tell them what to do and how to do it, I get the work out, but they never suggest anything." Often they added: "Workers either cannot or will not take the initiative to contribute suggestions or to start projects. They must be prodded to do so."

On the other hand, we found quite a number of managers who had the opposite experience. Their associates were not only capable of taking initiative but sought such opportunities.

Why the difference? In most cases, it depended upon management. If management from the CEO down the line encouraged workers to take initiative, they would. I found that many executives who decried their people's lack of initiative overtly or inadvertently inhibited it. By consistently rejecting ideas, by contending that the employee did not have enough know-how to initiate a project, by dogmatic insistence of following old procedures, they send a clear message: "We do the thinking; you do the work."

Poor communication skills. Several managers in the survey reported that many members of their work force do not have good communication skills. They cannot express themselves clearly and concisely in one-to-one conversations and freeze up when required to speak at a meeting. In cases where writing skills are required, they noted that even many college graduates cannot write a decent report or a clearly composed letter.

The upside of this complaint is that communication skills can be taught. There are some excellent courses available at community colleges, universities, and through private training groups to help people learn or improve their techniques of oral and written communication.

This is one of the areas in which I have been much involved. I have seen how relatively short duration programs can make significant improvements in the techniques and styles of the participants. The time and cost of such programs are insignificant in relation to the results attained.

"I can't depend on them." Several of the executives I interviewed felt that lack of dependability was probably a major complaint. One respondent commented: "I can't do everything myself, yet if I delegate it to others, I can never be sure it will be done right and done on time."

Yes, there are some people on whom you just cannot depend. Such people should be restricted to positions where they can be carefully monitored. However, most people can be depended upon if they believe you really trust them.

A woman I'll call Rosa Gomez, runs a successful printing shop in El Paso, Texas, and learned this the hard way. Gomez prides herself on the quality of her work. "I am a perfectionist," she says, "and I expect my people to put out perfect work." To assure that every order was filled with total accuracy, she would spend hours and hours proofing and reproofing copy. She did not trust anybody else to do this. In 1989, she collapsed at her desk. Her doctor insisted that she take an extended vacation and cut back on her work hours. She refused to take the vacation, but reluctantly delegated some of the proofreading. To her surprise, her people did excellent work. They knew that Gomez needed their help and they lived up to her hopes. A year later, she had enough confidence in their dependability to take her very first extended vacation.

In summary: establish high standards, train people to adhere to those standards, reinforce their successes with praise and have the confidence to allow them to do their jobs without looking over their shoulders.

They are unwilling to go that extra mile. Several managers reported that workers just won't stretch. They do what they have to do and no more. One manager reported that at 5 p.m., several of his people stopped work even though they had been told that the work had to be completed that night.

"I didn't expect them to put in another shift," the manager said, "just another half hour to finish the job, but it never occurred to them to volunteer to stay. Even after I reiterated the need to meet our commitment to the customer and politely asked them to finish the assignment, it was only with reluctance and resentment that it was accomplished."

Of course, there are many people who do put in that extra mile. My survey brought out that most companies have some workers and managers who willingly devote extra time and effort to their jobs, who put reaching company goals and achieving customer satisfaction on the top of their priority list—and the most successful companies have ingrained this attitude in their people.

QUOTES AND QUIPS

"When work is a pleasure, life is a joy.
When work is a duty, life is slavery."
Maxim Gorky, 1868–1936
Russian novelist

Yes, there are some people whose attitudes toward their jobs and their employers will always be negative. This may stem from deep-seated factors in their lives or bad experiences with other employers. But, my research has proven that this is not true of most men and women. Through training, trust, and motivation, people can be inspired to put out that extra effort and dedication that is the hallmark of successful organizations.

LOYALTY IS A TWO-WAY STREET

A great number of CEOs and other senior executives give talks and send letters to their staffs exhorting the importance of cooperation and trust, but their actions do not always follow their messages. For example, there are significant data available showing that customer and employee retention is a major factor in productivity and profits. Frederick F. Reichheld, a consultant with Bain & Co., made an extensive study of this and published the results in his book, *The Loyalty*

Effect.[11] Reichheld cites MBNA, a Maryland-based credit card company, as an example of a company which truly puts loyalty at the top of its agenda. He writes:

> MBNA has a wide reputation as a company that has mastered the art and science of loyalty-based management, but most managers look at MBNA's motto and fail to grasp its full meaning. Instead of systematically revamping their operation with customer loyalty in mind, most managers adopt ad hoc programs. They try to copy one or two of MBNA's practices. . . . They borrow MBNA's policy of delivering employee paychecks in envelopes labeled "Brought to You by the Customer" but fail to base bonuses on the enhancement of customer value and loyalty. Not surprisingly, the payoffs never materialize.

Loyalty is a two-way street. Management expects loyalty from employees, but they must show it by demonstrating loyalty to their employees.

Changing an organizational culture requires that senior managers take meaningful steps to show employees that they sincerely believe what they say and are committed to practicing what they preach. Such steps should show up in the form of compensation, working conditions, and the manner in which employees are treated on the job. Only then will everybody in the organization become truly involved in making the culture change work.

SUM AND SUBSTANCE

The type of organizational culture that is best for your company depends on many factors and must be tailored to the specific problems and needs you face, as well as the goals and vision of the organization. The environment in which each organization operates differs, but, based on the experiences of successful organizations, the foundation on which the culture is built should share the following characteristics:

• The zeal, excitement, and determination to reach the goals is shared by everybody at all levels of the organization. This is accompanied by a company-wide sense of pride, sincerity, and cooperation.

- A climate of creativity and innovation is ingrained in the organization. All employees are trained to be constructively discontent about all practices and procedures and are encouraged to critique the status quo, as well as suggest and implement improvements.
- The values and vision established by the organization are known, accepted, and practiced by everybody in all aspects of the company's activities. This includes developing and adhering to high expectations and standards of performance.
- Managers are not just leaders. They are ready and willing to take heroic steps to meet the challenges facing the company.
- Employees are rewarded for their contribution to the organization via equitable compensation and incentive programs.
- The organization celebrates its successes with recognition programs and group festivities.
- The "golden rule" is never forgotten when relating to employees, vendors, customers, and the public.

In addition, managers should be cognizant of the attitudes employees have about them and should take steps, where appropriate, to adjust their behavior so that the spirit generated by the new culture will be reinforced. Equally important, managers should carefully reevaluate their attitudes toward employees and work with them to resolve any differences.

REFERENCES

[1]Reported in *The Inc. 500*, 1998, p. 31
[2]Walton, Mary. *Deming Management at Work*. New York: Perigee Books, 1991.
[3]Adapted from "Managing by Values: Is Levi Strauss' Approach Visionary or Flaky?" *Business Week*, August 1, 1994.
[4]Boyett, Joseph H. and Conn, Henry P. *Workplace 2000*. New York: Penguin Books, 1991.
[5]Tyler, Kathryn. "Prepare Managers to Become Career Coaches." *HR Magazine*, June 1997, p. 100.
[6]Tyler, Kathryn, p. 101
[7]Koch, Jennifer. "Perpetual Thanks: Its Assets." *Personnel Journal*, January 1990, pp. 72–73.
[8]Manchester Consulting Research. Executive Briefing, Vol. 1, No. 4.
[9]Manchester Consulting Research. Executive Briefing, Vol. 1, No. 4.
[10]Manchester Consulting Research. Executive Briefing, Vol. 1, No. 4.
[11]Reichheld, Frederick F. *The Loyalty Effect*. Harvard Business School Press, 1996, p. 15.

CHAPTER 5

Getting Started

QUOTES AND QUIPS

"Changing the culture of an organization is certainly going to cause at least some uneasiness among managers, employees, subcontractors and, sometimes, vendors and customers. People are accustomed to working and living in one type of environment and resist changing to another. This resistance is often manifested by frustration, anger, cynicism, apathy, stress and even sabotage. Instead of ignoring or blaming those individuals who have difficulty in coping with change, we must create an organizational culture where people can face their fears, learn from their experiences and make the necessary changes to adapt in ways which will support their success."

Edward G. Verlander
President
E.G. Verlander & Associates, Inc.

The Change Agent: Internal or External?

The most effective way to assure that effective culture-related changes can be made is to first make the need to change a top priority of the organization. Once this is done, the first step is to assign the responsibility for its success to a *change agent*. The change agent should be one or a combination of the following people: a high ranking corporate officer, a team of top and middle managers, and/or an outside consultant.

There are both advantages and disadvantages to assigning the role of principal change agent to a member of management. The major advantage is that he or she knows the history and background of the company, is intimately aware of the personalities and idiosyncrasies of many of the employees, and the ramifications of changes that may be suggested. The major disadvantage is that the inside manager may be too close to the situation to view it objectively and may be blinded by his or her own prejudices, ambitions, or personal feelings about the direction the organization should follow.

Outside consultants, looking at the organization with unbiased eyes, can usually bring together divergent views and help members of the organization analyze problems more objectively. Because most qualified consultants have had experience in facilitating culture changes with other firms, they can provide expertise which internal managers may not possess. In addition, they can help resolve conflicts among managers and can design programs to assure that recommended changes are made.

However, there are disadvantages in using outsiders. Because they do not have intimate knowledge of the internal workings of the company, it will take them longer to pick up all of the subtleties that permeate the current culture. In addition, good consultants are expensive, averaging thousands of dollars a day.

The best course of action for most organizations is a combination of inside managers and one or more outside consultants. However, as previously noted, it is important that the team leader be a senior manager. Unless the change agent is a very high-ranking officer, the move toward a culture change will not be taken seriously.

QUOTES AND QUIPS

"There is nothing wrong with change,
if it is in the right direction."
Winston Churchill, 1874–1965
British Prime Minister

Attributes of an Effective Change Agent

The selection of the principal change agent is essential to the success of the program. In selecting this person, choose somebody who has the following attributes:

- *The change agent should be respected by people at all levels of the organization.* Title and position are not enough by themselves. A typical example of this occurred at Electronic Accessories, Inc., an electronics firm in New York. The CEO appointed his vice-president of operations as the leader of his change team. This doomed the project from the start. This vice-president, who was also the CEO's nephew, was looked upon by everyone as a sycophant and incompetent. The lesson: Unless the change agent has real influence in the organization and is respected by the staff, the project will not be viewed as a serious attempt to accomplish change.
- *The change agent must be an accomplisher.* He or she should have a record of getting things done. In many organizations there are people who talk a great game, but do not follow through with real achievements. Such people cannot lead the company to significant improvements. The person leading the team should be someone who has demonstrated the ability to bring about change on his or her own job.
- *The change agent must be a good communicator.* Doing successful things is important, but it's not enough. The change agent must also be able to communicate goals, information, instructions, ideas, and actions in clear, concise, persuasive ways. He or she must also be able to elicit ideas from others and be ready to accept good suggestions from persons at all levels in the company hierarchy.
- *The change agent should be a "people person."* He or she must be personable and have a history of working well with all kinds of people—colleagues, subordinates, bosses, vendors, customers, and the public. In short, this person should have a reputation of being a good, trustworthy, responsible individual who has demonstrated success in interpersonal relations.

Using a Consultant

As pointed out, the use of an outside consultant adds to the professionalism of the project and choosing the consultant who is right for you is key to the success of the operation. Consultants differ, however, and it is important that the person you select is the best person available for your project.

The first step is to determine just what role the consultant will play in the change process. Will he or she be part of a team or be responsible for the entire project? There are advantages and limitations to either role.

KEY POINT

Change agents should be
- respected by people at all levels
- have records of accomplishment
- be good communicators
- be "people people"

Let's look at two companies that chose different routes to changing their organizational cultures. The Adams Transport Corporation, a growing interstate trucking company, turned the entire process over to a consultant. Alan Adams, the CEO, recognized the need to make significant changes in his company culture if his firm was to make the kind of progress he envisioned. He realized that he had neither the time nor the expertise to do this alone. Each of his vice-presidents was a specialist in marketing, operations, finance, or human resources. None had the knowledge of the overall operation to function as a change agent.

To accomplish his goals, Alan had to find a consultant who could be the prime change agent. He felt that it would be an asset if the consultant he chose was thoroughly knowledgeable about the trucking industry. There are many experienced consultants who specialize in specific industries. Through trade associations, reading trade publications, and talking with other trucking company executives, Alan was able to locate prospects with trucking backgrounds.

The other company which had decided to make a culture change was Homeowners Savings and Loan Association. Although not tainted by the S & L scandals of the early 1990s, the company recognized the need to change its culture if it wanted to move aggressively into the 21st century. This dynamic financial institution required its staff to keep up with the latest developments through continuing education seminars, graduate degrees, and technological training. They had a ready-made cadre of competent people to make up a change team, but recognized the need for an outside consultant—not to lead the project, but to facilitate and coordinate the transition.

The consultant chosen by Homeowners S & L did not need experience or even knowledge of the finance business. The well-trained staff could provide all of this expertise. Here the chief requirement was the ability to facilitate the process. Most professional consultants do not have expertise in any one industry. Despite the attitude of many businesses that they are unique, most organizations are more alike than different. Professional consultants not only bring their own expertise to the process, but the experiences picked up from working with organizations with similar problems.

Choosing a Consultant

In choosing the right consultant for your organization, keep in mind the role he or she will play:

Members of the consulting team must be people you can talk to openly and honestly. Obviously, it's more important that consultants ask questions that will help them understand your company's problems than to come up with glib, easy solutions.

One of the prospective consultants interviewed by Homeowners S & L had an impressive brochure describing his background and experience. At the meeting with the culture change team, he boasted about all of his accomplishments, dropped names of prominent business leaders that he knew, and answered their questions with positive assertions about his ability to solve their problems. He was so sure he knew the answers to all of their problems, that he did not even ask pertinent questions. Despite his smooth presentation and impressive appearance, the committee realized he was not a person with whom they could relate.

They must truly listen. Effective culture change consultants are active listeners. They do not only sit or stand with ears open, but they follow up with additional questions about what is being discussed. They make sure they understand and seek clarification when needed. They do not listen only to you or other high ranking executives, but give equal attention to people at all levels who can provide insight into the problems.

The consulting group must have solid credentials. The consultant and his or her associates should have a combination of education and experience in organizational analysis, training and development and business management. In discussing their concepts, they should use clear, understandable language—not jargon and pseudo-psychological babble. If the principal consultant plans to delegate your project to subordinate staff members, make a point of meeting with the people who will be assigned to your firm. It is essential that each of them meet the criteria you have established for the assignment.

While the personal characteristics noted here are very important, the consultant must also have the technical know-how to do the job. Check on the academic and experiential credentials. Do members of the team have advanced degrees? Have they published books or articles in the areas related to the assignment? Have they worked on changing the culture of other organizations? Read their publications. Check carefully with previous clients.

The consultants should have a track record and solid references. If the claims made seem too good to be true or appear "gimmicky," be particularly skeptical. Ask other business people in your community or industry about their reputation.

You and your associates must feel comfortable with the consultants. Have those members of the firm who will be assigned to your company meet with several of the people in your organization with whom they will interrelate. Get the reaction of your associates to these consultants. Remember the success of the project lies with the employees and, unless the consulting group has their loyal support, it cannot succeed.

QUOTES AND QUIPS

"Confidence is that feeling by which the mind embarks on great and honorable courses with a sure hope and trust in itself."
Cicero, 106–43 B.C.
Roman statesman

The members of the group should be empathetic. They should demonstrate this by taking the time to get to know you, your company, and your associates. Before accepting the assignment, the best consultants should make an effort to learn as much as possible about your company, its strengths and weaknesses, and the problems you are most concerned about. Reputable consultants prefer to make their own needs analysis to determine objectively what steps need to be taken to identify and resolve the real problems that will be faced in the assignment.

They should have strong presentation skills both orally and in writing. During the process and after it is completed, results will have to be presented to managers, employees, and often to boards of directors or trustees. Oral skills can be measured by the manner in which the consultant speaks with you and your people. To evaluate written skills, ask for copies of nonconfidential reports or articles written about previous assignments.

They should have the capability to implement the program (if desired) or be available for follow-up and counseling if they do not participate in the implementation. Once the change project program is decided upon, it must be implemented. In many companies, the consultant continues working with the company until the entire culture change is completed. In other companies, the managers choose to implement the recommended programs on their own. Once the plan is approved, the consultants leave. The implementation is handled by an internal management team. How the plan is implemented will be discussed in Chapter 8. In such cases, it's a good idea to have the consultants come in periodically to check how things are going and to provide counsel when needed.

Where can one find such specialists? Probably most consultants are recommended by other firms that have been satisfied with their work. Let people in the business community know you are seeking a consultant and referrals will follow. Another good source is the academic community. Colleges and universities can recommend past and present faculty members and qualified alumni. Also, read business literature—often the author of an article or book is available as a consultant. Trade and professional associations and chambers of commerce usually know reputable consultants.

TACTICAL TIPS

To develop a list of potential consultants, attend seminars and trade or professional conventions and peruse professional journals. Keep a file of speakers and authors who impress you.

Communicating the Resolve

Once the decision has been made to institute a culture change, it is essential that this resolve be communicated at all levels of the organization. Here are some suggestions that will make this communication more effective:

- The announcement must emanate from top management. Remember, unless the CEO and the entire management group wholly support the project, it cannot succeed.
- The language must be straightforward and candid. Everybody should be informed of why change is needed, what results are anticipated and, equally important, what may happen if things remain as they are.
- It must be sincere. If the communication, be it oral or in writing, sounds phony or even lukewarm, it will not be taken seriously by those involved.
- A sense of urgency should be instilled, but not to the point of exaggeration. If employees feel that the company is on the brink of collapse if change does not occur *now,* they will be busy updating their resumes instead of cooperating.
- It should make clear who is responsible for each aspect of the project.

Techniques of Communicating

To see how one company initiated this aspect of the program, let's look at how the Consolidated Food Company, distributors of bulk food products to restaurants and institutions, began their culture change process. When it became clear that there was a need to make major changes in their ways of conducting their business, the executive committee formed a team to plan the change. The company consisted of two long-established food brokerage firms: Brown Groceries and Green Dairies, that had merged five years earlier.

The consolidation of purchasing, marketing, and much administrative work had been accomplished early in the transition period. However, there still existed a dichotomy between the "Brown group" and the "Green group."

Art Pastore, Consolidated's CEO, put together a team consisting of the two highest-ranking members of each of these groups, two middle managers who had been hired since the merger, and an outside consultant, Dr. Norman Roberts, a human resources professional.

Discuss the Goals with the Team

Pastore's first step was to bring his team together and discuss the goals they wished to accomplish. He took an active role in this discussion, but made sure to avoid dominating the group and to elicit ideas and suggestions from all the participants. He pointed out the importance of moving ahead rapidly on this project and assured them that this was a positive step forward and not a subterfuge for reorganization or downsizing.

Pastore pointed out that he would give the team his full support, but expected them to be the prime contributors. He introduced Dr. Roberts, who explained that his role would be that of a facilitator. Roberts noted that he did not have the answers to their problems, but he was skilled in asking the right questions so that they—the team members—could utilize their expertise in solving the problems.

It was suggested that each department head be briefed on the goals of the project and how it would proceed. They, in turn, would discuss this with their people, so no employee would be in the dark as to what was going on. This would eliminate rumors that might interfere with the accomplishment of the mission.

Send Preparatory Bulletins

Pastore also sent a bulletin to all employees stating the goals of the project, reinforcing his support, asking for the cooperation of all employees, and requesting that they make suggestions to the team. To develop excitement among the employees, a contest was held to name the project. The winning title, "Project for Progress," was suggested by one of the customer service representatives. Streamers and posters displaying this title were hung all over the facility.

Develop Plan of Action

To establish a sense of urgency, Pastore asked the team to develop a plan of action in the first week of their deliberations and to set a time table at which each step of the procedure should be accomplished.

Make Sure Everybody Understands Plan

To assure proper follow-through, Pastore met with Dr. Roberts privately to get his assessments of the progress made and periodically spoke to various team members for their input.

Conduct Informal Discussions and Regular Meetings to Keep Things Rolling Along

Weekly meetings of the entire team with Pastore gave him continuing insight into their progress and assured the team of his continued support.

Through carefully planned and meticulously executed communication with people at all levels in the organization, Consolidated's Project for Progress started auspiciously and moved forward with enthusiastic cooperation.

QUOTES & QUIPS

"All great changes are irksome to the human mind, especially those which are attended with great dangers and uncertain effects."
John Quincy Adams, 1767–1845
Sixth President of the United States

SUM AND SUBSTANCE

The choice of a change agent to lead a corporation's culture change is key to its success. This individual can be either a senior executive of the organization or an outside consultant, who specializes in aiding organizations in making culture changes.

Whether this person is chosen from internal or external sources, he or she should manifest the following characteristics:

Respect. If the change agent is chosen from internal managers, he or she must be a person who has earned the respect of employees by past actions. If the agent is an outside consultant, he or she must have achieved a reputation in the field which is communicated to the staff before the start of the program and is reinforced by the actions of the consultant from the very beginning of the process.

Communications. It is essential that the change agent be a superior communicator. Probably, the most important communication skill needed is listening. Culture changes cannot be started unless the agent and all others involved in the process truly listen to what is being expressed at all levels. In addition, the agent must be able to present concepts, information, and progress reports clearly, concisely, and in an exciting and inspirational manner to ensure continued enthusiasm about the program.

Empathy. The change agent should be an empathetic individual, who is sincerely interested in what people say and how they feel about what is going on in the company.

Once the change agent has been selected, a culture change team should be created which includes representatives of top management, middle management, and rank-and-file employees who will work with the agent to institute and implement the program.

If specific technical knowledge is needed that the change agent may not possess (particularly if he or she comes from outside the organization), persons with that specialized know-how should be assigned to work with the change agent.

CHAPTER 6

Designing the Strategy for a Culture Change

Once the diagnosis has been completed and the change agent is chosen, the next step is to develop the strategy to be used in accomplishing the steps that are needed for the organization to change from the as-is culture to the desired culture.

The first step is to discuss the results of the O-MRI with the CEO and other members of senior management. Without divulging sources, the results must be clearly described and discussed. This is the most difficult part of the culture change process. Often this group is shocked to learn how they are perceived by their staffs and their resentment can deter them from endorsing the program. The consultant must be prepared to make this presentation in a positive manner, indicating that most of us are so engrossed in the details of our jobs, it's easy to overlook some matters that had been revealed by the report.

This was illustrated in a recent experience of one of my colleagues. His client, a family-owned business, was still managed by the founder, a brilliant engineer, but a dogmatic manager. He listened carefully to the report and then turned to the consultant and said, "Nonsense. These people owe everything to me. I invented the product, developed the processes, hired and trained them, pay them well, and now they say *this* about me just because I demand excellence and refuse to coddle them."

Only after several days of meetings with the owner was the consultant able to persuade him to continue the process. "You hired me because you knew there were problems," the consultant maintained.

"The O-MRI identified the causes of these problems. Of course, they don't all result from your actions, but as CEO, everything that happens in this company is your responsibility. Your goal is to move forward. To do this you must accept that the 'as-is' situation cannot continue."

QUOTES AND QUIPS

"Show me a thoroughly satisfied person and
I will show you a failure."
Thomas A. Edison, 1847–1931
American inventor

THE THREE C'S

In order for a successful transition, a foundation must be laid by building into the organization what I refer to as *the three C's:*

THE THREE C'S

Confidence that the program to change the culture will really succeed.

Commitment of all the people at all levels of the organization to work together to achieve the desired goals.

Competence by developing the skills required to achieve these goals.

Building Confidence

Often one of the key problems identified by the O-MRI is lack of trust and confidence in management. It's not easy to restore this feeling, but it is necessary if the move toward a culture change is to start the program in a manner that will prove management is really sincere about making the change.

In short, confidence needs to be won back if the culture change initiative is to succeed. As this is an essential requirement in achieving the goal, the consultant and the team must take strong positive steps to develop renewed trust and confidence. It's not easy, but it can be done. In my experience, I have found that the following five steps are important in restoring confidence:

1. Release the Results of the O-MRI

In order to start solving problems, all concerned should know just what those problems are. However, the need to maintain confidentiality is essential. Information should be provided in as much detail as possible without identifying the names of persons who provided the information. This is not always easy to do since many of the reported factors relate to specific departments and members of management. Care should be taken to report them not as condemnations, but as areas in which improvement or change would help meet the new goals.

QUOTES AND QUIPS

"Truth is a gem that is found at a great depth; whilst on the surface of the world all things are weighed by the false scale of custom."
Lord Byron, 1788–1824
English poet

This information may be presented in oral and/or written form. Whether the report is presented by a member of management or by a consultant, it is important that confidentiality be maintained and that the employees leave the meeting feeling positive about the changes that will follow.

Usually this information is not released in a written memo or bulletin, but is presented to staff members at meetings, especially designated for this purpose. This enables the consultant or whoever conducts the meeting to explain aspects which may not be clear to some participants. It also enables him or her to get immediate reactions and to spot feelings of disbelief, opposition, insecurity, or other negatives that may be lurking in the minds of some people.

An effective practice is to start the meeting by thanking the participants for their cooperation in the conducting of the O-MRI and assuring them that what will be discussed is an overview of what has been learned and that the promise of confidentiality will be kept. It will be made clear that the purpose of the meeting is not to cast blame on anybody. In order to make changes for the better, it is necessary to understand where the problems exist so that everybody can work together to resolve them.

Give participants the opportunity to ask questions and express their feelings about the matters uncovered by the O-MRI. Point out that this meeting is not about solving problems (that will come later) but to inform the participants about what has been learned and to enable them to begin to think about what can be done to move ahead. Tell them: "You are an integral part of this process. Change cannot be made unilaterally by top management. For it to really work, every man and woman at every level in this organization must be involved."

2. Take Responsibility for What's Wrong

This does not mean asking managers to "confess their sins" and beg the forgiveness of their people. It does mean, however, that managers should admit that the approaches or tactics they had been using did not work and that they are ready to listen to suggestions for improvement.

Steve is a good example. He was a manager who had run his department like a military unit. Steve demanded absolute, no-questions-asked obedience. The turnover in the department was well above that of other departments and the morale of his group was low. After discussing the O-MRI results with the consultant, Steve was shocked. He had always assumed that his actions were "normal" and had considered himself to be a good boss.

After some private discussions with the consultant, Steve resolved to attend seminars and do some reading on supervisory techniques. At the departmental meeting in which the O-MRI results were discussed. Steve learned a lot. He was surprised to find that his staff felt unappreciated because he rarely praised their work. He had not realized that his management style was too dogmatic and arbitrary and, instead of resulting in greater efficiency, it caused resentment. Most important, he learned that his failure to seriously consider the ideas and suggestions made by members of his team stifled their creativity and, in the long run, the effectiveness of the department. Steve resolved that he would apply what he learned in managing his team.

TACTICAL TIPS

People usually respect those willing to admit their mistakes, especially when it is followed by a new attitude that indicates a sincere effort and resolve to change the aspects of their behavior that has caused the problem.

---

3. Develop a Reasonable, Digestible Plan of Attack

Many people are skeptical about formal plans. In many cases, they've undoubtedly seen numerous plans developed by consultants or internal managers that have cost much money, built up much hope, and then fizzled when attempts were made to put them into action. Many plans wind up as dusty notebooks on some high shelf, never to be looked at again.

The culture change plan must be different. It must be developed in the right way for the right reasons. It needs to be a living document that becomes a working tool for the entire organization. It should define the key areas that are to be addressed and provide realistic guidelines outlining the part each person will take in moving it forward. The plan should be a living document that not only guides, but inspires the members of the organization to commit their energies and emotions to its success.

In my own observations, plans that have been most successful follow these fundamental precepts:

They are simple. Written in clear, uncomplicated language, they are easily understood by the people who are responsible for making them work. Instead of theories and rationales, they provide common-sense approaches to dealing with the situations under discussion.

They move from the general to the specific. It is essential that everybody concerned with implementation of the program be thoroughly familiar with the goals and objectives. Each goal is carefully phrased to avoid misinterpretations. However, the basic plan does not include details. Strategies and tactics are left open to be developed as the plan moves along. This does not tie down the implementing group. It enables them to react with flexibility and encourages them to use their own creativity in fleshing out the plan.

Concentration is on immediate results. Although the long-term objectives are never out of mind, in order to build momentum and establish credibility, people want to see immediate results. By accomplishing specific changes early in the process, it encourages everybody to move upward and onward.

They stress the benefits. Unlike the traditional approach to planning, which concentrates on the "what," "where," and "how," the effective culture change plan emphasizes the "why." When people understand why what is planned will benefit the company and themselves, it reinforces their commitment.

KEY POINT

Successful plans for a culture change
- are simple
- move from the general to the specific
- concentrate on immediate results
- stress the benefits that will be derived

Constructing the Plan

Who should construct the plan? Inasmuch as the success of the program requires the confidence of everybody working in the organization, it is important that a variety of people have input into the development of the plan.

It cannot be reiterated often enough that unless senior management is fully involved in the culture change, the program will not succeed. But it is equally important to recognize that if the planning is limited *only* to senior managers, it cannot succeed.

The most effective method for constructing the plan is a two-phase procedure:

The executive retreat. Invited to this retreat are members of the senior staff. These are the men and women who are responsible for running the departments, divisions, and major staff activities. Their extensive expertise in their own specialties combined with their overall knowledge of the organization's problems enable them to contribute significantly to the plan.

Bringing them to a retreat, often in a hotel or resort away from the organization's facilities, removes them from day-to-day concerns and provides a relaxing atmosphere for creative thinking. The objective of the executive retreat is to build a sense of teamwork, trust, and goodwill among the senior staff and to develop a reasonably good sense of how the new culture should look and feel.

This group will provide the framework of the plan for change. They will identify major goals and objectives based on the results of the O-MRI. This might include timetables and general budget issues. However, specific strategies and tactics should not be part of this discussion. Those aspects will be dealt with later.

It is very important that retreats of this type be conducted by an outside facilitator. Usually, the culture change consultant, who supervised the first stages of the program, conducts the meeting. The main function of the facilitator is to keep things moving, to assure that the goals are met and that no one manager, no matter what the rank of that person, dominates the meeting.

One of the reasons that retreats have so often been effective is that it gives all participants the opportunity for social contact. In many organizations, people who work closely together on business assignments really do not know each other. Here is an opportunity for them to get to know the real human being hidden inside the corporate shell many people feel obliged to wear on the job.

Over golf or tennis, lounging before the fireplace, strolling through the gardens, relationships are built and solidified. As those of us who have experienced this have learned, this not only leads to better on-the-job rapport, but encourages a freer exchange of ideas both at the retreat and after it ends.

The multilevel retreat. The use of multilevel retreats for identifying the problems was discussed in Chapter 2. A similar retreat is often used as part of the implementation process. Participants will be drawn from various components of the organization. The agenda will be similar to that of the executive retreat.

As pointed out in Chapter 2, participants represent employees at all levels of the company and can express ideas and comments that may differ significantly from those developed in the executive retreat. These should be carefully listened to, evaluated objectively, and incorporated into the overall plan.

Once the problems that must be dealt with have been identified and accepted by the members of the organization, the final step in the planning process is to appoint a culture change committee. This group is made up of representatives of senior management, middle management, first-line management, and informal leaders of the rank and file workers. It is headed by the consultant. How this committee operates will be discussed in Chapter 9.

QUOTES AND QUIPS

"When people talk, listen completely. Most people never listen."
Ernest Hemingway, 1899–1961
American novelist

The Seven Basic Elements of a Good Culture-Change Plan

In evaluating the culture change plans used by a number of companies, I have compiled a list of the key ingredients that are common to those that worked the best:

- **A clear, accurate sense of the "as-is" situation**
  As pointed out earlier in this book, the first step in making any change is to have a clear picture of the current situation. A well-designed and administered O-MRI does this. It identifies the real causes and separates them from the symptoms. When executives hide their heads in the sand and hope problems will go away, no change can be effected. If the current culture is holding the organization back, the factors that cause the problems must be uncovered and accepted. Only then can the steps be taken that will lead to a culture change.

- **A clear, reasonable vision of the "should be" situation**
  Representative of senior management and those of lower levels should agree on what the new culture should look like. Using executive and multilevel retreats, goals should be developed that are attainable and acceptable to all.
- **Timetables**
  Timetables are established for the accomplishment of each phase of the program. These are agreed upon by all and every effort is made to meet them. Because it is not always possible to estimate how long it will take to accomplish many aspects of the plan, some flexibility should be built into the timetables, but every effort should be made to make it reasonable to meet them.
- **Budgets**
  Changing a culture, like every aspect of business, costs money. To avoid both the tendency to overspend and to avoid not having enough funds, a budget should be developed for the project. The consultant can be helpful in specifying what costs will be incurred.
- **A specific strategy to keep employees informed**
  As all employees—not just the management group—are essential to the plan's success, it's important that periodic progress reports are published. These reports will keep the employees abreast of developments, accomplishments, changes, if any, and thank-you's to people who were especially helpful.
- **A measurement system**
  To track progress, a measurement system should be created. One frequently used method is a *Gannt chart,* a simple chart on which actual progress is charted against the timetables as seen in Figure 6-1.
- **A process for continuing to solicit input**
  Plans to change a culture are dynamic. They are never truly final. Employees see new things, have new ideas, develop new approaches. Successful plans build in a process that encourages people to submit suggestions and recommendations. They may be in the form of the traditional suggestion system, through periodic idea-generating meetings, or through informal conversations with the consultant or other members of the team.

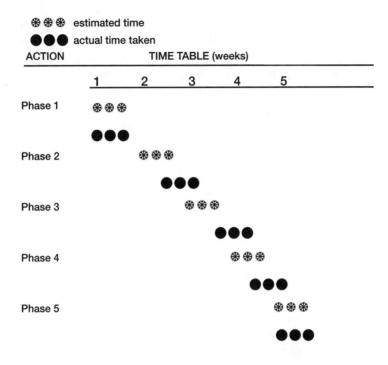

Figure 6-1. *Gannt Chart.*

Make Some Important Changes Early

Two of the most powerful motivators that I have found in initiating a culture change plan are first impressions and momentum. Both must be present to build initial and lasting confidence in the ultimate success of the endeavor.

The best way to accomplish both simultaneously is to announce and institute some significant changes in the first thirty days—or even sooner. It sends a strong signal to the entire organization that you mean business.

Remember the Excelsior Paper Company which was discussed in Chapter 2? When they finalized their culture change plan, the CEO, Douglas Stewart, instituted a new program to encourage upgrading the skills of all employees. The first step, commencing immediately, was to arrange for in-house skill training courses and tuition-reimbursement for employees taking courses at local colleges.

It was also announced that a series of additional programs was in the works and would be made available over the next several months. The reaction was gratifying. It was the chief topic of conversation among employees and the general attitude was: "I guess they really mean it when they say they are going to change things around here."

There is a danger, however, if the first changes are of a negative nature. The program at another firm was predestined to fail when its first move was to lay off marginal workers whom the managers felt might have become barriers to the program's success. Even though the lay-offs were justifiable, by terminating the workers at this stage, it sowed the seeds of distrust. If the culture change is associated with negative actions, instead of enthusiasm, fear is generated and instead of cooperation, distrust ensues.

Changes need not be dramatic. Even seemingly minor variations in procedures can have significant effects. Here are a few examples: a company, known for its adherence to strict dress codes initiated a "dress-down" day, another company eliminated reserved parking spaces for executives and a machine shop housed in an old building, redecorated the coffee-break room, and provided free doughnuts and bagels at break time. These may not appear to be important, but they send a message that things are changing for the better.

Communicate Your Successes Throughout the Organization

This can be done through the usual communication channels such as articles in the company newsletter, special bulletins, and other publications, as well as in discussions at meetings. However, more effective than formal channels is the spreading of the word via the grapevine. In every organization, this informal channel of communication proves to be more powerful than any other.

Few things will begin to reverse the flow of a bad culture and build confidence in the effort to change it than the honest and whole-hearted support of the informal leaders within the company. The best way to make this happen is to involve these informal leaders from the beginning. Identify and cultivate them early in the process. Meet with them off premises. Include them in the multilevel retreats and appoint them to the team. Always maintain their confidences and never make promises to them you can't keep.

I have found that the informal leaders are often loaded with ideas and suggestions on how to make things better. In a bad culture, management often looks upon informal leaders who do not agree with them as enemies to be suppressed. This usually causes them to go underground and become persistent thorns in their boss's sides. Instead of perceiving them as trouble makers, these influential men and women should be looked upon as intelligent, capable people who have much to offer. Instead of opposing them, include them in the change process. Bring them in as full partners.

KEY POINT

The key to making a good first impression and building momentum can be summed up in three steps:

1. Set immediate short-term goals—something that the O-MRI has indicated is important to the people.
2. Start implementing these goals as soon as feasible and accomplish them on or ahead of schedule.
3. Get feedback on how the changes you make are received. If they are not working, make changes—*fast*. If they are working, capitalize on the achievements by publicizing them and using them as stepping stones to additional changes.

Informal leaders feed the grapevine. If they are enthusiastic about what is happening, this will permeate the entire organization. By considering them as partners, you'll have converted opponents to sincere proponents and will have reversed the flow of energy. When this is compounded over dozens and perhaps hundreds of employees, it can be a powerful element in achieving the success of the culture change.

QUOTES AND QUIPS

"Confidence is the feeling by which the mind embarks in great
and honorable courses with a sure hope and trust in itself."
Cicero, 106–43 B.C.
Roman statesman

BUILDING COMMITMENT

The second "C"—commitment—follows logically the development
of confidence. Once confidence is established, it becomes relatively
easy to obtain commitment from those whose cooperation is essential
to the success of the culture change. The reverse, of course, is also true.
If people lose confidence, their commitment will wane. I have identified two key components in maintaining commitment to a culture
change: maintaining credibility, and focusing on results and benefits.

Maintaining Credibility

People working within troubled cultures are likely to be more cynical
and suspicious than those working within healthy cultures. They have
seen or personally experienced deceptions, broken promises, exaggerated statistics and overstated predictions. A good example of this was
experienced by my colleague, Dr. Arthur R. Pell, who was commis-
sioned to develop a full-scale human resources program for a medium-
sized hosiery company in Pennsylvania. Gary L., the CEO of the company, assured Dr. Pell that he was fully behind this program and had
budgeted sufficient funds to initiate and implement the program.

Pell's initial enthusiasm for the assignment was dampened on the
first day, when members of the management staff greeted him with
skepticism. "So Gary has another one of his 'progressive' ideas," they
commented. "Last month it was a move toward marketing research,
today its HR."

It didn't take Pell long to realize that even if Gary was sincere in
wanting to institute a human resources program, nobody in his management group really believed it. And, of course, they were right. Pell
learned that over the past several years Gary had grown hot and

cold about a number of projects, hired experienced managers or consultants to start them and, after a short time, dropped them. This curent plan was no exception. Within a few weeks, Gary lost interest, failed to show up at meetings concerning the project, and did not provide the support he had promised. Pell had no choice but to resign the account.

Unfortunately, there are many executives like Gary L. in the world of business. When good managers recognize this, they are reluctant to commit themselves to any of this person's ideas and often leave the company after a short time. Those who remain tend to be mediocre sycophants who probably do little more than perpetuate the whims and insincerity of the boss.

QUOTES AND QUIPS

The essential element in personal magnetism is a consuming sincerity—an overwhelming faith in the importance of the work one has to do."
Bruce Barton
Advertising executive

Ten Ways To Obtain and Maintain Commitment

Managers who lead successful culture change efforts stimulate their people and inspire them to commit wholeheartedly to the project. Over the years, I have noted ten precepts that outstanding managers apply to obtain and maintain the commitment of their associates:

1. **They only make promises they know they can keep.** Claude L., the vice-president of international business for a computer software company elaborated on this. "As a senior executive, I am often tempted to make promises to people based on what I am almost sure will occur. But, I know that if something develops which may make it impossible to fulfill that promise, even though it was made in good faith, it will reflect on my integrity. I make damn few promises and keep them all."

2. **They avoid exaggeration or overstatement.** A public relations executive told me that in order to promote her clients' organizations, it is very tempting to overstate information or stretch the truth—just a little. But, knowledgeable people will not be fooled and in the long run it will hurt the client.

3. **They set realistic goals—and then exceed expectations.** It always looks better to give more than is expected. Some managers set low goals so that it is easy to exceed them. This can be self-defeating because if goals are too low, not only will the results be mediocre, but the people working on the project will be unchallenged. Reasonable goals that can be attained with hard work stimulate people to commitment—and exceeding the goals makes the attainment that much sweeter.

4. **They tell the truth—even when it hurts.** The whole country saw an excellent example of this when McNeil Laboratories, manufacturers of Tylenol, discovered that several bottles of their product had been contaminated with cyanide. The CEO immediately announced that the company was recalling all the inventory and replacing it with new tamper-proof packages. To do this cost the company millions of dollars, but their forthright acknowledgment and action reinforced the reputation for integrity of McNeil and its parent company, Johnson and Johnson.

5. **They practice what they preach.** Many senior executives have climbed aboard the Total Quality Management (TQM) bandwagon and given speeches about the importance of empowering the people to make decisions, yet in their own companies, there is only lip service to this concept.

An example of a company that does practice what it preaches is General Electric, where truly empowered teams are committed to quality improvement. Jack Welch, GE's CEO, implemented an innovative management technique called "Work-Out" which encourages open communication and the sharing of ideas. Work-Out is essentially a forum where workers and management meet regularly to determine how they can solve problems at their company. Work-Out peels away layers of management and empowers workers to share ideas and reduce the amount of time it takes to get a quality product from the plant to the customer.

At GE's Lynn, Massachusetts, plant, Charles Reuter, a union leader, pointed out how the company's Work-Out forum had changed the attitude of the union and its members toward the company.

"People are listening," he said, "and the areas we disagree in are becoming smaller. Work-Out caused a culture shock in some of the old-line middle management, who used to say 'You're a grunt and I'm the boss so shut up and do it my way.'"[1]

QUOTES AND QUIPS

"Managing better means managing less. The old 2-by-4 style of management is dead. . . . We don't have a prayer of winning pr surviving without a self-confident workforce that comes to work every day searching for a way to succeed."
Jack Welch
CEO, General Electric Co.

6. **They admit their mistakes—quickly.** As the old adage says, "to err is human." We all make mistakes. Failure to acknowledge that one is wrong only compounds the situation.

The managers that I most admire don't make excuses or try to rationalize decisions that didn't work out as planned or for programs or concepts that did not meet expectations. They investigate the reasons for the problem, and work to make the necessary corrections and adjustments to bring the program back on track.

When Coca Cola changed its formula to the "New Coke" several years ago, it made the change after months of market studies and experimentation. Despite the tremendous amount of work and money spent in planning the revamped product, it was not accepted by the public.

Coca Cola's management could have rationalized that the market studies were right and all that was needed was time to get the customers used to the new taste. They could have attempted to justify their decision by pointing out the statistics, analyses and "scientific" studies that had been made. But they didn't. Roberto Goizueta, Coke's CEO, immediately reintroduced the old standard product, re-christened it "Classic Coke" and turned what could have been a major catastrophe into a marketing coup.

7. **They do their homework.** Instead of relying on hunches or superficial information, successful managers get all the facts before making decisions. They are not reluctant to ask for help from others including subordinates to obtain ideas and suggestions. They "benchmark" what other organizations have done when faced with similar problems.

8. **They are superb communicators.** They engender enthusiasm for the concepts they present, whether directed to their own people or to outsiders. They encourage others to bring out and develop their own ideas. Their enthusiasm is contagious.

This was illustrated when Lee Iacocca was appointed CEO of Chrysler. The company was in serious trouble and in order for Chrysler to survive, major steps had to be taken. How Iacocca persuaded Congress to provide financial support and how he rebuilt the company has been written about in many articles and books. The key to his success was his skill in communicating. His sincere enthusiasm for his company, his people, and his products resulted in bringing Chrysler back to a major position in the automobile industry.

9. **They relate to people at a human level.** Organizational changes start with the people in the organization. The change agent must understand the psychology of the people with whom he or she is dealing. People differ and what is important to one may not be to another.

10. **They always follow up and follow through.** Richard L. is an example of a man who didn't follow-up. When he was appointed vice-president of operations of his company, he gave the three department managers who reported to him a great deal of autonomy.

"They are trained and competent managers," he said. "Together we developed goals and objectives and I can depend on them to fulfill their assignments."

Richard concentrated his efforts on planning future programs and left the day-to-day operations to his managers. He assumed that they would carry out what had been agreed to. It didn't quite work out that way. By failing to follow up to determine if the work was on target, errors were made and decisions taken that delayed timely completion of the assignments.

TACTICAL TIPS

Follow up does not mean "micromanage." Set established points for completion of key phases of a project. These are not surprise inspections. Each participant is aware of these points and both manager and associates always can check on the status of the project.

Focus on Results and Benefits

In the beginning the enthusiasm of the initiation and the excitement of the change agent(s) keep the flow of energy going in all those involved. But as time goes on, and the program becomes more routine, employee enthusiasm may begin to wane.

The effort to maintain the enthusiasm for a culture change must be kept on the front burner so that it's always in the forefront of everyone's thoughts. This can be done by building right into the design strategy a provision to track and log the results that are accomplished along the way. Then tie those results into the tangible benefits that are of interest and concern to employees.

Top salespersons understand and apply this concept all the time. They know that in order to persuade a prospect to buy, the prospect needs to see clearly how it will benefit him or her—how it will make his or her job easier, increase the likelihood of something good happening, or reduce or eliminate a thorny problem. Successful salespeople make a strong effort to make the connection clear. Managers leading a culture change should do the same.

Show Employees the Benefits of the Culture Change

In the summer of 1998, I made an informal survey of companies which were in the process of changing their cultures. My objective was to learn what steps were being taken to show employees how the specific changes being made would benefit them. Here are some of the results of that survey:

Personnel staffing: An important goal of the culture change in most respondent companies was to attract and retain high quality employees. To accomplish this, it had to be made clear to the current staff and to prospective employees what specific changes were being instituted to meet this goal so that they could realize the benefits they would derive. Some of these changes reported were:

• Introducing a profit-sharing program
• Opening a day-care center for children of employees
• Improving health benefit plan
• Upgrading 401K plan
• Extending maternity leave
• Redecorating cafeteria and break areas
• Making Friday a dress-down day.

But staffing is not limited to recruiting good people; an essential part is the manner in which new associates are screened and finally accepted. How this can be accomplished will be discussed in the next chapter.

Getting greater commitment of employees to high-quality performance. Obtaining commitment to achieving goals is obviously more than just giving pep talks and motivational speeches. Employees had to understand what such commitment would mean to them. These included:

• Developing more meaningful job descriptions geared to results expected rather than vague standards
• Creating several new training programs
• Improving educational tuition reimbursement programs
• Instituting more timely annual reviews
• Making career counseling available

It took months of persuasion for Alex K., a Human Resources vice-president, to convince his boss at Topical Pharmaceuticals to allow him to implement some of the programs noted above, but it truly paid off. Once new and more meaningful job descriptions were created and training programs put into place to enable employees to attain added skills, there was an immediate improvement in morale and a significant improvement in performance. Over the next few months, employees began to suggest innovations, as well as request training to prepare them to perform more complex assignments and to take on responsibilities they had formerly shunned.

Encourage more employee participation and cooperation. Employee attitude surveys had indicated that a good portion of the employees were reluctant to become involved in what they had always perceived to be "the manager's job—not mine." To help overcome this attitude, the responding companies pointed out some of the benefits that employees would derive. Among them were:

- Easier access to higher level managers
- Elimination of objectionable executive perks (e.g., special parking spaces and executive dining rooms)
- Better designed employee attitude surveys, followed by faster actions based on results of these surveys
- Management commitment to empowered teams
- Greater utilization of teams on major projects
- Increased training in team dynamics

Recognition of employees as individuals and as achievers. Many of the respondent companies had implemented employee recognition programs to which they attributed much of the success in obtaining the enthusiastic support of their staffs. Some of these were:

- Awards granted for years of service
- Recognition of birthdays
- An employee-of-the-month program
- A revised suggestion system with higher awards and more recognition
- Articles in the company paper about employees who contributed over and beyond the call of duty on the job or in some outside activity
- Encouragement of supervisors (and others) to take courses in interpersonal relations
- Introduction of systems in which employees were provided with the tools to recognize another employee's special contributions. One program that several firms used was a variation on the "You Made My Day" form (see Fig. 6-2). Any employee could acknowledge the special help of an associate by completing this form and sending it to that person with copies to the supervisor and the Human Resources Department.

YOU MADE MY DAY

Date _____

To: _____ Dept. _____

From: _____ Dept. _____

What you did: _____

_____

What it meant to me: _____

_____

Signed: _____

Copy to HR Dept.

Copy to team leader

Figure 6-2. *Sample of a form that recognizes an employee's special contributions.*

The actions that were reported in the survey only skim the surface and some of the items may appear to be superficial. But in the companies in which they were instituted, they met a need that had not previously been addressed.

These are only the first steps, but they represent an important beginning of the effort to project to the entire staff that the organization is taking its culture change seriously and intends to keep a steady focus on how all changes and improvements benefit employees.

KEY POINT

Make some significant changes early in the culture change process. It shows to the entire organization the benefits that have been promised have begun to accrue.

Driving Out Fear

Fear saps the energy of an organization. This has been proven over and over again, yet many managers still manage by fear. If the energies of staff members at all levels are centered on protecting themselves from dominating bosses, they'll have neither spirit nor motivation for innovation and progress.

Is this an exaggeration? I don't think so. I have studied many organizations run by domineering bosses. Keen observers of the management scene all agree that when people are fearful, they behave in ways precisely opposite of people who work in strong, positive cultures. They pull back when they should push forward, and play it safe when they should be taking calculated risks. They are so concerned about their own job security that they miss opportunities and avoid challenges, making decisions based on what they think the boss wants rather than what is best for the company. They hide bad news and spend incalculable amounts of time and energy "protecting" their jobs. These actions often result in lost opportunities and, in some cases, in total disaster.

Carl S. is an example of a dogmatic manager who almost ruined his company. Like many autocrats, Carl was a charismatic person. Handsome, well polished, educated at the best schools, he was the prototype of the movie-role business executive. He spoke and wrote brilliantly, and easily won the admiration of board members and stock holders.

After receiving his MBA, Carl joined a prestigious management consulting firm. Although his work was not outstanding, his charm won over his clients. After a few years with the consulting firm, Carl accepted a senior management position with one of his clients, a manufacturer of men's clothing.

After two years as assistant to the president, Carl was promoted to vice-president for Administration and two years later to executive vice-president and a member of the executive committee. Carl was a skilled manipulator. He wooed his fellow executive committee people, made the right moves, and when the president/CEO decided on early retirement, Carl was appointed to that position.

Now for the first time, Carl was in complete charge. Perhaps because he had always gotten by on his political savvy, he did not have the keen know-how needed to actually run a business. But that didn't stop him from setting policies and making decisions on every aspect of the business.

Instead of calling on his excellent staff of manufacturing, marketing, and financial executives for their expertise, he felt that he knew more than they did and made all the decisions himself. He did not tolerate dissension and ruled by fear. "It's my way or the highway" was his credo.

Over the first few years, Carl forced out several key people who did not agree with him and caused others to voluntarily leave. When queried by his board, he criticized the departed executives as not being team players. He filled their jobs with sycophants, on whom he could depend to agree with him. He dubbed this group his "dream team."

What happened to the company? New and creative marketing plans were vetoed because he did not originate them. Instead, he instituted poorly designed programs suggested by his "dream team," that cost the company vast amounts of money and were never really successful.

Innovative competitors took advantage of this situation. They persuaded key customers that their products were more in line with current trends resulting in the loss of a significant part of the company's market share. After three years of continuing declining sales and profits, Carl was forced out of his job by the Board. It took several years and a tremendous influx of capital and energy for the company to regain its market share.

QUOTES AND QUIPS

"No passion so effectively robs the mind of all its power of acting and reasoning as fear."
Edmund Burke, 1729–1797
English statesman, orator,
and author

So, What's The Answer?

The logical first step is to identify and remove tyrants, liars, politicians, and frauds from decision-making positions. Obviously, this is easier said than done. Often these people have strong positions in an organization and political clout with higher-level managers or the board. But if an organization is committed to building an esprit de corps that will truly exponentialize results, the fear issue must be tackled.

Such despots are like a cancer eating away at the soul of an organization, sapping its energy, and consuming attention and resources that should be used constructively. If ignored and unstopped, it can eventually devastate a firm.

When consultants trade horror stories, it often centers on such tyrants. Many progressive management thinkers have made serious attempts to change the psyche of dogmatic managers, but few have succeeded. Management by fear is too deeply seated and can only be excised by moving such people out of positions of power.

My colleague, Dr. Daniel Matthew, described such a situation. The tyrant in this case was Edwin, who was the brother of the president and sole owner of the firm. Edwin had held a variety of jobs in the organization and had failed in all of them. Eventually his brother appointed him vice-president of corporate affairs—a nebulous position created to keep him busy. The president had hoped that this would place Edwin in an innocuous position where he could not interfere with the real work of the company. Edwin, however, had other ideas. Knowing his brother's travel took much of his time, he insinuated himself into every department, stalling decisions that had to be made, and threatening department heads if they did not accede to his wishes.

The best solution would be to remove Edwin from the scene. His brother, out of filial feelings, was reluctant to do this. Only after much pressure from his advisors and his board, he compelled Edwin to take early retirement. From the minute he was gone, the company began the turn-around that has resulted in increased profits and market share.

It is never easy to terminate people with whom you have a close relationship and who have wielded power in an organization, but it is often the only sensible course of action. There is nothing more effective and more successful in changing the mood and pace of an organization—literally overnight—than to identify and replace tyrants who have abused their authority by stifling the initiative and independence of their staffs.

The effects of doing this have often astounded me. Reaction has ranged from audible sighs of relief when the word got out to full-blown parties celebrating the event.

One manager-victim described it in vivid terms: "It was like being released from a torture chamber. I had been so miserable and the only thing that prevented me from quitting was my own financial situation. It was like being given a whole new opportunity to really be all that I could be. My energy and enthusiasm, that had almost faded away, was now restored."

But, the real pay-off comes later as the men and women who had been stifled for so long, apply themselves with renewed vigor to their jobs and to the company. The result: productivity, morale, and enthusiasm for the business, along with the level of commitment to the culture change effort, often soars.

QUOTES AND QUIPS

"I have found that the men and women who got to the top were those who did the jobs they had in hand, with everything they had of energy and enthusiasm and hard work."
Harry S. Truman, 1884–1972
33rd President of the United States

Develop an Attitude of Constructive Discontent

Many people in positions of leadership, although not despots or tyrants, may resent disagreement and may subtly repress ideas that differ from theirs. Although they don't manage by fear, they do not encourage opposing views. Such managers have to be sold on the importance of listening to other opinions and being open-minded.

Organizations sincerely desirous of changing from an authoritarian to a more participative culture make a conscious effort to invite dissent, dissatisfaction, and disagreement. They view it as part of a process of continuous improvement. They recognize that it leads to breakthroughs and exponential effects. They believe it is essential to the long-term interests of the business. As pointed out in Chapter 4, this phenomenon is called *Constructive Discontent*. One of the basic elements of culture change is to foster this attitude throughout the organization.

In my own experience in helping companies change their cultures, I have synthesized 16 ways to accomplish this:

1. **Let people know that disagreement is not a capital offense.** Not only will one not be punished for dissenting, but it will be looked upon as a plus by supervisors and company management.

2. **Managers and supervisors should treat all viewpoints with respect.** Even if you think the idea is not valid, let the proposer know it will be seriously considered. And do consider it. Your initial reaction may have been biased, based on inadequate information, or just plain wrong.

3. **Never ridicule the opinions of others.** Even if an idea appears to be trivial, not well thought out, or downright ridiculous, treat it as an honest effort. When you reject it, deal with it in the same way you deal with more serious suggestions.

4. **Hold no grudges.** Sure, some people may appear to always oppose your ideas. Don't consider this a personal matter. Remember that only through open disagreements can ideas be brought out and evaluated.

For example, you may have an employee like Marilyn K., who disagrees for the sake of disagreeing. Such people can be nuisances, but if they see that you are serious about listening to their ideas and are not riled by their continuous disagreements, they will often stop trivial dissents. Marilyn told me that she got a kick out of irking the boss. When she realized that her manager was not annoyed by these dissents and indeed, encouraged disagreements, she channeled her thinking into more constructive avenues.

5. **Don't let your pride of authorship or ownership keep you from seeing other people's viewpoints.** Many managers become defensive about protecting their own ideas. Just because the idea being discussed was suggested by you, don't resent disagreement. It is especially important that you keep an open mind. The goal is to do the best for the company—not to aggrandize you or anybody else.

6. **Don't play favorites.** It is tempting to accept ideas from favored employees and reject those of others. People who may not appear to be as bright or as diligent as others in the group, however, may still come up with winning concepts.

7. **Put the emphasis on doing *what's* right—not *who's* right.** In evaluating suggestions, the focus of your analysis should be on the *content* of the material—not on the *source*.

8. **Train yourself and your people to keep these two questions in mind concerning everything you do: Is what we are doing the very best way to deal with this situation? If not, in what ways can we improve it?** Methods change, management concepts change, organizational goals change. These two questions should be asked periodically to assure that what you are doing is on the cutting edge of the current technology.

9. **Accept the fact that there are no stupid questions.** Even questions that appear to be irrelevant can often identify problems that may not be obvious to you.

10. **Listen.** Develop the techniques of being an active and empathetic listener. By your actions and reactions when people discuss matters with you, you can turn them on or off. Be the person people want to talk to because they know you truly listen.

11. **Value the diversity in people and in their perspectives, opinions, and perceptions.** People from different cultures, different levels of education, and different types of backgrounds bring with them varying viewpoints. We can learn much from seeing things through their eyes.

12. **Keep encouraging people to explore their opinions.** Help them evaluate the merits and limitations of their ideas. Provide them

with the tools they need to do this—such as access to data, research materials, and books and articles in the areas involved.

13. **Don't kill the messenger.** Managers must know the truth and the truth is not always pleasant. Mistakes cannot be corrected or compensated for unless we know that they have been made—and know it as soon as possible. In a culture where people are blamed for being the bearers of bad news, employees who perceive problems will be afraid to report them. Unless managers know about problems that develop, action cannot be taken to correct them until it may be too late. Encourage people to be forthright in presenting information—good or bad.

14. **Give recognition to people whose application of constructive discontent has resulted in positive changes.** Consider tangible rewards where appropriate. Make it a point to acknowledge their contributions at department meetings. If you have a company newspaper, publish stories about the changes made and those who contributed to them.

15. **Strive to create exponential effects.** Let people know that real progress does not have to be incremental—that jumping over several steps rather than taking one at a time can result in dramatic improvements. Give examples of such moves. Encourage people to discuss with you radical changes they believe will accelerate progress.

16. **Establish a climate in the company or the department that stimulates cooperation, collaboration, and teamwork.** Managers and team leaders at all levels should be trained to become participative leaders instead of dogmatic bosses. Training in good communications, creative thinking, and collaborative actions should be on-going and reinforced in the day-to-day workings of the entire organization.

COMPETENCE—THE THIRD "C"

Competence, which will be further discussed in Chapter 7, can be achieved through improved recruiting and selection followed by superior training and coaching, enhanced by programs that will assure continued loyalty and motivation of employees. Among the areas that must be included are fair compensation packages, a sense of job security, and programs that will offer opportunity for career advancement.

QUOTES AND QUIPS

"Planning is the open road to your destination. If you don't know where you are going, how do you expect to get there?"
Basil S. Walsh, 1878–1943
Insurance executive

SUM AND SUBSTANCE

In order for a transition to a new culture to succeed, the organization must first lay the foundation for building into the organization the three C's: *Confidence, Commitment,* and *Competence.*

To develop *confidence,* it is important to release the results of the O-MRI, take responsibility for what is wrong, and develop realistic plans to improve.

A well designed plan of action will include studying and fully understanding the "as-is" situation and having a clear concept of the changes that the organization wishes to achieve. The plan must include realistic timetables, a budget that will enable the company to financially support the implementation of changes, and a measurement system to keep tabs on progress. In addition, an on-going method of communicating results to all involved should be in place.

One way to assure that everybody knows that the organization is taking the culture change effort seriously is to make some important changes early in the process.

Equally important to the development of confidence is the building up of *commitment* of all employees who are involved in the culture change. An important step that managers must take to ensure that their commitment is earnest is to set realistic goals and then communicate them throughout the organization. This can be reinforced if managers:

- Practice what they preach
- Keep their promises
- Keep the staff fully informed—not only about successes, but also about failures and disappointments
- Work cooperatively and collaboratively with all people

If any significant improvement is to be made, all elements that may cause fear or otherwise discourage the suggesting of change or expressing opinions that may be different from a boss must be removed. Tyrannical managers should be replaced by people with true leadership capabilities. A spirit of constructive discontent should be fostered.

REFERENCE

[1]Brotherton, Hal., "GE Employees, Management Work-Out Together to Make a Better Company." Lynn, Mass. *Daily Evening Item*, November 15, 1991.

CHAPTER 7

Building Competence

The third critical component during the strategy design phase of a culture change is developing a staff of highly knowledgeable, strong-minded people who can implement the needed changes. The key components of this effort are:

Hiring well. Employing the best possible people for all positions.

Training well. Establishing training and development programs that will hone skills at all levels.

Promoting well. Developing a career advancement program that will motivate potential leaders.

Retaining well. Keeping the best people and weeding out the less efficient.

Let's examine what organizations can do in each of these areas to assure that their move to change their cultures will be effective. In this chapter we will discuss Hiring Well, Promoting Well and Retaining Well. Training Well will be discussed in the following chapter.

Hiring Well

It's more than just a cliché to say that people are the life-blood of any organization. Yet, many companies spend more time and money choosing the company logo than they do in recruiting and selecting key people. Studies show that the most common source for filling a job is personal contact. Executives hire friends, people in their network of business contacts, referrals from customers, vendors, and social acquaintances. While there is nothing wrong with using these sources, too many companies accept such referrals without careful evaluation and screening. Remember, if an applicant is referred by somebody you respect, it doesn't necessarily mean that he or she is right for your company.

Sometimes a company may become so desperate to fill an opening that they take the first "qualified" applicant. Although this person may meet the basic requirements for the job, he or she may not be the right person for the job. It is not uncommon for employers to be overly impressed by the candidate's appearance or charm and base the hiring decision on these superficial factors rather than on an evaluation of his or her true qualities.

Unless recruitment and selection are high-priority functions and given the attention they deserve, the results can range from disappointment to disaster. The cost of high turnover, poor performance, personality problems, and the other tangible and intangible results of poor hiring practices can be catastrophic.

It's not easy to get the right person for a job. It involves careful research to determine the qualifications that are really needed. Time, money, and expertise must be committed, and that starts with the development of a meaningful human resources program.

QUOTES AND QUIPS

"Executive ability consists of getting the right people in the right places and keeping them willingly at top notch."
Herbert G. Stockwell, 1866–1936
Management consultant

One of the most undervalued activities in many organizations is that of the human resources (HR) department. Too often, this department is looked upon as a necessary evil—to keep the company out of trouble with the Equal Employment agencies, to handle the red tape with medical insurance carriers, to deal with labor unions, and to do the routine recruiting and initial interviewing for personnel.

More and more companies, however, recognize that this function is essential to the success of the organization. Let's look at just one function of the human resources department—recruiting and selecting personnel—and see how companies have used this function to obtain (and retain) high quality people.

Recruiting and Selecting Personnel

To assure that an organization's recruiting and selection is effective, the process should start with a clear concept of what jobs entail and the development of realistic specifications that will enable managers to match applicants' backgrounds to job requirements. This should be followed by careful screenings of candidates through well planned interviews, reference checks, and in some instances, testing. A compensation package should also be designed to attract highly qualified candidates. In this section we'll examine the hiring process.

Developing Realistic Job Descriptions

Unless you know exactly what the job you wish to fill involves and what qualifications are needed to fill it, you can't even start a job search. Rather than the traditional job description, which focuses on duties, I recommend a *Job Results Description (JRD)*, which focuses on results. Let's look at a typical situation.

When the controller of Allied Merchants left the company, the CEO retained an executive search firm to fill the job. He handed them a copy of the job description, which had been written a few years earlier, as a guide. This description emphasized the accounting aspects of the job and may have been accurate at the time it was written.

Fortunately, the account executive assigned to this search, did not accept it at face value. He investigated, studied what the controller actually did, learned from the CEO some of the functions he would like the new controller to be able to implement, and rewrote the description to represent what was really needed.

The revised Job Results Description is shown in Figure 7-1. Note that is divided into several Chief Result Areas (CRAs). These are the major aspects of the job that must be accomplished by the person(s) holding it. Each is then supplemented by a list of standards on which performance will be measured—the results that the person performing the job is expected to accomplish.

CONTROLLER

OVERALL GOAL: To establish and implement policies and procedures that will maintain the financial health and continuing growth of the organization.

Chief Result Area 1: Financial Planning

The functions of this area will have been satisfactorily performed when:

a) the executive committee has been provided with long term financial goals that are realistic and attainable
b) relations with investment banks, security houses, and other outside financial sources are effective and profitable
c) annual budgets are submitted on time and approved by the executive committee

Chief Result Area 2: Accounting

The functions of this area will have been satisfactorily performed when:

a) the general accounting, cost accounting, credit and collections, and payroll departments are operating at optimum capacity
b) systems and procedures for accounting operations are developed and implemented to meet the changing needs of the department
c) audits by our CPA firm confirm the accuracy and effectiveness of our accounting procedures, reports, and other activities

Chief Result Area 3: Money Management

The functions of this area will have been satisfactorily performed when:

a) short-term cash surpluses are invested for optimum returns
b) loans for short-term cash requirements are obtained when needed at favorable rates
c) favorable credit lines are available when needed

Figure 7-1. *Job results description.*

Chief Results Area 4: Taxes

The functions of this area will have been satisfactorily performed when:

a) all federal, state, and local taxes are paid as scheduled
b) consultation with tax accountants and attorneys are maintained to assure best tax advantages

Chief Results Area 5: General Administration

The functions of this area will have been satisfactorily performed when:

a) all positions in the office are satisfactorily filled
b) employees are fully trained to perform their jobs
c) performance of all employees in the office are regularly evaluated
d) the central filing system is functioning effectively
c) office equipment and supplies are purchased when needed and properly maintained

---

Figure 7-1. *Continued.*

Job Specifications

These are the requirements that the successful applicant should possess. The first set of these requirements are tangible aspects such as education, experience, and skills. Note that these must match the chief results areas. In addition, there are intangible aspects such as personal characteristics, ability to communicate, interpersonal skills, and others.

One of the dangers in developing the job specifications is setting the requirements too high or too low. Standards should be high enough so that candidates with mediocre backgrounds would not even be considered, but not so high that truly qualified people will be passed over for the wrong reasons. On the surface, it may appear smart for a company to require the highest standards possible, but that can sometimes can work against you.

For example, the CEO of Allied Merchants listed being a CPA as a requirement for qualifying for the controller's job. When asked why he needed this certification, the CEO responded that the controller had to deal with their auditors and it would be an advantage to be at their level. The recruiter pointed out that this was a secondary aspect of the job and although it might be useful, it was not essential and would eliminate some excellent candidates who may not be CPAs, but met all the key requirements.

The intangible aspects of the job specification are extremely important, but often are too vague. Too often they are expressed in generalities such as: "The candidate should be trustworthy, loyal, honest, helpful, etc." Of course, we do want people to have these characteristics, but to make the intangible job specifications meaningful, they should be related to the job and should be measurable. For example, an important requirement of most management jobs is the ability to express oneself fluently orally and in writing, This is a specific management trait and can easily be determined through interviews and tests.

It is important for team leaders to have the ability to obtain the cooperation of people. This can be determined by good interview questions and reference checks.

Figure 7-2 shows the job specifications for the controller's position.

JOB SPECIFICATIONS

In order to perform the job of the controller effectively, the successful candidate should have the following qualifications:

Education:

- Bachelor's degree in Accounting
- MBA in Management
- Equivalents will be considered

Experience:

- Long-term financial planning for a medium or large company
- Development of complex, multiunit budgets
- Liaison with investment bankers and/or securities firms

Figure 7-2. *Sample job specifications.*

- Has held top accounting position (controller or chief accountant) in multimillion dollar corporation
- Good background in EDP systems and procedures
- Responsibility for bank relations and money management
- Thorough knowledge of federal, state and local tax laws
- Office management, including supervising diverse clerical staff

Special Skills

- Written communication: Superior ability to write letters, memos, and reports
- Oral communication: Ability to make presentations to internal and external groups
- Statistics: Thorough knowledge of statistical techniques
- Computers: Experienced with IBM or compatible computer programs. Lotus 1-2-3 a plus

Personal Characteristics:

- Ability to work under pressure—and sometimes extreme pressure
- Team player
- Leadership. Should have a proven record of leadership on previous jobs or other aspects of life
- Integrity. Past record must stand up to intensive scrutiny.

Figure 7-2. *Continued.*

QUOTES AND QUIPS

"The intangibles that make for success on a job are just as important as education, skills and experience. In making a job analysis, be as diligent in determining the intangible factors as you are in specifying the tangible factors."
Paul J. Mackey
Management consultant

Sophisticated Screening Techniques

Probably the most frequently used screening technique is the job interview. Many interviewers conduct the interview as a friendly conversation. Yes, it's important to be friendly, but in order for the interviewer to obtain meaningful information, it must be carefully structured.

Some interviewers fail to ask applicants about key aspects of their background. For example, when Arlene R. was interviewed for the marketing manager's position at Consolidated Distributors, she expected to be asked in-depth questions about her philosophy of marketing, her experience and knowledge of the latest developments in her field along with probing questions that would bring out aspects of her personality. Instead, each of the people who interviewed her, including the CEO, asked superficial questions that had already been covered in her resume and spent much of the interview time telling her about the company and bragging about their own accomplishments.

Arlene reported to me that they had learned nothing about her, but she had learned much about the culture of that organization. "It wasn't the kind of company I'd be comfortable in," she related.

By applying the techniques developed by human resources specialists, behavioral scientists, and successful business executives, organizations can increase their chances of hiring people who will not only succeed in their work, but will also interact with their colleagues, subordinates, and managers in a synergistic manner.

Some of these techniques include:

Carefully structured interviews. An interview should not be a casual conversation about the candidate's job qualifications. In order to assure that the applicant meets the job specifications, questions should be designed to bring out the related experience and knowledge that the applicant offers. Seek specific examples of what the candidate has accomplished. Insist that people who spout generalities and vague concepts back them up with specific examples about what they actually have done.

Ask questions about management philosophy. Elicit information about their techniques of dealing with the type problems that are likely to be faced on the job. An applicant for a marketing job might be asked to detail the steps taken in introducing a new product; a candidate for a Research & Development position should describe his or her approach to product development. Applicants for supervisory positions should be queried about their techniques of motivating people.

Plan the questions in advance so that every point will be covered. Most of these interviews are conducted on premises, but many managers find it advantageous to meet with candidates informally for a meal or in a social environment to obtain a different perspective of that person.

All personnel who conduct interviews, whether they be line supervisors, staff specialists, or senior managers should be trained in interviewing techniques. Generic training programs in this area are available through management training organizations like the American Management Association, Dun & Bradstreet, and others. Your own human resource experts or consultants retained by the company can tailor programs to the special needs of the organization.

TACTICAL TIPS

Before making a hiring decision, have two or more people who will work closely with the applicant interview the prospective job candidate.

Assessment centers. Some companies have used assessment centers as a means of evaluating current employees to determine their advancement potential. This approach can be adapted for screening applicants for important or sensitive positions.

Here's how it works. If after several interviews with key executives, there is a serious interest in the candidate, he or she may be invited to participate in the assessment process. Members of the assessment group are usually drawn from key executives, some of whom have already interviewed the candidate and others who have not. A human resources manager or consultant facilitates the meeting. Some companies may bring in specialized consultants to contribute to the evaluation. For example, a marketing, technical, or financial expert may be utilized when assessing a person in one of those fields.

Assessment center programs are not just a repetition of the individual interviews by the panel. Candidates will be questioned by the panel on various aspects of their background or their views, but this is just the beginning. Most assessment center programs go much deeper.

There are many variations of this process. Some include a series of situational exercises in which candidates must respond to real-life problems likely to be faced on the job. They may be asked to prepare and make a presentation of a new project, to study a situation, make recommendations, and then defend their position.

Some companies assess several people in the same session. They may be rivals for the same position, candidates for differing jobs, or current employees being considered for promotion (not necessarily for the same jobs.) In these cases, one of the goals of the assessment program is to study the way the various participants interact. The assessors note which people take leadership roles, come up with the most creative ideas, cooperate with the others, and also study what personality traits are manifested.

Although assessment centers provide useful information, often not easily attainable through other sources, they are expensive to conduct and should probably be reserved for key positions.

Psychological evaluations. Many companies retain industrial psychologists to evaluate candidates. Psychologists may administer a battery of tests to identify characteristics that may impact positively or negatively on performance. This is followed by an in-depth interview in which the psychologist brings out facets of personality that may be difficult for lay people to identify.

In choosing a psychologist, it is important to check his or her credentials. Over the years there have been many people and organizations claiming magic formulas that predict the success or failure of potential employees. Some of these have been around for years and boast provable records of success. Others are fly-by-night. If you choose to include psychological evaluations in the screening process, use a certified psychologist who has a record of success with substantial companies in your community.

QUOTES AND QUIPS

"The effective interviewer:
INQUIRES: Is probing
Asks open-ended questions
What? Why? How?
LISTENS: Is receptive
Keeps an open mind
COMMENTS: Is responsive
Follows up to obtain more information."
The Psychological Corporation
San Antonio, Texas

Reference checks. Shakespeare's words, *What is past is prologue,* probably can be one's best advice in screening applicants. What a candidate has accomplished in past jobs, in school, in community activity is a likely indicator of what they will do for you.

Interviews tend to bring out what applicants wish to tell you about their accomplishments. Although most people tell the truth, exaggeration is not uncommon. A thorough reference check can be the most valuable tool in the screening process. Unfortunately, it has become difficult to obtain information about prospective employees. Many companies, afraid of lawsuits, will verify only dates of employment and other basic information.

To overcome this, particularly in screening candidates for key positions, special steps should be taken to obtain as much information as possible. Here's how Ellen D., HR manager of a chain of women's casual clothing stores, checked the references of candidates for the position of training manager. After she had narrowed the choices to two apparently well-qualified people, Ellen personally visited their former employers and was able to pick up considerable information that letters or phone calls would never have uncovered. Her personal sincerity and ability to establish easy interaction with the managers enabled her to pinpoint key aspects of each candidate's strengths and weaknesses—important to her final decision.

Another source of verifying and obtaining information is to retain investigative services. The most effective of these services hire personnel who are skilled in interviewing and in digging up hidden information. If you choose to use an investigative service, be sure to provide specific aspects of the applicant's background that you want checked. For example, if you want information about how the candidate relates to subordinates, they will speak to his or her subordinates and others who have seen the candidate in action.

Keep in mind that there are laws governing the use of such investigative services. Federal law requires that you notify candidates that such an investigation may be made and that they have the right to request copies of the report. Some states have additional restrictions. Check with your legal advisor before using such an investigation.

Setting the Compensation Package

As in every other aspect of business, one gets what one pays for. Money may not be the primary concern of most executives, but it is a significant factor. Determine early in the process what the salary range should be. This can be ascertained by salary surveys and your firm's compensation policies. Be flexible. It may be to your benefit to exceed the range for a given individual. Often one good individual at a higher salary will produce more than two mediocre employees.

Compensation usually includes benefits and perks in addition to salary, and, in some cases, profit sharing or stock options. Total package should be presented to the job candidate so there is no misunderstanding about the arrangement.

Making the Offer

Once you have made your selection, make an offer as soon as possible. Good people are in demand and, by stalling, you may lose the best candidate. Be sure that the person you pick views the job in the same way you do. If the new employee has only a vague concept of what you expect, it will lead to trouble. The final step in the hiring procedure should be a thorough review of the Job Results Description with the candidate at that time to reiterate the company philosophy, clarify the chain of command, and answer the many questions he or she may have.

Promoting Well

The opportunity to advance in one's job and career is a major motivator for most people, but that is not its only benefit. By promoting effective employees to positions in which they can utilize their skills and expertise, the organization gains many advantages. It reduces turnover by retaining good workers. It enables management to fill important positions with experienced men and women who have proven themselves on the job. Most important, it builds a growing team of proven associates to assure the successful continuity of the organization.

But there is a downside to promoting employees. Promotion should be based on competence and potential, yet too many companies promote people for the wrong reason. Let's look at some of these:

Seniority. When an opening for a supervisor occurs in a department, rather than go through the complexities of seeking the best possible candidate, too many organizations often still follow the archaic policy of promoting people based on years of service.

Productivity. The person chosen to be the new supervisor is the best producer in the department. What is overlooked, however, is that she or he might not have the personal characteristics that make for a good manager.

Sycophants. "Yes men" and politically astute people are selected rather than the truly competent and creative men and women.

Here's an example of how such a promotion can destroy an organization. Peggy L. was bright and competent, but she was often unethical and dishonest in her quest for power in the organization. In her first position as a marketing assistant, she identified the people in her department who were most likely to be her competitors for advancement. She took every opportunity to discredit them, to downplay their ideas to the marketing manager, and to subtly sabotage their initiatives. She maneuvered her work assignments so she would be involved with those activities that she knew were her boss's pet projects.

It didn't take Peggy long to be the "teacher's pet" and it paid off. Within a year she was promoted to project manager—jumping over more capable and productive people. In order to advance further, she found excuses to meet with the company CEO to discuss situations that should have been discussed with her boss, the marketing manager.

In time, she ingratiated herself with the CEO, who was so impressed with her that he created a new position just for her. Her new job, director of corporate services, gave her control over a variety of projects. In this position, for the first time, she had real power—power to make policy decisions, power to transfer or fire personnel, power that could affect the bottom line. And she used it.

At first, her ideas and changes appeared to be dynamic and productive. Her dogmatic style, however, her unwillingness to listen to the ideas of others, and her intolerance of disagreement resulted in the resignations of some key people, the institution of poorly thought-out policies, and antagonism of customers and distributors.

Despite all this, she maintained the confidence of the CEO and persuaded him that the problems that had arisen were temporary adjustments needed to reach long-term goals. It took him three years to realize the true picture and let her go. The damage Peggy had caused, however, would take years to repair.

Personal friendships. When the decision to promote is based on personal friendships, the "old boy network," and on nepotism, the company will almost always suffer. It will suffer in the short run by poor performance. It will suffer in the long run by discouraging truly good employees.

Competency-Based Promotion

The best competency-based promotion systems have three things in common:

A well-designed job results description. When people are aware of the results expected of them and know that they will be evaluated on the basis of results achieved, they will have confidence in the fairness of the system.

Consideration of intangible characteristics of the person(s) being considered for the promotion. This includes such factors as judgment, problem solving ability, technical competence, creativity, and the level of trust and respect generated by the person.

One way of measuring this is the assessment center discussed earlier in this chapter. Organizations which have used this technique for many years in evaluating candidates for promotion report that it enables them to identify many of these intangible facets. Based on objective factors and observations by people who are not personally familiar with the candidates, it minimizes the effects of personal bias and political maneuvering.

Consideration of leadership abilities—as determined by the ability to enlist the willing cooperation of others to achieve desired results. As more and more companies become flatter and more team-based, the importance of working as part of a group has become key to success. Choosing team leaders requires a different perspective than selecting more traditional managers. By careful observation of men and women as team members and by 360-degree assessments—evaluations by peers, subordinates, supervisors, and others, this ability can be determined.

TACTICAL TIPS

In making decisions about promotions, ask yourself:
"Is this the best possible choice for the advanced position?"
If not, keep looking both within and outside the organization.

RETAINING WELL

William Bennett, Secretary of Education in the Reagan administration, and author of the best selling *The Book of Virtues,* when discussing the difference between democracy and communism, said: "One only needs to observe where people go when the barriers come down to know which is better."

The same can be said of companies. The bad ones are loaded with turnover and poor performers. The rush is to leave. The incompetents stay and continue to perform marginal work. The best recognize that their talents are being wasted and move on to more rewarding opportunities.

One of the diagnostic tools I find most helpful when examining a company's culture is studying the flow of people—talented and not so talented—into, out of, and within the firm. These statistics speak volumes about the current state of the organizational culture.

According to management consultant, Frederick Reichheld, as reported in *Newsday*[1], American companies lose half of their employees every four years and half of their customers every five years. Reichheld points out that retaining an extra five percent of customers a year can double a company's profits. He comments that customer retention is directly related to employee loyalty. You cannot retain loyal customers without loyal employees—and the best employees prefer to work for companies that deliver the values that build customer loyalty.

This was confirmed in a survey made by Manchester Partners International of 378 companies. Turnover was running more than 20 percent at one out of every three companies surveyed, and 52 percent said the rate at which they were losing workers was going up. Replacing a worker cost more than $10,000 at a third of the companies surveyed, and between $5,000 and $10,000 at another third.

What are these companies doing to try to retain their best people? Figure 7-3 indicates some of the more commonly used approaches and the percent of companies using each tactic:

Percentage of Companies Using Each Retention Tactic			
	Senior Execs.	Middle Mgrs.	Front-line Workers*
Better pay and benefits	67%	61%	50%
Stock options	52%	32%	N/A
Profit sharing	27%	23%	17%
Retention bonuses	16%	27%	7%
More careful selection in hiring	47%	54%	57%
Tuition reimbursement	23%	41%	47%
Improved training programs	N/A	N/A	45%
Flexible hours and schedules	18%	25%	33%
Casual dress code	22%	31%	38%

N/A = not applicable
*includes office, production, and retail sales workers
Source: Manchester Partners International Survey of 378 companies

Figure 7-3. *How companies try to keep employees.*

Recognize and Nourish Talents

Good people, productive people, and creative people need a climate in which their talents will be utilized and appreciated. One of the best ways of retaining those people who can contribute most to an organization is to create such an atmosphere.

This was demonstrated when Yuri Popov, a chemical engineer, emigrated to the U.S. in 1985. He was hired by a manufacturer of water purification systems. A highly competent engineer, Yuri was handicapped by his limited knowledge of English. The company recognized his talents and arranged for additional schooling in English. His boss spent hours with him helping him master the technical terminology.

After a few years, Yuri, now virtually fluent in English, was offered a much higher paying job by a larger company, but he rejected the offer. "This company went all out for me," he said. "They appreciated my technical talents and helped me learn English. They stuck with me when I needed it most and now it's my turn to show them my appreciation and loyalty."

Redeploying Good People

When companies restructure or downsize, employees with good potential are let go because the jobs they hold are eliminated. Often the companies had expended thousands of dollars to recruit and train them. Many companies, however, have salvaged these people by redeploying them within the firm, sometimes even training them to perform in different skill areas.

There are many advantages of redeploying employees:

- You know the work record, work habits, accomplishments, and personality of these people . . . clearly a head start in getting them productive rapidly in the new assignment.
- By the company and the employee jointly choosing the assignment based on company needs and the employee's goals, chances for success in the new assignment are enhanced.
- Companies which have redeployed workers have found that it takes about half as much time to train them in the new job than training outsiders.
- It raises morale—not only among those who have been retained and retrained, but often throughout the organization as well.
- It saves money as the cost of retraining is usually less than the cost of hiring and training new people for these spots.

QUOTES AND QUIPS

"It's a fine thing to have ability, but the ability to discover ability in others is the true test."
Elbert Hubbard, 1856–1915
American author and editor

Provide Equitable Compensation

The salary earned by an employee is more than just the purchasing power it gives that person. It represents his or her status in the organization. In the recruiting process, money does attract good people and, once employed, it is a significant factor in retaining them.

A common practice when companies downsize is to fire the highest paid people because it reduces payroll rapidly. This is often shortsighted. I have seen many cases where companies have laid off productive $80,000-per-year workers and lost much more productivity than if they had laid off two workers earning $40,000 each.

As the culture changes, the methods of determining compensation must also change. Today in many companies, salary increments are based on three factors: job classification, length of service, and performance. All jobs are classified into ranges; compensation for people in a classification falls within the range.

Most workers start at the bottom of the range and salary increments come annually. Employees on the payroll for that year automatically get a raise. In some companies, the amount of the increment may vary. Even poor workers get the minimum annual raise, but better performers *may* get more than that minimum. Tenure dominates, and performance is secondary.

The trend in far-sighted companies is the move away from this traditional approach to compensation. The emphasis shifts from paying for time to paying for performance. This does not mean reverting to piece work—the nineteenth century system in which workers were paid per unit produced—or to the quota system devised by the industrial engineers of the 1920s and 30s.

Base salaries will be modest—enough so that people need not worry about meeting the family budget, and probably adjusted periodically to account for cost of living changes. Substantial reward for superior performance will be in the form of bonuses. The bonuses may be determined by team productivity, contribution to company profits, or some other formula tied directly to the person or team's effectiveness.

Hammer and Champy, in their book *Reengineering the Corporation*, take this one step further.

> Paying people based on their position in the organization—the higher up they are, the more money they make—is inconsistent with the principles of reengineering. Traditional point schemes, in which the size of a person's salary is a function of the number of subordinates that person has working for him or her and the size of his or her budget, also does not fit into the process-oriented environment. . . .
> In companies that have been reengineered, contribution and performance are the primary basis for compensation.[2]

Often, when senior executives are counseled that performance and not rank should determine compensation, they react with shock and skepticism. "How can I pay a person more than his or her supervisor? It will destroy the command structure."

The truth is that it can be done and, indeed, has been done in many types of situations. Consider professional sports. The star players are almost always paid much more than the coach or manager. Movie superstars are usually paid much more than the director. In many sales organizations, the top salespeople make more money than the sales manager. So why can't this be expanded to other departments?

"But," executive argue, "managers have more responsibilities than the rank and file." Do they? In the team oriented company, the traditional manager has been replaced by the team leader. The entire team takes responsibility for performance. The team leader may be entitled to a slightly higher base pay, but his or her major compensation, as is that of all the team's members, should be based on the team's performance. Companies that have instituted this approach have found that, in the long run, everybody wins. The collaborative team activities lead to more earnings for team leaders and team members alike.

Employee Stock Option Plans (ESOPs)

Another trend in tying compensation to productivity is to give employees more of a financial stake in the company. One approach is the introduction of Employee Stock Option Plans (ESOPs). These programs enable employees to purchase shares in the company at favorable prices. In some of these plans, the employees may actually own a major portion of the stock. In others, ownership remains with the general stockholders, but as employees are a significant group of these stockholders, they share in the profits and participate in stockholder meetings.

The resultant employee commitment is palpable. Instead of employees complaining and griping, they pitch in to solve problems. Instead of evading assignments, saying, "It's not my job," they seek out areas in which they can contribute.

Another approach to financial incentive is open-book management. Its goal is to get *everyone* to focus on helping the business make money.

The traditional approach in which the bosses run the company and employees do what they are told is replaced with empowered teams. After being given all the facts and figures needed, employees and management collaboratively make decisions and are rewarded for their successes through profit sharing bonuses. Of course, they must also accept the risks of failure and the ensuing lower income.

In his article *The Open-Book Revolution,*[3] John Case presents three essential differences between an open-book company and traditional business:

1. Every employee has access to numbers that are critical to tracking the company's performance and are given the training and tools to understand them.
2. Employees learn that, whatever else they do, they must never lose sight of the goal to move those numbers in the right direction.
3. Employees have a direct stake in the company's success. If business is profitable, they share in the profits, if it is not there are no profits to share.

Of course, there is a downside. Since most employees do not have the accounting knowledge truly needed to understand the figures, the "open book" concept will be meaningless to them. Companies who choose to use this approach must take the time and effort to provide the necessary training.

An example of this occurred at the Beta Machine Tool Co., a small company dominated for years by a dogmatic owner. After three years of increasing losses, the owner was convinced that the only course

open to him to save the firm from bankruptcy was to cut costs by lay-
ing off about 20 percent of his employees.

Fortunately, the owner sought advice from a consultant, who
pointed out that the solution was not cutting costs, but increasing
productivity. Out of desperation, the owner agreed to try this new
approach. The consultant suggested that they institute an open-book
management program. For the first time, the staff understood why
they had not had a raise for three years, and why some of their
actions had curtailed productivity instead of enhancing it. The
employees subsequently learned what steps they could take to save
the company and their jobs. Within six months, the company began
showing the results and was on its way back to profitability.

Test Your Retention Quota

Adequate compensation is basic to retaining staff, but it is generally
accepted that money is not the only or even the main reason people
leave their jobs. Examine your personnel practices to determine some
of the reasons that your retention rate is not as high as you would like.

Ask questions like:

- Is the company's compensation program (salary + benefits) at
  least at a par with competitors for the same types of personnel?
- Do you make employees feel that their work is vital to the company's success?
- Do you provide training to keep your staff at the cutting edge of
  the technology needed in their work?
- Do you send employees to professional development programs
  on a regular basis?
- Do you keep in mind employees' personal goals and provide
  opportunity for them to achieve these goals?
- Do you encourage employees to contribute their ideas and suggestions?
- Do you provide opportunity for employees to assume more
  responsibility—and pay them accordingly?
- Do employees see the career paths open to them and the steps
  you are taking to help them move along those paths?
- Do you give both private and public recognition to each person's
  accomplishments?

• Do you sense a feeling of pride in the work and the company among the employees?

Review your responses. Any "no" answer is an indicator of a problem that may lead to the loss of some of your good employees.

The Separation Interview

Too often, companies do not know why they lose good employees. Exit or separation interviews are designed to probe for the real reasons people leave a job. I have witnessed a number of exit interviews in which the questions were of such a superficial nature, that no significant information was developed.

In order to get meaningful information that will enable you to identify and correct problems that have caused turnover in the organization, you must conduct a well-structured interview. Just as in an employment or appraisal interview, it is best to start a separation interview by building rapport. Questioning should begin with a general type of question that will not put the employee on the defensive. The question on why he or she is leaving the company should never be the first one asked.

A better start might be to ask about the kind of work the employee had been doing in his or her most recent assignment. This will start the conversation going, but will also enable you to evaluate whether this is the kind of work one might be expected to do in this particular job. One reason people leave jobs is because it was not what they expected to do. A market researcher, for example, might be spending all her time on statistical compilations, when she expected to be doing depth analyses.

TACTICAL TIPS

An unbiased, objective separation interview shouldn't be conducted by the team leader or supervisor of the employee who is leaving. The interview should be conducted by a member of the Human Resources Department, another management level person, or an outside consultant.

Here are some important questions that should be asked in a separation interview and some clues as to what you should look for to interpret the responses.

Questions About the Job

What did you like most and least about the job? Are these job factors or personal factors? You can obtain insight into the job by the pattern of answers you get from people who leave it.

How do you feel about your compensation? Many people leave their jobs for another with higher pay. Others feel they should have made more money even though they were being paid the going rate for the work. Taking this into consideration, evaluate the answers to this questions in the light of the equity of their pay scale, along with the methods used to give increases as compared to other companies in your area or your industry.

How do you feel about the progress you've made in this company? A good number of people claim they have left their jobs because of lack of opportunity for advancement. Often this masks the real reasons for leaving. However, it's important to examine what a person might have expected in terms of growth in your company and relate it to the real opportunity for advancement in the job she or he held.

How do you feel about working conditions? Companies have picked up information from this question about matters that were unimportant in their eyes, but that annoyed employees to the point of causing them to leave. Often these are easily correctable.

Questions About Supervision

What did you like most (and least) about your supervisor's style of managing? As many of the problems existing in organizational life are due to problems with supervisors, it's important to probe this factor, particularly if there is a large turnover in that department. You can learn if the supervisor is dogmatic, stubborn, or authoritarian. Does he or she encourage participation?

Probe further to learn about how the supervisor dealt with complaints. Some supervisors tend to be defensive and take any complaint as a personal affront; others take time out to talk about even the most far-fetched grievances.

It also helps to learn the good points of each supervisor so that they can be reinforced when reporting back the information to the supervisor.

Does your supervisor tend to favor some employees or act unfairly to others? Favoritism on one hand and bias on the other are major causes of discontent. The question can also point up blatant areas of cronyism or, at the other extreme, prejudice and discrimination. If this bias is based on racial, religious, national origin, gender or age factors, it might alert you to potentially serious legal problems and give you a chance to correct them.

Questions to Sum Up the Interview

If you could discuss with top management exactly how you feel about this company, what would you tell them? This open-ended question often results in some interesting insights. Let the employee talk freely, and avoid leading questions that might influence the response. Encourage him or her to express real feelings, attitudes, suggestions, problems, fears and hopes about the organization.

If the applicant has accepted a job with another company, ask: *What does the job to which you are going offer you than you were not getting here?* The answer may repeat some of the facts already brought out, but it may also uncover some of the ways your firm failed to meet the employee's hopes, goals, or expectations.

If the above questions have not been solidified in your mind, the true reasons for the employee's leaving, ask specifically: *Why are you leaving at this particular time?* Some of the problems that have come out at the interview have been in existence for a long time. Some of them have seemed unimportant until now. Find out what precipitated the resignation at this time. Have things become worse? Is there anything you can recommend to management which will prevent them from becoming even more serious and causing more turnover?

A good separation interview can take an hour or so of your time, but it can provide insight into how employees in your firm really feel about the organization, and how you can overcome the negatives or reinforce the positive aspects of your work environment. In short, it's time well spent.

SUM AND SUBSTANCE

The components of building competence are to hire, compensate, train, promote, and retain employees effectively.

Hiring well starts with the development of realistic job specifications. Once it's made clear what it takes for a person to succeed on the job, the next step is to screen applicants to determine which one(s) meet those specifications. To do this requires skilled interviewing, supplemented by testing and careful reference checks. Many organizations have found that by having candidates interviewed by several people they will improve the chances of picking the best qualified applicants.

Once employed, the key to bringing the new person to optimum performance is the type, quality, and effectiveness of the training. No matter how experienced the new associate may be in the technical aspects of the job, training in how the work is performed in your organization and in the ramifications of the corporate culture must be made clear. One way to accomplish this is the Skill Development Process. This includes:

- Trainees should be oriented to expect and accept changing their behavior. They must be given a clear picture of what is involved, and how they will benefit from the training. Excitement about the training should be engendered by demonstrating how it will enable them to improve and grow.
- The material that is being presented should be presented in a manner that utilizes as much participation as is feasible.
- Coaching-supported practice should be an integral part of the process.
- After the formal training is completed, it should be reinforced by regularly scheduled follow-up activities.

Another important facet of developing competence is to offer opportunity to employees to advance in the company and in their careers. The process of promotion should be based on performance—not on favoritism, tenure, or the arbitrary whim of a higher-ranking manager.

Companies who retain their people are far more likely to be successful than those with high turnover of personnel. Every effort must be made to develop programs of recognition, compensation programs based on individual and team performance and bonuses and profit sharing programs that involve employees at all levels.

REFERENCES

[1]Caulkin, Simon. "Loyalty More Profitable than Ruthless Cutbacks." *Newsday*, August 18, 1996, p. F15, (regarding a review of the book *The Loyalty Effect* by Frederick F. Reichheld. Harvard Business School Press, 1996).

[2]Hammer, Michael and Champy, James. *Reengineering the Corporation.* New York: Harper Business, 1993, p. 75.

[3]Case, John. "The Open-Book Revolution." *Inc.*, June 1995, p. 26.

CHAPTER 8

Training Well

According to a survey made by *Training* magazine, expenditures for formal corporate training grew from $55.7 billion in 1996 to over $60 million in 1998.

A good deal of the money spent on training is often wasted on ineffective and sometimes gimmicky programs that do not result in lasting impact. At first they appear to be effective. Lights flash, bells ring, but no real training takes place. No wonder so many line executives tend to discount the value of training. They see little, if any, return on their investment.

Yet, the training function is critical if companies are to thrive—and even survive—in the dynamic economy in which we live. Training must be a central focus, however—an integral component of the corporation's mission and vision.

Properly developed training programs can have a dramatic, lasting, invigorating effect on a business, and show an enormous return on investment as individuals increase their current skills and develop new ones. This results in an increase in innovative ideas, and more creative approaches to solving problems.

In addition to training in specific occupational and professional areas, training in the soft skills—leadership, communications, and interpersonal relations— provides tools and techniques that lead to closer and more meaningful relations with coworkers, subordinates, supervisors, customers, vendors, and the public.

QUOTES AND QUIPS

"Training people is often a one-way process. The teacher presents information and you hope the student absorbs it. When training is replaced by *learning,* the emphasis is on developing the capability of trainees to identify and solve problems; seeking knowledge; and taking the initiative in continuing self-development."
Erwin S. Stanton, 1930–1996
Psychologist

The Skill Development Process

A good part of my work has been devoted to the design and development of training programs. Over the years, I have synthesized a highly successful formula that has been implemented in the training endeavors of not only the clients with whom I have been directly involved, but in many other organizations. It consists of a four-step procedure intended to not just dispense content, but to actually change behavior.

The four steps are:

1. **The Attitude Conditioning of Learners.** Unless the training participants are properly oriented so that they're receptive to learning, the chances of success are minimal. Not only must minds be open to receive and accept new information and ideas, but they must become excited about it.

   To accomplish this, a thorough orientation of training participants becomes an essential prelude to the actual learning. The following steps should be included:
   * *Give participants a clear picture of what's involved.* This includes an overview of what will be taught, the reasons for its importance, and a preview of the techniques and methods that

will be applied. For example, if workshops, interactive team projects, or brainstorming sessions will be used, let participants know about this in advance. Get them interested and excited about using these training tools.

- *Help participants understand how they will benefit from the training.* Demonstrate how it will enhance their careers, make the work easier, and allow them to work smarter rather than harder.
- *Remind participants that they participated in determining their own training needs.* Their input weighed significantly in the design of the program as it stemmed from the O-MRI, in which they were important participants.
- *Get the participants excited about what will be learned and the satisfaction they will get from participating fully in the training process.* Motivate them to be active participants. Let them know that learning can be fun.
- *Demonstrate to the participants that they can change, grow, and improve.* Describe how the change process has succeeded in the past. If possible, use current examples from the organization. Supplement this by describing similar successes in other firms.
- *Be enthusiastic about the entire process.* By your enthusiasm and that of others in management, make everyone enthusiastic about beginning the process.

2. **Presentation and Demonstration of Content.** It has been long established that the key to successful training is the active involvement and participation of the entire group. Real learning begins when all participants are drawn into the process. Unless the members of the group are fully involved in the training, only superficial knowledge can be obtained.

Active participation through case studies, role plays, simulations, working assignments, and similar exercises make the material come alive, leading to better learning and long-lasting retention. Demonstrations of what is being taught in the classroom and on the job give learners a chance to apply what they are learning to their actual work.

All members of the group should be encouraged to engage in discussions, debates, disagreements, and deliberations. Dissenters should be encouraged to express their opinions. Only when doubts are resolved can full consensus be reached and the new learning be absorbed and accepted.

The trainer must resist the temptation to be a preacher-teacher. He or she should assume the role of facilitator, helping the trainees through the process, not spoon-feeding information to them, but enabling them to examine, evaluate, think about, and truly learn the new material. The best trainers are active listeners and observers, who are alert to the actions and reactions of the trainees, and provide feedback.

KEY POINT

The Success Development Process consists of four steps:
1. Participants must be conditioned to accept that training will involve change in their behavior.
2. Content of training should be presented and demonstrated in an interesting, participative, and dynamic manner.
3. Participants must practice what has been learned.
4. The training must be followed up and the new behavior reinforced.

---

3. **Practice.** The classroom training is just the first step in the learning process. Unless class members try what they have learned on the job, it cannot be determined if the learning has taken hold. We cannot wait until after the training has been completed to measure this. Errors and misunderstandings must be corrected immediately before they become bad habits.

Successes must also be acknowledged immediately to give the program participant positive reinforcement. One way to do this is by starting each session with a reporting period at which everyone reports on what they've learned in the previous session and how it was applied, as well as the results.

Recently I was conducting a sales training program for a client in which some new approaches to selling the firm's service were introduced. Participants were asked to use at least one of the techniques learned in the first session during the week between the first and the second session and to report on how it worked.

When the reports were given, the entire class critiqued each participant's experience. All of us benefited. The reporter received feedback on his or her performance; all class members learned from the experiences of each of the participants; and I, the facilitator, learned in what areas I had succeeded in providing learning and how I could make the training even more effective.

4. **Follow-up and reinforcement.** I have often come across organizations that bemoan the failure of their training programs, complaining that all of the money they spent was wasted because, after a short time, participants reverted to their old habits. The complaint, valid as it may be, is usually not the fault of the training program, but the lack of proper follow-up. Just as a muscle will atrophy if not exercised, knowledge and skills will be lost if not used.

To overcome this, follow-up programs should be incorporated into the training plan. The first meeting is usually 30 days after the completion of the training sessions. This meeting, designed in an exciting and motivational format, reinforces and remotivates participants. Included are reports of progress, opportunities to ask questions and discuss problems that have arisen on the job, and motivational exercises so that everybody leaves with the enthusiasm to assure continued commitment. Subsequent meetings are spaced 30 to 60 days apart for as long as desirable.

It's essential that representatives of top management show their support for the program. By word and deed they let all involved know that the application of the new skills, as well as the changes in attitudes and culture based on the training, is paying off in its impact on productivity, progress, and profits.

QUOTES AND QUIPS

"I find the key to learner interest is his or her active—not passive—participation in the learning process. As learners state their attitudes or their actions—and their reasons for these— then and only then can they be helped to see their present habits and attitudes and do something about them."

Allen A. Zoll
Management consultant and author

COACHING

Trainers must not only utilize the most effective techniques of instructing, but must also be good coaches. A coach has the ability to recognize each trainee's strengths and limitations and work with each to maximize his or her potential.

Good coaches are expert motivators. They bring out the best in others. They instill self-confidence by reinforcing the strengths of the team members and their determination to succeed. They also provide the tools, the plans, and the techniques that will enable people to achieve their individual goals and the goals of the team. Above all, they're role models. They practice what they preach.

Coaches do not have to be skilled in every aspect of the jobs they supervise. Some workers on a job may be better performers than their supervisor. The ability of the coach lies not in his or her ability to excel in every aspect of a job but in bringing out the best in team members.

TACTICAL TIPS

A coach:
- Motivates the team
- Helps team members develop self confidence
- Teaches tangible and intangible techniques needed to do the job
- Is a role model for the team

Mentoring

Mentors are valuable resources in developing the skills of their protégés—and equally important in orienting them to the organizational culture. Most organizations don't have a formal program to encourage mentoring. Some managers want to share their knowledge and experience with newcomers; others take a special liking to a new employee and become his or her mentor; some young people take the initiative and ask managers they admire to become their mentors.

I am an advocate of a formal mentoring program that systematically identifies and trains managers on the techniques and subtleties of the art of mentoring and then pairs up mentors and protégés. This not only assures that younger employees will obtain mentoring, but gives the opportunity to managers to participate in the program.

QUOTES AND QUIPS

"A manager might say, "Here's what you need to do." A coach says, "Let me ask you some questions that can help you get a different view—one that might reveal more options."
Kim H. Krisco
Management consultant

Executive Coaching

In many companies, coaching has been restricted to helping workers become more effective in their jobs or in preparing junior employees to move up to more responsible positions. In recent years, companies have found that even senior members of their staffs can benefit from coaching. Often the characteristics that helped a person move up the ladder are different from the characteristics needed to succeed as a managing executive.

According to a Manchester Consulting[1] survey of chief executive officers, 45 percent said senior level executives need coaching in new management skills and techniques. In another Manchester Consulting survey of human resource executives, poor communication skills was regarded as the number one problem in how managers *manage* people. Poor interpersonal skills was cited as the number one problem in how managers *relate* to people.

In addition, the surveyed CEOs revealed that the skills they most want to develop in members of their executive teams are team building, strategic thinking, leadership, the ability to motivate others, entrepreneurship, and well-roundedness. Executive coaching is one way of developing these special skills in individuals.

In an article in *The Manchester Review*[2] Dr. Lewis R. Stern describes the four-phase step of an executive coaching process.

Our coaching process is customized for each client but has four phases within which tailoring is completed: pre-assessment agenda setting, assessment, coaching, and evaluation of progress/follow-up. Pre-assessment always follows an informal process of identifying the overall goals for the coaching sessions and agreeing on the ground rules, roles, and sources of assessment data. In almost all cases, a tailored assessment is structured within what is referred to as the DIAS[3] methodology.

"DIAS cubed," as it is referred to, ensures that three sources are brought together for a full perspective of the executive. These three sources include historical perspective (based on lengthy career influences interviews with the executive), normative assessment (based on the executive completing a series of tests/surveys—the scores being based on comparative placement along scales of national norms), and 360-degree feedback (based on the coach conducting extensive, structured feedback interviews and distributing a Leadership Behavior Study® with the executive's superiors, peers, and subordinates).

Special coaching techniques are utilized to fit the personalities of the individuals involved and the areas where improvement is desired.

Stern identified the ten most common skill deficits where coaching was indicated. They are listed in the order of frequency starting with those mentioned most frequently.

1. **Supervision.** This includes clarity of the assignment, holding employees accountable, providing direction and support, facilitating consensus and providing mentoring, trust, recognition, and rewards.
2. **Active listening.** This includes talking less and paying more attention when others talk. In addition, asking the right questions, not interrupting too much, showing enthusiasm and emotion, balancing seriousness with humor, good body language, and smiling.
3. **Cross-functional collaboration.** This includes reaching out to develop relationships, treating people consistently, building alliances, networking, maintaining a win-win attitude, and mingling with others.

4. **Conflict management.** This includes constructively confronting others as conflicts arise, giving clear, direct feedback presented in a non-aggressive fashion that demonstrates respect and support.
5. **Positive attitude toward others.** This includes considering other viewpoints with an open mind, demonstrating enthusiasm, focusing on positive solutions rather than negative problems, and presenting opposing views with a win-win approach.
6. **Self-confidence.** This includes taking reasonable risks without being overwhelmed by fear of failure or becoming defensive, and taking tough stands in a decisive, forceful way.
7. **Demonstrating respect for others.** This includes how to approach others with a belief that they can make a valuable contribution, and how to demonstrate a true respect for other's viewpoints without appearing to be condescending or arrogant.
8. **Strategic leadership.** This includes viewing the business from a big-picture, long-term perspective, building strategic plans, articulating ways to implement these plans, and developing strategic initiatives.
9. **Setting priorities.** This includes time management, setting reasonable standards and priorities, and driving oneself and others with an appropriate level of perfectionism, attention to detail, and holding people accountable without micromanaging them.
10. **Managing up.** This includes communicating the big picture to your boss, knowing his or her priorities, pushing back when you know you are right and promoting your accomplishments and advocating for the people you lead.

Stern concludes that there was no "one size fits all" solution when it comes to coaching methodology. The coach must use an approach that fits the style and needs of the person being helped.

He comments that coaching has a significantly positive impact on executive job performance and promotability. "Executives can change how they work and interact with others. It is not a matter of being 'good' or 'bad' managers. Almost all executives are talented leaders with great potential as well as having some areas to be changed and improved upon for greater success."

QUOTES AND QUIPS

The question often arises, can people ever really change? But if we think about it for a moment, almost everyone knows someone who has changed significantly and sometimes quickly. History and literature are replete with examples from Moses and the burning bush to Ebenezer Scrooge. The more relevant question is why do some people change and under what circumstances? Fortunately, modern psychological research is beginning to provide some major answers.

Raymond P. Harrison
Management consultant

Transformational Coaching

It is often the most seasoned and successful executives who have the most difficulty in making the change. They have a vested interest in maintaining their past success patterns and often have strong personalities which make it difficult for them to change their behavior.

In addition, they have built up a reputation within the organization of being tough, often abrasive leaders and small incremental changes in their management style is likely to be either ignored or considered a minor aberration of their usual style. It tends to be unnoticed and therefore not reinforced. This leads to their reverting to their old behavior and no real progress is made.

At Manchester, Dr. Raymond P. Harrison has developed a process to overcome this. He refers to this process as *transformational coaching*[3] which is outlined in the following eight principles:

Principle #1: *Capitalize on Teaching Moments*

There are certain times in the lives of all executives when you have their attention about management style issues. These may be times of triumph, disappointment, personal crises, leaps in levels of responsibility, demotions, etc. These periods of heightened emotionality and vigilance are also opportunities for learning because, as these people flounder to regain balance, they will also be receptive to new ideas and suggestions from others.

Principle #2: *Organizations Arrive at Impressions about People as a Result of "Critical Events"*

Many executives have reputations that precede them, which were founded on specific events observed by others. The key question is, "how do we know what we *think* we know about the executive?" In most cases it can be traced to some specific events that led to the creation of the perception. People come to conclusions about another person as a result of specific interactions with them or observations of them interacting with others.

Principle #3: *Memory for Critical Events Is Notoriously Faulty*

A fundamental technique of most executive coaching interventions is that you talk to the executive about problematic things that have happened in the past, what might have been done differently, and what needs to happen differently in the future. Some of the basic problems with this approach is that people often lie, have selective memories, distort the recollection, or unconsciously create events that never happened.

The practical implication is that it isn't sufficient just to get critical events about an executive's behavior; it is also necessary to get descriptions of the events from several sources. We call this the *Roshomon technique,* in tribute to the ancient Japanese story of the same name about a robbery and attack told from multiple perspectives. Hearing a specific event described from the perspective of several participants and observers gives it more depth and reality, causing the executive to deal with the collective perceptions.

Principle #4: *Practice to Mastery*

Practice to mastery refers to learning an activity not just to the point of competence, but to where the behavior can be produced easily and automatically. Think of learning to drive a stick-shift car. Once it is mastered, you do not think about shifting gears, it occurs virtually automatically.

When an activity is practiced and learned to the point of mastery, it is also more likely that *transfer of training* will occur. For example, if one masters a four-speed transmission, he or she can usually master a five-speed easily.

Practice to mastery facilitates transfer of training to related situations that cannot be anticipated by the executives or their coaches. For example, if one fully masters the techniques of giving employees accurate, specific, and constructive performance feedback, it will be much easier to use the same techniques with a subordinate who seeks career guidance.

TACTICAL TIPS

Activities must be overlearned and practiced to the point where the individual can reproduce them easily. Once learned, they must be put into practice immediately in the workplace, Failure to practice will lead to regression to the former ways.

Principle #5: *Behavior Drives Attitudes*

Changes in ideas, assumptions, and attitudes as well as emotions and motivations are critical if lasting change is to occur. So how can attitudes be changed? Surprisingly, direct methods of verbal persuasion have often been shown to be useless. Studies in smoking cessation, for instance, have shown that when subjects are given lectures or films about the evils of nicotine, they are even less likely to stop than groups receiving no treatment at all.

Psychologists now understand that, when verbally coerced to behave in a certain way, people react to the threat of diminished personal choice with silent counter arguments, becoming even more entrenched in their positions than before.

Attitude change must *follow* behavioral change. In this smoking cessation example, it was discovered that interventions—like asking subjects to role play picking up a cigarette, putting it away, or refusing an offer of a cigarette—resulted in a greater likelihood of subjects giving up smoking.

Research in this field have shown that changes in ideas, attitudes, and values will result in long lasting behavioral change, but this is likely to be preceded first by actual changes in behavior.

Principle #6: *Stakeholder Analysis And Action Planning*

Executives do not just work alone, they are constantly interacting with others: superiors, peers, subordinates, and customers. Analyzing who the key stakeholders are and developing productive relationships with them is essential for success. Once this key constituency has been determined for the executive being coached, initiatives need to be taken with each stakeholder.

Gene Boccialetti[4] has developed a conceptual scheme for analyzing and planning stakeholder initiatives: *distance, deference,* and *diversion.*

Distance refers to the amount of intimacy and informality in a relationship. Executives who are high on the distance factor favor relationships at work characterized by formality, little self disclosure, and a no-nonsense task orientation.

Deference refers to the degree that an individual feels comfortable in voicing or receiving opinions from others. Executives high in deference tend to be good soldiers who want structure and who will follow orders. In their relations with peers, they are not likely to volunteer ideas in their peers' areas of responsibility about how work could be done more effectively.

Divergence refers to the degree that one sees his or her goals in competition or opposition with others in the organization. Executives who are high on this factor are likely to view their relationships with colleagues as competitive and adversarial.

Let's say that one of the problems the executive who is resisting the culture change has is peer relationships. It may be that he is too distant in his relations with them. In this case, specific activities such as inviting peers to lunch or arranging informal meetings might be suggested. If deference is the problem, the executive needs to work on listening to the opinions of others as well as volunteering opinions in a non-aggressive manner. If the problem is divergence, the basic business strategy and goals should be discussed and the differences between the goals of the executive and that of the organization must be resolved.

Principle #7: *Measure What You Want To Change*

Feedback about one's performance is critical to any kind of on-going learning. An essential aspect of feedback is that if it is to be helpful, it must be fairly immediate, allowing for quick corrections.

Whatever methodology is used, selection of the specific behaviors needed for change is essential. The executive who resists the culture change because of fear of losing power over others needs to identify specific critical events with peers that have contributed to their negative perception of him. With the help of the coach, that person must devise new behaviors which will begin to challenge those perceptions followed by timely and accurate feedback.

Principle #8: *Reward What Has Been Changed*

People need reinforcement for the changes they make. This is best accomplished by a systematic reward program. This may take the form of tangible rewards, such as bonuses, salary increases, and profit sharing; or intangible rewards, such as special recognition.

However, to make this effective, the reward must tie in specifically with the things that are changed in the management behavior of the executive.

It starts with a clear discussion between the executive and his or her boss outlining the behavioral goals and how and when they should be attained. Then the behavior should be monitored, deviations pointed out, corrections made and followed through. Unless the executive involved truly changes, no reward should be given—and, indeed, failure to change should be considered a serious negative factor in that person's next performance review.

If these steps are implemented, not only will the individual involved have a very good chance of making a dramatic and rapid change in behavior, but a powerful message will have been sent to the entire organization about what is really required for executive success.

QUOTES AND QUIPS

When teaching adults:
- Encourage independence. Adults want control over how they learn.
- Link learning to daily work life. Minimize theory; emphasize practicality.
- Focus on the learner, not the lesson.

Malcolm Knowles
Educator and author

Measuring the Effectiveness of Training

Is the time, energy, and money spent in training really worthwhile? Until relatively recently, there were few tools available to enable organizations to evaluate the effectiveness of their training activities.

Over the past few years, much research has been done in this area. Because training is so important in the changing of an organization's culture, it seems logical that determining its value is a critical factor in the culture change process.

Over the years, many senior executives have been skeptical about the value of training because they could not quantify the results. Attempts to measure the effectiveness of training programs were generally done superficially, usually by asking each participant to fill out a questionnaire reflecting his or her reaction to the program.

QUOTES AND QUIPS

"The expense is not what it costs to train employees.
It's what it costs not to train them."
Philip Wilbur
President, Drug Emporium, Inc.

Donald L. Kirkpatrick, now professor emeritus at the University of Wisconsin, first proposed a model for measuring training programs in 1959. This model was recently revised and updated in his book, *Evaluating Training Programs: The Four Levels.*[5] The four levels described by Kirkpatrick are:

Level 1: Using the traditional trainee evaluation forms. Although not very sophisticated, immediate feedback by class members serves the function of determining their reaction to the program including such important aspects as the trainee's feelings about course content, instructor effectiveness, and whether the course met trainee's expectations.

Level 2: Determination of what the trainee learned. Just as schools have always tested students as to what they learned in class, this level may take the form of a written or oral examination, or a demonstration of skills acquired.

Level 3: Evaluation of behavioral changes and application of learning on the job. This can be a significant tool in determining the value of training. Has the training been effectively applied on the job? This is easy to measure in training in such areas as reduction in number of rejects and increase in productivity. However, this is much more difficult to measure in less tangible areas, such as attitudes, interpersonal relationships, communication skills, and leadership styles—usually referred to as the soft skills. Some examples of how this is accomplished will be discussed later in this chapter.

Level 4: Tying training to organizational impact. Did the training result in a measurable improvement in business results? This level focuses on the actual results the program achieves in the organization when the program objectives have been met successfully.

To these four levels, Dr. Jack J. Phillips, a leading consultant in training program evaluation, has added:

Level 5: ROI (Return on Investment). This focuses its attention on whether the monetary value of the results exceeds the cost of the program. This may be the most valuable measurement and it will be discussed in depth later in this chapter.

Implementing the Kirkpatrick-Phillips Model

Level 1 evaluations are used by most organizations. They are usually obtained by getting feedback from participants through questionnaires and evaluation reports immediately or shortly after the completion of a training program. Level 2 evaluations (what has been learned) can be accomplished by written or oral tests prior to and right after the program.

Techniques to implement Levels 3 and 4 have been more difficult to develop and apply. Let's look at how this has been accomplished in some companies.

Level 3—Application. Probably the best example of measuring the application of new skills is that developed by Motorola University.

Motorola created its university in the 1980s to institute continuous learning as an integral part of its company culture, as described in more detail later in this chapter.

To assure its success, they developed a Level 3 evaluation program. According to Karen Neuhengen, Senior Training Evaluation Specialist at Motorola University, the first step was to determine the specific behaviors that represent a soft skill such as leadership and then track the changes in behavior the trainees exhibited.

One of the techniques used is the 360-degree evaluation. Surveys were sent to trainees, their bosses, and their subordinates, in which the trainees were rated on the frequency in which they displayed those behaviors that relate to leadership. This was followed by quarterly discussions between trainees and their bosses to reinforce the principles of the leadership programs. Their primary concern was whether the courses result in the behavior changes that they have been designed to develop.

The Motorola evaluation program has been adopted by several other organizations including the Ford Motor Co., Texaco Refining and Market, Inc., Caterpillar Construction and Mining, Goodyear Tire and Rubber Co., and the Internal Revenue Service.

Level 4—Tying training to organizational impact. A few years ago, 26 companies joined in a task force to develop a means of Level 4 evaluation. The result is the Training Valuation System (TVS). It starts with an in-depth situation analysis and concludes with the dollar value added to an operation by training or other factors. Through this approach, specific, current, and potential values can be identified before training is conducted. It then measures the value obtained after training. If the training fails to produce the anticipated results, it helps to determine why.

After Alberta General Telephone, Ltd. of Edmonton, Canada, decided to save training expenses by shortening the entry-level training program for customer service representatives from two weeks to one, they tracked the effect of the decision.

By using the TVS model and performance measures already in place, it was found that reps who completed two weeks of training were able to complete a call in an average of 11.4 minutes. Those completing only one week of training took 14.5 minutes. The extra time required to complete calls cost the company more than $50,000 in lost productivity in the first six weeks. In addition, the cost of lost quality due to increased errors, increased collectibles, and service-order errors brought the added cost to $100,000. Management quickly decided to restore the two-week training program.[6]

QUOTES AND QUIPS

"Most organizations conduct evaluations to measure satisfaction; few conduct evaluations on an ROI level. Both are desirable. Evidence shows that if measurements aren't taken at each level, it's difficult to show that any improvement can be attributed to the training."

Jack J. Phillips, President
Performance Resources
Organization

Level 5—A New Approach: Measuring Return On Investment

With the increase in the amount of money being spent on training, questions have been raised as to whether this expenditure is really justified. Until recently there were no studies available concerning this critical area.

In 1994, the American Society for Training and Development (ASTD) published the first of a series of articles describing specific company experience in measuring ROI.[7] The author, Dr. Jack J. Phillips, describes the process as follows:

Two common formulas for calculating return on investment are the benefit cost ratio (BCR) and ROI. To find the BCR, you divide the total benefits by the cost. In the ROI formula, the costs are subtracted from the total benefits to produce the net benefits, which are then divided by the costs.

For example, a literacy skills training program at Magnavox produced benefits of $321,600 with a cost of $38,233. The BCR is 8.4. For every $1 invested, $8.4 in benefits were returned. The net benefits are $321,600 − $38,233 = $283,367. The ROI is $283,367 divided by $38,233 × 100 = 741 percent. Using the ROI formula, for every $1 invested in the program, there was a return of $7.4 in benefits.

Typically, the benefits are annual—the amount saved or gained in the year after training is completed. The benefits may continue after the first year, but the effects begin to diminish. In a conservative approach, long-term benefits are omitted from calculations. In the total cost of a program, the development cost is usually front-loaded and prorated over the first year of implementation. Or, you can prorate development costs over the projected life of the program.[8]

The basic steps in measuring ROI include:

- **Collection of data.** The information that is needed in order to measure effectiveness includes:
  Hard data—Production output (units produced, forms processed), quality (scrap, waste, rejects, returns), equipment downtime, employee overtime, training time, and costs (overhead, sales expense, accident costs)
  Soft data—Employee absenteeism, turnover, tardiness; employee grievances, discrimination charges, job satisfaction, loyalty; and employee development (promotion, training programs attended, performance rating, skills acquired)
- Isolate the effect of training from other factors that may have contributed to the results. This includes:
  Changes in the overall economy
  Changes in the industry
  Changes in management
  Installation of new equipment
  Installation of new processes
  Significant changes in personnel
- Convert results into monetary benefits.

Phillips suggests five steps for converting data into monetary values:

Step 1: Focus on a single unit. For hard data, identify a particular unit of improvement in output (such as products, services, and sales), quality (often measured in terms of errors, rework and product defects or rejects), or time (to complete a project or respond to a customer order). A single unit of soft data can be one employee grievance, one case of employee turnover or a one-point change in the customer-service index.

Step 2: Determine the value for each unit. Place a value on the unit identified in Step 1. That's easy for measures of production, quality, time and cost. Most organizations record the value of one unit of production or the cost of a product defect. But the cost of one employee absence, for example, is difficult to pinpoint.

Step 3. Calculate the change in performance. Determine the performance change after factoring out other potential influences on the training results. This change is the output performance, measured as hard or soft data, that is directly attributed to training.

Step 4. Obtain an annual amount. The industry standard for an annual performance change is equal to the total change in performance during one year. Actual benefits may vary over the course of a year or extend past one year.

Step 5. Determine the annual value. The annual value of improvement equals the annual performance change multiplied by the unit value. Compare the product of this equation to the cost of the program, using the formula: ROI = net annual value of improvement – program cost.[9]

As you can see, the making of ROI evaluations takes considerable time and money. The ASTD study found that it was not feasible or necessary to subject every program to Level 5 evaluation. Many organizations required all of their training programs to be evaluated at Level 1, and 40 to 70 percent of the training activities at Level 2. Both of these levels are relatively easy and inexpensive to utilize.

Level 3 (on-the-job application) takes more time and expense to perform and was used on only 30 to 50 percent of programs, Only 10 percent of programs were evaluated at Level 4 (business results) and only 5 percent at Level 5 (ROI) as both of these processes require significant resources and budgets.

Examples of Good Training Programs

Many companies have highly successful training activities. Among such organizations are:

Walt Disney World Resorts

Disney University is not a campus but a process for training all employees of this enterprise. Jayne Parker, director of Training and Development for Disney University, commented: "Our training exercises reinforce the basic foundation of what Disney is and what makes us different as an organization. The first thing we want our people to understand is the culture of Disney and our values. That way, all employees, regardless of the positions they hold, can communicate them to guests through their work."

The first week includes a workshop called "Traditions," in which, using multi-media techniques, the participants are given an overview of Disney history and culture and the vision of the organization. The facilitators for the sessions are a variety of cast members (the generic term for all employees of Disney theme parks, whether they get into costumes or not). Professional facilitators lead only technical and executive sessions. The cast members share with the trainees their own interactions with guests (the Disney term for customers).

What makes this program really unique is that the trainees mingle among the visiting crowds at the parks to observe and study cast members in action. Parker says, "We are witnessing people who are experiencing their one fantasy day of the year. Our training helps each of us understand that, whether we are in costume, at a desk, or back in the laundry, we are all here to help serve the guest, which is our business."

The result: The attrition rate at Disney is only 15 percent compared with 60 percent for the rest of the hospitality industry.[10]

Saturn Co.

To manufacture the Saturn, General Motors created an entirely new organizational structure. The use of teams is the key to this structure. An important facet of the training program for all employees is Saturn University whose function is to teach employees to operate as continuously learning, fully independent work teams.

The first part of the program involves training or retraining in quality, finance, and other areas. This is done in a traditional classroom format. Gary High, manager of resources development, states: "Teams learn from day one where they fit in the overall process. They know who are their upstream suppliers in production, and who are the customers of their production. They also learn what the ramifications are if their customers expect one hundred parts, but receives only ninety-five. They must understand the consequences of that."

Once the basic training is completed, the teams become responsible for their own development. High noted: "As a team they're running a business. They manage their own budgets, order their own materials, and gauge their own educational progress."

Each employee is responsible for creating his or her own training and development plan. It may be brushing up on current skills or acquiring new skills. It can include attending seminars, completing computer-based training programs, even teaching a training session or cross-training a team member.

Half of all training is in the soft skills. High says: "People make a difference here—not technology. These are highly intelligent, motivated people doing their jobs every day, and we have to support them and provide a nurturing environment."

Saturn guarantees that each employee will receive a minimum of 92 training hours, while on the job; however, the average for most workers is 170. Gary High says: "Our definition of a leader is someone who teaches." The best example of Saturn's commitment to education is that all executives, including the CEO, teach at Saturn University.[11]

GTE

A few years ago, GTE, the fourth largest telephone company in the United States, serving both commercial and residential customers, had undergone a merger, including a major reorganization, and a substantial downsizing. Proposed changes in government regulations were in the offing. Employees at all levels were experiencing the effect of these changes with no end in sight.

An employee opinion survey in 1996 showed that satisfaction ratings of hourly employees on a broad range of workplace issues were falling. To correct this, GTE formed a Culture Council made up of employees from a cross-section of the firm. Its function was to seek ways to share information, encourage employee involvement, demonstrate leadership commitment, and reward achievement.

The first step involved benchmarking successful culture changes in other organizations. The Council studied how the practices of these firms, taking into account the differences in their work environment and that of GTE. From this, they developed the Culture Initiative, a comprehensive culture change program consisting of the following elements:

- **Coaches' clinics.** These one-day meetings were geared for front-line supervisors for information sharing, problem solving, skills development, and training.
- **Jumpstarters.** Structured meetings in which cross-functional, multi-level teams raise and resolve issues.
- **Continuous process improvement.** A process to improve cost, quality, and time measures for nine key business processes.
- **Employee zealots.** This program introduced the principles of *appreciative inquiry.* This is a method of studying what gives life to an organization to enhance its vitality and effectiveness rather than emphasizing what's wrong with it. Using this approach enables an organization to discover the best of its past and present and to design its future. It involves a detailed, four-part process:

    (1) **Discovering.** Understanding and appreciating the "as-is" situation.
    (2) **Dreaming.** Imagining what might be.
    (3) **Designing.** Determining what should be.
    (4) **Delivering Results.** Creating what will be.

- All of these were fueled by a training course for frontline employees to learn about GTE's business, recent industry developments, and the utilization of the principles of appreciative inquiry as it applies to day to day work.

One of the early results of this program is that GTE has a renewed recognition of the importance of employee understanding and support of the company's business direction. A performance measure now is in place that tracks how well employees understand the business direction and how well they think information is shared within the company. In just one year's time (1996–1997), employee's support for GTE's business direction jumped 50 percent and their perception that information is shared openly rose nearly 140 percent.

One example of the result of the training was increased employee participation and innovations. This was demonstrated in the work of the collections process team. In one year (1996), the team improved

GTE's credit verification process, resulting in the collection of $3 million. They streamlined the payment process saving $7–8 million annually, and they developed a new way to automate the insufficient funds process, saving $4 million.

As a large company with more than 60,000 employees, GTE could commit significant resources to its Culture Initiative—$4.2 million in 1997. But any organization can adopt these elements:

- Creating cross-functional teams to identify internal and external factors affecting the organization's culture
- Using benchmarking to discover the best problem-solving techniques used by other organizations such as training, continuous process involvement, and including all employees in a positive way in performance management systems
- Establishing a common set of principles to bring all employees into the change process.

GTE's program was recognized in 1997 as one of the winners of the American Society for Training & Development's Excellence in Practice award.[12]

QUOTES AND QUIPS

"Be not afraid of growing slowly, be afraid only of standing still."
Chinese Proverb

SUM AND SUBSTANCE

As corporate cultures change, employees will often be required to handle more and more functions and tasks. The only way this can be accomplished is through total commitment to training and development at all levels.

The Success Development Process consists of four steps:

1. Trainees must be conditioned to accept that training will involve change in their behavior.

2. Content of training should be presented and demonstrated in an interesting and dynamic manner.
3. Trainees must practice what has been learned in the class and on the job.
4. Training must be followed up and new behavior reinforced.

Trainers must not only utilize the most effective techniques of instructing, but must also be good coaches. A coach has the ability to recognize each person's strengths and limitations and work with each to maximize his or her potential.

Mentors are valuable resources in developing the skills and or their protégés—and equally important in orienting them to the corporate culture.

It is often the most seasoned and successful executives who have the most difficulty in making the change. They frequently have a vested interest in maintaining their past success patterns and often have strong personalities that make it difficult for them to change their behavior. An effective way to deal with this is "transformational coaching."

A company's training investment is most likely to pay off best when training is held accountable for results, used only when it is the appropriate tool, and linked to the company strategy.

The Kirkpatrick-Phillips Five Levels of Measuring training are:

Level 1: Using the traditional trainee evaluation forms. Although not very sophisticated, immediate feedback by class members helps determine their reaction to the program, including such important aspects as the trainee's feelings about course content, instructor effectiveness, and whether the course met expectations.

Level 2: Determination of what the trainee learned. Just as schools have always tested students as to what they learned in class, this level may take the form of a written or oral examination, or a demonstration of skills acquired.

Level 3: Evaluation of application of learning to the job. This can be a significant tool in determining the value of training. Has what the trainees have been taught been applied on the job?

Level 4: Estimating impact. Did the training result in a measurable improvement in business results?

Level 5: Return on Investment (ROI). This focuses attention on whether the monetary value of the results exceed the cost of the program.

REFERENCES

[1]Manchester Consulting Research, Vol. 1, No. 2.

[2]Stern, Lewis R. "Five Types of Executives in Search of Coaching." *The Manchester Review*, Vol. 3, No. 2, 1998, p. 14.

[3]Harrison, Raymond and Edward, Betov. "Transformational Coaching: A New Paradigm for Rapid Executive Change." *The Manchester Review*, Vol. 1, No. 2, Fall 1996, pp. 17–24.

[4]Boccialetti, Gene. *It Takes Two*. San Francisco: Jossey-Bass, 1995.

[5]Kirkpatrick, Donald L. *Evaluating Training Programs—The Four Levels*. San Francisco: Berrett-Koehler, 1994.

[6]Fitz-Enz, Jac. "Yes, You Can Weigh Training Values." *Training*, July 1994, pp. 54–58.

[7]Phillips, Jack J. "ROI: The Search for Better Practices." *Training and Development*, February 1996, pp. 42–47.

[8]Phillips, Jack. J. "ROI: The Search for Better Practices." *Training and Development*, February 1996, pp. 60–61.

[9]Phillips, Jack J. "How Much is Training Worth?" *Training and Development*, April 1996, p. 22.

[10]Carey, Robert. "Five Top Training Corporations." *Successful Meetings*, February 1995, pp. 58–59.

[11]Carey, Robert., p. 60.

[12]Cheney, Scott and Jarrett, Lisa L. "Up-front Excellence for Sustainable Competitive Advantage." *Training and Development*, June 1998, pp. 45–46.

CHAPTER 9

The First
Thirty Days

The planning is done. The organization is now ready to begin implementing its strategy to transform its culture. Not surprisingly, the first thirty days are the most critical. It is during this time that the support and enthusiasm for the initiative will either grow or begin to show signs of decay that may infiltrate the foundation and eventually cause the effort to crumble. Your ability to show and communicate results during this critical time is essential to long-term success.

You are now ready to get the program off the ground—to rumble down the runway for the takeoff. This takes hard work and it starts with well-thought-out steps for the initiation of the process.

Getting Off to a Good Start

One exciting way to get everybody enthusiastic about the culture change is to start with a major event—*a kickoff rally*. Who should be invited? Everybody! This means everybody from the CEO to entry-level employees. Invite their families, too.

To make everybody feel welcome, post bulletins and colorful posters announcing the event. This should be supplemented by a letter from the CEO sent to each employee's home, clearly stating the reason for the gathering.

Some people will greet this with skepticism. They may think: "What are they trying to pull on us now?" This cynicism can be mitigated by a series of bulletins issued before the rally explaining the reasons for the proposed changes and describing what the company plans to do to identify problems and assure employees that the organization is committed to resolve them. The purpose of the rally is not to tell the staff for the first time that the corporate culture will be changing, but to establish a start-off date for the actual changes.

How *Not* to Do It

Last year, I was invited by a friend to attend a formal dinner that his company was giving to initiate the start of their culture change efforts. "My boss," he told me, "really takes culture change seriously and he is starting it with this banquet so we all know that he means business."

As I looked around the room, I saw men and women, dressed in their finest clothes, chatting over drinks before the dinner service was announced. My friend introduced me to several of them—all middle- and high-level managers. "Where are the workers?" I asked. "Oh," answered my friend, "this dinner is for the key people—those who have to get the program moving."

That was the first mistake. Unless everybody is involved in the program from the start, the program will be perceived as just another management gimmick.

At the dinner, the CEO gave a ponderous talk about his commitment to changing things. He provided no specifics about what was going to be done, who would do it and when it would occur. He then introduced a guest speaker, a college professor, who gave an erudite talk on the history of corporate culture. Although he made some interesting comments, his speaking style was so dull that he lost the audience after the first five minutes.

Several months later, my friend reported that the program was moving along very slowly and that no real progress had been made.

The Human Resources manager of another company told me that his boss, over his objection, decided to charge a "nominal" fee of five dollars per person to cover the costs of the culture change kick-off rally. Most of the managers attended, but few rank-and-file workers showed up. The HR manager was not surprised. He told me: "Even though it was a small amount that everybody could easily afford, it was looked upon as small-minded and cheap." This is not the way to develop the enthusiasm and support needed to reverse a troubled culture.

Make It Fun

A good approach to that opening event is to treat it more like a football rally than a formal affair. The objective is to get everybody excited and enthusiastic to get the program underway. Decorate the cafeteria with bunting and balloons. Even better, have the event off-site. Hire a hall. Instead of a dinner, have a buffet. Perhaps, have a theme party with everybody coming in costume. One company's "circus" party is still being talked about several years later. It could be a picnic or a barbecue. Make it fun. Make it memorable. Make it exciting.

Instead of formal talks, the CEO and other managers should let their hair down and mingle with the staff. Talk up the program informally all through the event. Bringing in an inspirational speaker such as a sports or entertainment figure also helps add to the excitement and a sense that positive changes are on the horizon.

QUOTES AND QUIPS

"Nothing great was ever achieved without enthusiasm."
Ralph Waldo Emerson, 1803–1882
American essayist and poet

Use the event to reinforce the intent of the program and to address the concerns that some people may have about the changes to be made. Games, contests, and children's events should be arranged to make the party move along without snags. Everybody should be given a good time so they'll remember the rally as a highlight of the year.

The Kickoff Follow-up

After the party is over, keep the momentum up and running. I visited one company about three months after their kickoff rally. Pictures of the rally graced the bulletin boards. Photos of the employees with their families taken at the party were displayed on many desks or posted above workbenches. People were still talking about the event.

About a month after the kickoff, they showed videos taken at the party in the lunchroom so people could relive the experience. The result: the prolonged excitement reinforced the momentum.

Six Ways to Keep Your Culture Change Moving Forward

Too often, activities that start with a big bang end in a whimper. To avoid this, real results must be achieved from the very onset of the program. Here are six ways that have enabled organizations to achieve early successes:

1. Promise Some Early Changes—and Make Them Significant

Rita R., CEO of Flagstaff's Department Store, did this by making a major change in the compensation system as a first step in their culture change program. She and a team of people drawn from managerial and nonmanagerial personnel took a year to study the current policies and practices before initiating the program.

At the opening-gun rally, Rita promised her people that a major change in compensation would be announced later that week. For the next few days, the entire staff eagerly awaited the announcement. Would it be some superficial adjustment to make people think real changes would be made or would it be a really significant move?

The news was announced in a bulletin that was distributed to the employees when they reported to work on Thursday morning. As in most traditional department stores, Flagstaff paid most clerks a straight salary; salespeople in some departments, though, such as in jewelry and men's clothing, were paid on commission. Although their incomes varied, they could generally make much more money than those paid straight salaries. Salespeople in other departments resented this and felt they should have the opportunity to make more money if they sold more merchandise.

Rita announced that a new plan in which *all* employees would be paid on a salary-plus-productivity bonus would be put into effect at the start of the next month. Nobody would make less than they were currently earning; and all had the opportunity to earn more.

This reinforced in the minds of the employees that the store was serious about changing what they had been doing and looked forward to other changes that the organization would soon be making.

TACTICAL TIPS

Significant changes made early in the culture change process reassure employees that the organization is serious about changing the status quo.

---

2. Make a Conscious, Public Effort to Share Credit

As previously noted, the success of a culture change program is directly dependent upon the participation of everybody in the organization. Particularly in the early stages of the program, make a big fuss over every improvement, every good idea, every accomplishment—and do it publicly.

Although tangible rewards such as bonuses or awards for suggestions are important, recognition does not have to be financial. Awarding certificates and plaques, reporting successes in the company house organ, and sending press releases to local papers about special contributions of employees all work to inspire others and maintain enthusiasm.

One of the most effective and least expensive ways of recognizing achievements is a note of thanks. You can have a "thank you" form printed, dictate letters of thanks, or send a "thank you" fax or e-mail. The most effective method, however, is a personal hand-written note.

To make that thank-you really meaningful, be sure to specify what that person has done to earn your thanks. "Thank you for a good job" is okay, but far better are such comments as the following, made by the CEO of a New Jersey utility company: "Thank you for that extra time and effort you put in to get our project out on schedule. I was particularly impressed by your creative ideas that enabled us to take new approaches in dealing with the problems we faced. This was a fine example of how collaboration among the staff members at all levels resulted in successful accomplishment of a difficult task. Your work on this assignment is greatly appreciated."

Make sure everybody knows about these accomplishments. Place comments on bulletin boards, announce it at staff meetings, and talk about it in informal conversations with others in the company.

QUOTES AND QUIPS

"Praise the slightest improvement and praise every improvement. Be hearty in your approbation and lavish in your praise."

Dale Carnegie, 1888–1955
American pioneer in personality
development and motivational
author, including How to Win
Friends and Influence People

3. Plan Some Nice Surprises

Most people worry when the boss calls a meeting. Their first reaction is: "What did we do wrong?" "What trouble are we in now?"

Wouldn't it be a nice surprise if, when they come to the meeting, they are greeted with good news—something like: "This meeting has been called to congratulate you on the great work you did in meeting the deadline on the XYZ project."

Everybody likes pleasant surprises. If you can make it a practice to find such good news from time to time, it pays off in good will, increased cooperation and increased enthusiasm for the program.

4. Make Some Key Personnel Changes

As pointed out earlier in this book, often the serious problems that plague an organization stem from arbitrary management practices by people who have the clout to steer the company in directions that may be exactly opposite of where the organization plans to go. So long as these people are in influential positions, a culture change will never take place.

Stella M. is a good example of how one person can poison the atmosphere of an entire organization. Stella had been secretary to the president of Consolidated Rubber Products for 20 years. When the founder, Rodney R., died, his son and successor, Sidney, inherited the presidency, and with it, Stella.

Rodney had been an old-school tyrannical boss and like many boss's secretaries, Stella often acted for him and imitated his autocratic style. In his last years, when illness kept him away from the office for long periods of time, Stella was the *de facto* president. She treated everybody with disdain and was feared and loathed by all.

When Sidney took over the presidency, Stella dictated to him how he should conduct the business. Any changes he proposed were denigrated by her with the comment, "That won't work. Here's how your father would have handled it." She would "misinterpret" his orders when passing them on to subordinates. She treated him as the not-too-bright son, who didn't quite fit into his father's shoes.

Once Sidney had settled in as CEO of Consolidated, he realized that major changes had to be made if the company were to meet the challenges it now faced. He also realized that so long as Stella held a position of authority, it wouldn't be possible to institute such changes.

Stella rejected his suggestion that she should retire now that his father had passed on. She would suffer no financial loss by retiring, since her pension and an early retirement bonus would allow her to live comfortably. Sidney pointed out that now she could spend more time with her family and grandchildren. Stella, however, rejected the notion of retirement.

Sidney recognized that people like Stella wield great influence in many companies and their continued presence inhibits change. To accomplish the planned changes, such people must be removed from power. He dealt with this forthrightly. He told Stella, that although she had been an excellent secretary to his father, he wished to retain the secretary who had worked with him before his promotion.

As he could not force her to retire, he created a new job for Stella, handling special projects. In this position, she would work on her own and was given no authority over anybody in the company. He placed her in an office in another part of the building where she had little interaction with the other employees.

The resultant increase in morale was palpable. Without Stella's interference in their projects, department managers began to initiate ideas, and professional staff became more creative. Within a few months, Stella became frustrated with her lack of power and accepted the offer of early retirement.

QUOTES & QUIPS

"When it comes to people and their quirks, idiosyncrasies, and personality flaws, the manager's aim is to keep these human beings from clogging up the workings of their group."
Andrew S. Grove
CEO, Intel Corp.

5. Improve the Physical Surroundings

One suggestion often made by psychologists to depressed patients is that they redecorate their homes. By brightening up your physical surroundings, you'll also be brightening up your life. This philosophy also works as a morale booster in an organization. Changing the color of the walls from dull gray to a light pastel shade can not only brighten the room, but also uplift the spirits of the employees. If a color change is not appropriate, a fresh coat of paint may do as well.

An example of how changing the "scenery" affects morale was demonstrated a few years ago at the Lincoln Discount Corp. in New York City. As you looked around the office, you were faced with a sea of desks, each with its computer terminal, book rack, telephone, and chair. On some desks were photos; on others were plants. Around clusters of four or six desks were six-foot partitions separating them from other cubicles. This is typical of most offices—dull and unimaginative.

About two weeks after management commenced the culture change program, all employees were requested to clear off their desks on Friday and to take off anything posted on partitions. When they returned on Monday morning, they were delighted to see a new set-up. Gone were the partitions. Each cluster of desks was surrounded by planters plush with greenery. This change in the working environment was not only a morale booster, but was an indication that steps were actually being taken to implement the culture change the company had initiated.

6. Track and Report on Progress

One of the strongest reinforcements to the continued enthusiasm for culture change is keeping everybody involved and informed on the progress that has been made. Bulletins, newsletters, letters from the CEO all have been used extensively and do the job well.

The art of communications has advanced so much in recent times that even more exciting techniques are available. A computer systems manufacturer, located in Silicon Valley, employs a videographer, whose only job is videotaping progress reports. This involves interviewing managers and workers about what they are doing, videotaping manufacturing processes before and after changes have been made and making video records of every aspect of the culture change process.

Each week, the videographer edits the tapes and provides videos of that week's work which are then shown in the company lounges and are available to be taken home by employees. Many employees do take them home, especially when they're in the video. This has the added benefit of getting their family's support. The kids can now see what Dad or Mom is doing and why he or she sometimes can't be home in time to see the school team play or attend the school play.

TACTICAL TIPS

Keep everybody informed of the progress of the program. Let them exult in the successes and be aware of problems. In this way, they will truly be a part of the process.

Building Speed and Momentum

Enthusiasm alone is not enough to get your program down the runway and off the ground. It needs concrete actions. Momentum must be built, brick by brick, in a systematic way. To do this, I recommend the creation of a series of *action teams* to provide guidance, assistance and direction in the critical areas needed to keep the culture change effort alive and kicking. Inasmuch as everybody in the organization must be involved for successful results, members of the teams should be people who are respected by both the formal and informal organization.

Who should choose these team members? In one company whose culture change program is greatly admired, the Culture Change Committee, which organized the activity from its inception chose the team leaders for the operating teams. The team leader, in turn chose members of his or her team. To avoid some of the pitfalls that often develop when a leader picks the team members, the following guidelines were set:

- No more than two team members can come from the same department.
- Each team must consist of members from middle management, first-line management, and rank-and-file employees.
- Team leaders should not just choose people with whom they work comfortably. Surrounding oneself with "yes-men" defeats the purpose.
- Team leaders should pick people who have a reputation of thinking creatively, putting ideas into action, and working cooperatively. Avoid people who tend to dominate or intimidate.

I recommend that organizations begin with three key teams. A team should not have fewer than five nor more than twelve members, depending on the size of the organization.

The OFI Team

OFI stands for *Opportunities For Improvement*. Its goal, as the name suggests, is to seek out and serve as a gathering point for ideas and suggestion that either identify an area or issue in need of strengthening or a solution of a known problem.

Note the words: *seek out*. It is not the function of this team to investigate problems and brainstorm ideas. It is to encourage all people in the company to put their observational skills and brain power to work to identify and report pertinent problems. This can be done through a variety of means. Some of the more successful techniques that have been used include:

Internal advertising. One company used a series of colorful and imaginative posters challenging employees to find areas where improvement was warranted. Another had their advertising agency develop a full-blown marketing campaign to stimulate action.

Suggestion systems. These traditional programs can be jazzed up to generate more ideas. By awarding one-time special awards for ideas for improvement made during the first month of the program, one company received ten times the number of suggestions made in any one previous month.

Idea fairs. At a medium-sized printing plant in Grand Rapids, Michigan, the OFI team persuaded the CEO to open the plant on a Saturday for an "idea fair." All employees and their families were invited. During the three-week period prior to the fair, employees were deluged with bulletins, announcements over the PA system, and posters encouraging them to come to the fair with at least one idea on what and how things could be improved. Refreshments were served in the cafeteria. Booths were staffed by team members. It resulted in a large number of good suggestions.

When ideas are submitted to the team, they should be either investigated by one or more of the team members, or if the idea is of a technical nature beyond the scope of any of the team, it should be assigned to a competent specialist for evaluation. There may be employees who feel uncomfortable in submitting ideas that may be divergent from company practices, so the option of submitting suggestions anonymously should be available.

Follow-up is essential. Unless the persons who submit ideas are kept informed as to the status of their suggestions, the whole program will collapse. Formal letters of acknowledgment should be sent. In addition, team members should meet informally with people who submit ideas to ask questions, get clarification, and let them know what action results.

The Recognition and Awards Team

In order to provide recognition to employees who contribute to the culture change, many companies have opted to form an R & A team. R & A stands for "Recognition and Awards." The function of this team is not to select persons for awards, but to set up a system in which anybody in the organization can recommend another for recognition.

QUOTES AND QUIPS

"The best way to inspire people to superior performance is to convince them by everything you do and by your everyday attitude that you are wholeheartedly supporting them."
Harold Geneen
Former CEO, IT&T

More and more companies are looking at their employees as internal customers and internal suppliers. For example, if Mike, a punch-press operator, supplies assemblers with parts, the assemblers are Mike's customers. Inasmuch as customer satisfaction is the overall goal, the punch-press operator's goal is to satisfy the assemblers. Let's look at how this works in action.

A deadline is approaching and the assemblers are under pressure to complete the job. They're running low on parts. Mike, always alert to the status of the parts' inventory, skips his lunch and works overtime to meet the assemblers' need. The deadline is met and the assemblers nominate Mike for special recognition. He has performed above and beyond the call of duty to satisfy his customer.

This is where the R & A team steps in. By developing a procedure to give such awards and administering it in a fair and equitable manner, they contribute to the success of the program.

The R & A team encourages their internal customers at any level to recognize an internal supplier's special help by sending her or him a "You Made My Day" certificate (Figure 6-2).

Companies that encourage peer recognition by using the "You Made My Day" form or some other approach have augmented the process by presenting awards to employees who have received peer recognition. Such awards vary from plaques and framed certificates to monthly luncheons to which employees who received recognition are invited.

The Communications Team

The Communications team is charged with developing an ongoing program of providing truthful, properly balanced reports on the progress of the project so that everybody is kept informed on both the successes attained and any problems. The key to success of a communications team is that it should be free to operate without too much control from senior management. It must be able to "tell it like it is."

Hiding unpleasant information may seem like a good way to keep up morale, but sooner or later, it will come out and the damage caused by the cover-up will be far greater than any immediate consequences of the bad news. More likely, bad news may serve as a stimulant to get things moving back on track.

Feel the Pulse

As part of the O-MRI, an employee attitude survey has been taken. Now's the time to take another study to measure how the inception of the culture change activities are viewed by the employees. This survey will assess the state of their morale and determine if the first steps are really working.

Questions should be asked that will elicit opinions about the extent to which people are now starting to realize that things are really changing and beginning to get better. It's a bit too early for progress to be measured as the program has just started. The objective is to send another signal to employees that you are really interested in what they think and feel about what's going on.

Make Mid-Course Corrections

Keep in mind that if you are going to ask people for their opinions, you must be ready to take criticism with an open mind and demonstrate a willingness to address issues brought to your attention. This is a learning process for the culture change team. From what is learned, action must follow. If nothing is done to correct faults, adjust misconceptions, solve problems, and learn from early mistakes, your credibility will be diluted and the entire program put in jeopardy.

This is what happened at a wholesale lumber company in Rumford, Maine. The owner of the company was committed to instituting a culture change and appointed a three-person team to implement it. When the first reports pointed out that some first-line supervisors refused to conform to the new concepts, the team's reaction was: "Give them time and they'll come around." But the reaction of the workers was: "The company talks big, but our supervisors still do what they always did."

Let's remember that *perception is reality in the mind of the perceiver.* It is up to the leaders of the culture change, *by their actions,* to dissolve poor perceptions and reinforce in the minds of all of those involved that this is a worthwhile, attainable, and beneficial endeavor.

Get Vendors, Suppliers, and Subcontractors Involved

Few organizations are totally self-sufficient. Most companies are dependent on outside sources for materials, supplies and, often, other aspects of the work. Unless these outsiders are taken into the picture, it will have a negative impact.

This was displayed at Freeport Contractors, a construction company in Rhode Island. Since this organization does not have a drafting department, they subcontract drafting requirements to a specialized design and engineering firm. Freeport Contractors was hired to build a multi-unit warehouse and office building complex—a three-year project. They subcontracted the drafting to a local firm, Construction Drafting Associates (CDA), which sent a contingent of design and drafting personnel to work on the project in Freeport's offices.

At the start of the second year of the project, Freeport retained a consultant to help them institute a culture change program. An Organizational MRI was conducted and steps were taken to implement the program. But almost from the beginning, problems developed. The culture of CDA was quite different from Freeport's. Their designers and draftsmen worked under autocratic supervisors who allowed no diversion from their rigid system. Inasmuch as CDA employees were working in close relationship with Freeport's own people, conflicts in approaches rose from the beginning.

To deal with this situation, a meeting was arranged with the president of CDA, the owner of Freeport Contractors, and the consultant. To illustrate the steps Freeport was taking and why it was being done, a role-playing session was prepared in which a team of Freeport workers demonstrated how decisions were made before the changes were instituted and how they now were approached. Several employees also "testified" on what this new process meant to them and how it had motivated them to become more creative and more committed to the job.

It was pointed out that the process would be even more successful if the CDA people who were on the premises became full participants in the program. Inspired by the demonstration, the president of CDA agreed to cooperate. The teams were restructured with CDA personnel as participants and the program moved forward smoothly. So well, in fact, that CDA is considering instituting a similar program for themselves.

While suppliers and vendors do not have as much influence on culture change programs as subcontractors, they should be made aware of the program and how it affects their relationship with the organization. They should be shown how they can participate in the program, and they should be invited to join appropriate team discussions.

On the following pages is an ACTION CHECKLIST. Use this as a guide to the implementation of your program.

ACTION CHECKLIST	
Action	**Check when done**
Before the start of the program:	
Prepare for the kickoff affair	
Appoint manager responsible for kickoff rally	
Prepare and distribute announcement of kickoff rally	
Prepare and post notices, bulletins, and posters	
Arrange for catering and decorations	
Determine overall objectives:	
Policies, personnel, special awards, etc.	
Appoint team participants for the OFI, R & A, Communication, and other appropriate teams.	
First action week:	
Host the kickoff affair	
Explain objectives of the culture change program and the plans to activate them to employees	

Get initial feedback from employees

    Preliminary survey

    Walking around

    Meet with "informal" leaders

Plan early changes

    Policies

    Physical environment

    Personnel

Key committees begin functioning

<u>Second and third weeks</u>

    Review feedback from managers and committees on current results

    Make necessary adjustments to stay on track

    Implement changes planned during first week

    Meet with subcontractors and vendors to bring them into the picture

    Reinforce enthusiasm generated in first week at a meeting in each department

    Reinforce commitment of employees by letters of recognition from supervisors and team leaders

    Initiate program of peer recognition, such as "You Made My Day" certificates

<u>Fourth week</u>

    Get reports from all committees on progress

    Get informal feedback from supervisors, managers and the culture change consultant on progress

    Conduct employee survey

        Determine from all of the above:

        Specific changes in policies and practices that have already been implemented

        Changes of attitude of employees

        Employees' perception of changes made to date

        Employees' desires of changes still to be made

    Plan for the next phase of the program

SUM AND SUBSTANCE

In order to get the culture change program off the ground, it should start with a bang. One way is to begin with a kickoff rally—an exciting event for the entire organization. Once the program is underway, the excitement should be reinforced by a series of immediate actions that show all associates that the organization takes the program seriously and is committed to its success.

One way of doing this is to make some significant and dramatic changes early. Among these might be key personnel changes, alterations in some systems and procedures, improving physical environment, and similar moves that are easily seen and understood by everybody. Reports on progress should be made frequently with recognition given to those who contributed to its success.

Several teams should be formed to work on the various aspects of the culture change. In addition to the main culture change team, which is responsible for the entire process, additional teams might include:

- **An OFI (Opportunities for Improvement) Team,** to set up programs that will encourage all employees to seek and present suggestions for improving any company activity.
- **An R & A (Recognition and Awards) Team,** to provide a system of recognition for associates whose work or contributions are outstanding.
- **A Communications Team,** to set up a continuing program to keep people informed on the progress of the program—not only its successes, but its failures and shortcomings as well.

By also including vendors, suppliers, customers, and subcontractors in the culture change activities, a synergism develops which enriches the entire process and benefits all parties both within and outside of the organization.

CHAPTER 10

Gaining Speed and Momentum

In order to stay viable, your culture change efforts must be continuously reinvigorated. One reason for this is that the pressure to succeed is in itself a cause of failure. When people are overly stressed, they often lose their enthusiasm and may even burn out. Early failures are inevitable. You try new things and it's unlikely that everything you do will work. This creates doubts about the entire project. Instead of looking to a rosy future, people begin calculating the odds of success against the cost of failure.

Experienced culture change agents prepare for this. They are ready to give the nay-sayers that extra shot in the arm to renew their enthusiasm and commitment. This cannot be accomplished by a superficial pep talk or a hyped-up rally. Now that the effort has been undertaken, the proof of its value must be evidenced in action and results.

KEY POINT

To pass through this phase unscathed is to simply continue to do the things you planned, work out the kinks, make adjustments and keep going.

Fly by the Instruments

There may be times when we are not sure what the problems are. Perhaps they're hidden behind clouds of vagueness or confusion. The true situation may not be obvious, so we have to dig deeper. Like a pilot who flies into a cloud bank and cannot see the ground, we turn to our "instrument panel" to guide us. The pilot uses gyroscopes, radar, compasses, and sophisticated electronic instruments to keep the plane on course. As managers, we must develop equivalent tools to keep our programs on course.

Institute a Monitoring System

When the matter involved is quantifiable, monitoring systems are easy to install. Such systems can be as simple as charts which compare actual performance with projected goals to highly complex statistical process control systems.

However, there are aspects of a culture change that are conducive to this type of monitoring. In some instances, the immediate increases or decreases in sales volume, production, and quality may well be indicators of the effects of the new changes on the business itself. Turnover, absenteeism, and tardiness statistics are often meaningful monitors of employee morale.

By determining baselines for each of these factors—often department by department or project by project, you can measure how they change week by week as the change effort progresses.

QUOTES AND QUIPS

"Monitor—yes. Micromanage—no! When you micromanage, you stifle creativity and prevent team members from working at their full potential."
Robert J. McCarty
Executive coach

Because so much of culture change involves interpersonal relations and other soft skills, there are few objective monitoring programs available. Other than well-designed and administered employee surveys, managers have to depend on their eyes and ears to spot symptoms of problems before they arise and to take the steps needed to alleviate the situation, correct errors, shore up the beams, and fill up the cracks before the entire plan begins to falter.

Be Alert

Let's look at some of the ways a manager can keep alert to potential problems:

- *Encourage well-designed reports.* Honest reporting on the status of the vital signs of an organization: sales, cash flow, inventories, production, payroll, etc., will enable managers to keep their fingers on the pulse of the organization.
- *Walk around.* You cannot know what is really going on by secluding yourself in your office. Walk around. Talk to the men and women who are doing the work. Get their input on how things are progressing.
- *Be a keen observer.* Look for signs of discontent. Observe where pressure or stress is affecting work or morale. Look for changes in attitudes among the employees, such as their reluctance to talk freely about problems, more frowning than smiling faces in the workplace, as well as a general lack of enthusiasm.
- *Meet regularly with team leaders and supervisors.* Get progress reports on every project. Discuss any deviation from expectations immediately. Take action to correct them.
- *Cultivate the informal leaders.* They can tell you things your supervisors and mid-level managers may not even be aware of.

Key Point

Keep alert to potential problems by
- Designing and using meaningful reports
- Walking around and carefully observing
- Meeting regularly with team leaders
- Cultivating the informal leaders

Signs of Trouble

Consultants report that when they've been called in to rescue culture change programs that have faltered, they've found that almost all of them experienced several of the following situations:

The reality did not match the promises made. Organizations often start out looking like an champions, but soon begin to look more like also-rans. Why? The hype and hullabaloo of the inception of the program gave the rank-and-file employees high hopes, but these hopes were dashed when the program took longer than expected to get off the ground, and many of the promises made were not fulfilled.

To prevent this, make sure you do not oversell the program. Yes, get everybody excited, but not by creating hopes that cannot be met within a short time. By pointing out that these are long-term goals and will take time to accomplish, disillusionment can be avoided.

Missed deadlines. One of the more subtle ways in which people express discontent is by slowing down. If a pattern of missed deadlines shows up, study what really is going on in that department.

This happened at the Sweet Sixteen Cosmetics Company. Two months after the inception of their culture change plan, Meredith M., the program coordinator, noticed that the market research department had missed deadlines on their last three reports. She made discreet inquiries and learned that, as a result of the initial discussions of the culture change in their department, the analysts had expected their computers to be upgraded.

When several reminders to management were ignored, the market research team lost its enthusiasm and just didn't stretch to get the work out on time. Once the market researchers were assured that the upgrade was definitely scheduled for the following month, they returned to their former support and enthusiasm for the project.

Early failures or setbacks. Yes, there will be failures—particularly in the beginning when you're still feeling your way. Expect them. Learn from them and don't let them get you down.

When a culture change program was initiated at a printing plant in Connecticut, most of the managers and staff of the company were excited and optimistic about the changes that were proposed. One significant change required close coordination with a subcontractor. Unfortunately, this firm failed to provide the services that had been promised. This delayed a major phase of the program.

Two middle-level managers whose original skepticism had been temporarily assuaged by the overall enthusiasm of the group used this failure as an indicator that they had been right all along. Not only did these dissidents have to be brought back in line, but the "I told you so" attitude that they were spreading to other employees had to be reversed.

Correcting the service problem with the provider was much easier than reselling the program to these managers and the people they influenced. It took patience, persuasion, and demonstrations of the successes that had already been achieved to win them over.

QUOTES AND QUIPS

"When dealing with people, let us remember we are
not dealing with creatures of logic.
We are dealing with creatures of emotion."
Dale Carnegie, 1888–1955
American motivational author

Sometimes you can anticipate potential problems and can develop contingency plans. For example, it is always a possibility that a key person may become incapacitated, or for some other reason cannot continue to function in the assignment. Just as the star of a Broadway play has a stand-in ready if needed, it's a good idea to have another manager trained and available to take over if something unexpected develops. In addition, as computers or equipment may break down, replacement sources should be lined up to fill any gap.

Cybercorp, a manufacturer of state-of-the-art electronic components in southern Florida, was faced with this type of emergency. They were well into their change from centralized management to team-based management when Hurricane Andrew severely damaged their facility. The first reaction of top management was to take charge as they had in the past, get the damage repaired, and put aside the changes until things were back to normal.

Their culture change agent, however, convinced them that instead of looking at this calamity as a setback, they should use it as a challenge to the new system. By establishing teams to deal with each of several matters that had to be accomplished, they not only got back into production rapidly, but solidified the collaborative concept that had been the main goal of the culture change.

Diversions caused by other issues. A common problem faced by organizations that run into problems in the early stages of their culture change is that they lose focus. The key players in the culture change program become so bogged down with putting out these fires that their thoughts and energies are diverted from the long-range objectives.

Management by crisis is not unusual. When crises develop, they must be addressed. By careful planning and foresight, though, many potential problems can be resolved before they reach emergency proportions. If a crisis does occur, of course, it must be dealt with. But it's essential that the energies of management be redirected to the culture change program once the emergency is resolved.

Too much left to lower-level managers. As pointed out earlier in this book, a culture change cannot succeed unless senior management takes an active, wholly supportive role. If the change agent is an internal executive, he or she should be at least at the vice-president level. If a consultant is the prime change agent, a member of senior management should be assigned as the liaison officer.

Although representatives from various levels of management should be included in the culture change team, unless the key person heading the endeavor is close to the CEO, it may not be taken as seriously as it should.

Procrastination in making tough decisions. When making major changes in a corporate culture, decisions must be reached that may not be welcomed by some key people in the organization whose power and influence may be affected. As such people may wield considerable clout in the organization, the project committee may be afraid to make decisions that affect these managers. This often results in failure to take significant steps that are essential to the culture change.

Because decisions that may curtail the influence of these managers are often key to the success of the project, they must be made without fear of repercussions or the entire project may be stalled or even derailed. The committee should have the power to make these decisions or, if more expedient, to recommend them to the CEO, who can issue and implement them.

Don't stall when it comes to matters that are key to the culture change. Procrastinating only makes changes harder to accomplish. It leaves the impression that you may not do what you plan to do and what others expect you to do. Make the decisions and implement them immediately so you can move the project forward.

QUOTES AND QUIPS

"While we are postponing, life speeds by."
Seneca, 55 BC–40 A.D.
Roman philosopher

Regression. Despite early commitment to making significant changes in the corporate culture, there are many examples of companies who give up too soon. This may be because of early failures or the loss of passion for the program by senior managers. This can often be countered by the renewed efforts of a dynamic culture change leadership.

Such a regression occurred at the Galactic Moving and Storage Co. Happy with the success of their TQM program, the company felt that, as a follow-up, it would reevaluate the total corporate culture and institute changes that would, as stated by Galactic's CEO, "bring the firm into the 21st century."

A committee was formed to lead the program and steps were taken to initiate and implement a systematic approach to the culture change. For the first few months, the program moved along at a quick pace, but then things slowed down. Some of the early changes instituted did not work out as expected, causing several key managers to lose their enthusiasm. They noted that the TQM program had moved along more rapidly and had shown immediate results, while the culture change program had thus far made little real impact. This disillusionment spread rapidly and the CEO chose to defer further implementation until he could study and evaluate the progress made.

Over the next few months, nothing was done and it was assumed that the program was discontinued. However, a few of the managers recognized the long-run value of making changes in the company's culture and persuaded the CEO to renew the program. They formed a new culture change committee and retained a consultant, who had recently completed a very successful culture change program for another firm in their community. The program was started afresh with new leadership, new ideas, and new enthusiasm.

TACTICAL TIPS

Keep the momentum going. When things slow down, enthusiasm is lost. Reinvigorate things via new thinking, new actions and renewed leadership.

Organizational politics. There's no doubt that in most companies, politics—both internal and external—affect the culture. Sometimes it's pressure from an influential stockholder; sometimes it is from valued customers who may feel that the changes made affect them adversely. Most often, it's from members of the management group who feel that they have much to lose.

It is not always obvious who the really influential people are. Sure, employees know who they are, but outsiders can be misled by just looking at an organizational chart. For example, if you were to study the organizational chart of Discount Merchandisers, (Fig. 10-1), a man I'll call Keith Johnson does not have a position that appears to be one of power. As administrative coordinator, his box is well below those of vice-presidents and department managers.

Organizational charts can be misleading, however. Johnson is one of the most influential people in the company. His boss, the vice-president of administration, a largely ineffective manager, has given Johnson far greater scope of authority than his job normally provides. Over the years, Johnson has used this power to make decisions that should have been made by his boss. Even more important, this has enabled him to become a confidant of the CEO and influence many of his actions.

When the culture change program was initiated, Johnson supported it. He assumed that he could exert the same type of influence on the committee as he had on his boss and the CEO. As the committee moved ahead and the program got off the ground, however, Johnson's efforts to intervene between the committee and the CEO were frustrated. He came to the realization that the only way to consolidate his power was to oppose the program.

Over the next few months, in his dealings with the CEO, Johnson bad-mouthed the work of the teams that were implementing the changes, found fault with every decision made, exaggerated the fail-

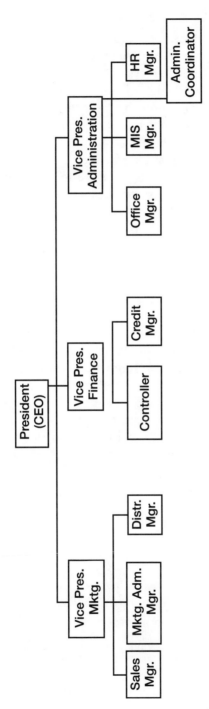

Figure 10-1. *Organizational Chart Discount Merchandisers.*

ures, and mocked the advances. His political skills and his clout with the CEO had their effect. The CEO became disillusioned with the progress and just as it was beginning to make a real difference, canceled it and reverted to the old system.

The point: There are Machiavellian schemers like Keith Johnson in many organizations. To counter the effects, a strong committee, an influential group of other managers and/or a no-nonsense consultant will be needed.

Failure to obtain the necessary support. One of the added values of using a consultant in a culture change effort is that he or she has probably already faced most of the problems that are typically encountered. In truth, such problems are rarely unique. The consultant, having worked with other organizations that have met and conquered these obstacles, can apply this knowledge when dealing with related situations in your firm.

As pointed out earlier, consultants also provide both the technical and psychological support to management and the change committee, which enables them to get underway, helps them jump the hurdles and builds up morale when things don't go right. They act as impartial arbiters in resolving conflicts among participants. When teams go off course, the consultants are there to identify why and guide them back.

A dynamic consultant can move things forward when they bog down, can intervene with top management when support is not forthcoming and, above all, can keep everybody focused on the main goal—to change the organizational culture so that everybody in the organization can work together more effectively.

QUOTES AND QUIPS

"Once the culture program gets underway, it's essential that it be carefully monitored so that it doesn't bog down and that it will move along steadily toward its goal."
Dr. Arthur R. Pell
Consultant, Human Resources
Development, and author

SUM AND SUBSTANCE

A systematic approach to keeping tabs on the progress of the culture change process should include well-designed reports that will enable managers to keep current on the effect of the program on production, sales, costs, profits, and other vital statistics.

Reports alone do not always tell the whole story, however. To get the "feel" of how the program is being accepted by the staff, members of the culture change team should become active observers. They should walk around and talk to team supervisors, informal leaders, and the rank-and-file workers. In this way, they can keep their fingers on the pulse of the organization and identify problem areas before they develop.

Some signs of incipient trouble that may develop in the early weeks of the process are:

- The reality does not meet the expectations. Promises may have been made that are not being kept. Progress in key areas of the program is slower than was anticipated.
- Deadlines on key aspects of the process are not met.
- Setbacks and failures in one or more aspects of the process may discourage participants.
- Managers are distracted by extraneous issues.
- Senior managers leave too much of the responsibility for implementing the program to lower-level associates.
- The program is sabotaged by internal politics.

In order to overcome these problems before they get out of control, the culture change team and/or the consultants involved must take proactive steps to keep the process on track and moving along.

CHAPTER 11

Special
Circumstances

As we have seen in previous chapters, changing the culture in which an organization has operated is never easy. It becomes even more complicated when special circumstances exist that must be especially addressed. In this chapter, we will look at three areas which often are of particular concern: Recognizing and accommodating for diversity in the workplace, the cultural changes that occur when one company acquires another, and the unique problems affecting family-owned businesses.

Diversity in the Workplace

There have been federal laws prohibiting discrimination because of race, religion, national origin, age, sex, and disability in existence for over 30 years. In addition, presidential orders, federal agency and court rulings, plus a variety of state policies have appended the laws with additional factors. These include affirmative action programs that require companies to give favorable treatment to people whose opportunities in the workplace had been limited because of these factors.

Despite these governmental edicts, according to a study made by the U. S. Dept. of Labor of over 16 million workers, white males held 51.7 percent of executive and administrative jobs. While women held 42.9 percent of these jobs, most were in the lower end of the administrative position category. Only 6.7 percent of these jobs were held by African-Americans and 4.9 percent by Hispanics.

Changing a culture to accommodate for diversity is more than just complying with the laws on equal employment. According to a 1987 study issued by the Hudson Institute, by the year 2000, only 15 percent of the people entering the work force will be American-born white males, compared with 47 percent in 1987. This has enormous implications for the future of American industry, and it's imperative that steps be taken to recognize the values that this diverse population can bring to an organization. Steps must be taken to adjust the culture of the organization to deal with this.

The main cause of this change in the demography of the United States was the passage of the Immigration Act of 1965. Prior to this law, a quota system existed that favored immigration from Western Europe. The new law abolished these quotas. This allowed a significant number of immigrants to enter this country from Asia, South America, the Caribbean, and Africa.

Despite the "Americanization" of immigrants, cultural traits from their native lands persist for generations. Instead of America being a "melting pot," social scientists now look upon it as a "salad bowl" in which each group maintains significant aspects of identity. This diversity affects all institutions within the United States—the schools, the communities, the workplace, and the marketplace.

Many companies have recognized this and have approached the situation by instituting programs to sensitize employees to racial, ethnic, and gender differences. Often, however, these programs are superficial and just don't work. In fact, some companies found they had a negative effect, causing friction between minorities and women with the white males that they perceived were the cause of the inequity.

Unfortunately, many organizations that have invested in diversity training programs have not received a fair return on their investment. Compared with other initiatives, such as total quality management, reengineering processes, and moving into teams, much diversity training has not shown results. Part of the reason for this is that the capacity of employers to change the way people think and feel is limited. Changing attitudes is a major undertaking.

In addition, companies rarely pursue diversity programs with the same commitment as other programs that have direct effects on the bottom line. Lip service is given to diversity and little money or effort supports it. For a diversity program to work, training is only the first step. It must be supplemented by actions fully endorsed by top management. Change must be made measurable and managers must be held accountable for their implementation and then rewarded for their successes with bonuses and recognition.

QUOTES AND QUIPS

"The greatest revolution in our generation is the discovery that human beings, by changing the inner attitudes of their minds, can change the outer aspects of their lives."
William James, 1842–1910
American psychologist

Such companies as IBM, Corning, and Honeywell have made dealing with diversity part of the changes in the total corporate culture by linking diversity to business objectives, and holding managers responsible for meeting them. The goal is to create a culture that enables *all* employees to contribute their full potential to the company's success.

Barbara Coull Williams, vice-president for human resources at Pacific Gas and Electric Co., reported that one way they have moved diversity beyond sensitivity training on race and gender issues was to groom more qualified minorities and women through active succession planning.

For senior executives down to lower-level managers, PG&E identifies candidates with potential and helps them acquire the skills needed to compete. They have instituted a mentor program so that higher-level managers can work with potential high achievers to give them the benefit of their expertise and to share insights into the way the company operates.

Another company that has successfully dealt with diversity is Polaroid. Emphasis is on giving women and minority employees opportunity to acquire skills that will enable them to move up in the company. Polaroid, Ameritech, and Dow Chemical are examples of companies that reach out to the community for help. They work with community groups, schools in the inner cities, and other groups representing women, minorities, the disabled and others to monitor their policies and keep them on track in their efforts to change the organizational culture in this area.

One of the most effective programs was instituted by Ceridian, a Minneapolis-based company, engaged in both electronics manufacturing and providing technical informational services. Ceridian provides internships to students at inner-city schools and recruits at predominantly black colleges. Every year, managers set diversity goals and 10 percent of their bonuses reflect whether these goals are met.

A succession planning system also assures that high potential minorities and women are given help in developing their skills. The result: Of Ceridian's 7,500 employees, 50 percent are women and 19 percent minorities. At the managerial level, 36 percent are women and 10 percent are minorities.

Resistance to diversity programs by white males in the organization has caused problems in many companies. Lectures and even one-to-one counseling have had limited success. Honeywell, Inc. took overt steps to bring white male employees right into the heart of the process.

In the early stages of the diversity program, special groups such as the Honeywell Women's Council and the Black Employee Network, had been established to give women and minorities a means to present their views to management. Another group, The Minneapolis Technical Operations Council—that was predominantly white and male—was already in existence. To assure that the diversity program would receive full support, Honeywell established a 20-member Diversity Council made up of the leaders of these three groups. Working together to resolve problems that arise has greatly facilitated the change of culture in this area.

Levi Strauss has taken this concept a step further. Its Diversity Council consists of groups representing African-Americans, Asians, Hispanics, gays, and women. Not only is this group concerned with the special problems of diversity, but it is part of the entire culture change process. Levi Strauss has spent more than a year, at a cost of $12 million, in planning and implementing the total culture change.

Minorities and women still complain that there will not be a truly diverse organizational structure until it is reflected in top management. There are still very few women and minorities at the helms of major corporations. Even at Levi Strauss, with its commitment to diversity, the executive committee consists of seven white men and only one white woman. No other segments of the population are represented. CEO Robert Haas feels this will change over time.

The company has doubled the percentage of minority managers to 36 percent and woman managers from 32 percent to 54 percent since 1984. The downside is that there has been some grumbling among white male employees and the company has no easy answers to this. It is Haas' aim to eliminate the "old-boy" network as a factor in promotions. Such decisions will focus on performance and contribution.

Understanding Diverse Cultures

People brought up in cultures that are different from the traditional American standards often view their lives and jobs from a different perspective than their coworkers and bosses. To help them reach their full potential requires that managers understand their cultures.

For example, in many cultures it is considered immodest to point out one's accomplishments. In companies where employees are expected to apply for advancement or to participate in their own performance reviews, people who have been conditioned to keep silent about their achievements may be overlooked when it comes to promotion or assignment to better or more challenging jobs.

In other cultures, people may be so intimidated by authority figures that they are reluctant to seek help when needed or to even ask questions to clarify areas of misunderstanding. Knowing the attributes of the various cultures from which employees come, such as attitudes toward authority, communication styles, and work habits can facilitate effective interaction.

This knowledge must always be balanced by understanding that people even from the same culture differ one from the other. Stereotyping people from a specific culture is just as bad as ignoring their cultural backgrounds. The effective manager of a diverse work force must be able to not only understand the employee's cultural backgrounds, but recognize each person's individuality within that culture.

QUOTES AND QUIPS

"Decision makers must learn to accept the reality of diversity. This calls for abandoning traditional stereotypes about people. Energies should be directed toward designing work systems that utilize the varying and unique qualities of a diverse work force."

Dr. Arthur R. Pell
Consultant in human resources
development, and author

Breaking Through the "Glass Ceiling"

Proctor & Gamble provides a good example of how a company transformed its culture to stem the tide of losing some of its best female employees. In 1991, a study of employee turnover indicated that two out of every three good performers who quit were women. At P & G, all higher-level jobs are filled from within, so retention was a critical issue.

To deal with this problem, they created a Female Retention Task Force, and they attacked the problem in the same way they would a marketing problem. First, they conducted a survey among current and former female employees to determine the reasons for their leaving. The results were surprising. Of fifty women who had left, only two had dropped out of the work force. The others had gone to other high-stress jobs—often working more hours than they had at P & G.

The assumption that women leave companies chiefly because of family responsibilities was incorrect. The main reason was rooted in the company's restrictive culture. The women felt that because they worked best with a consensus-building leadership environment, they were perceived as being indecisive. In addition, the surveyors learned that the women did not mind working the long hours typical of P & G executives, but they wanted a more flexible time schedule—not part-time work that would slow down their opportunities for advancement.

They approached this problem by using the "brand manager" concept that has made P & G the top marketer in its field. In the marketing areas, this is done by targeting market share goals for the sales of products. By applying this concept, the task force's approach to stop the high female turnover was to set a "market share" goal of 40 percent women at each level of brand management by the year 2005.

The task force brainstormed for innovative ideas to help build the female work force. The most important was a mentoring program which reversed the usual process. Instead of senior men mentoring junior women, the women became mentors to their seniors on issues affecting women. This enabled the women to change the P & G culture literally one manager at a time.

In addition, family-friendly benefits were expanded and better communication about these benefits instituted. Internal advertising campaigns have been instituted to sell woman on working for P & G and encouraging other women to join them.

Over the six years that the program has been in effect, the exodus of women has been reduced to the same rate as that of men. Employee attitude surveys show women's job satisfaction is up 25 percent since 1994, and women now account for nearly one third of the vice-presidents and general managers in the brand management ranks—up from only five percent in 1992.

TACTICAL TIPS

Establish conditions and activities in the organization that create an environment where people can achieve their fullest potential, regardless of the many ways they may differ from each other.

Guidelines to Success

As a result of my research and my own experience in working with companies having instituted diversity programs, I offer the following guidelines:

1. Not only must all senior managers be committed to the success of the program, but they must take an active, visual role in its institution and monitoring.
2. The organization must seek and cultivate the best talent for all positions from all segments of the population.
3. Career planning should be an integral part of the human resources function and should include all employees.
4. Diversity programs should be much more than sensitivity training seminars or videos. It should be incorporated in every phase of employee orientation and training, management development, and in the actions taken in the day-to-day operations of the organization.
5. The implementation of diversity policies by managers should be a *chief result area* in their job results description and should be included in their performance evaluations.
6. Persons who contribute to the success of the program should be rewarded both financially and by recognition and publicity.

7. In companies where employees are drawn from different countries with different cultures, managers must take steps to learn the differences in diverse cultures and adapt their management style to accommodate them.
8. Avoid packaged programs that offer gimmicks or quick cures. Diversity is a long-term process that must be continuously renewed and applied on an ongoing basis in all aspects of the organization's activities.

Mergers and Acquisitions

When a company acquires another organization or when two companies merge, the corporate culture of the dominant company usually replaces that of the subordinate firm. Not only may this cause considerable discomfort among employees of the acquired company, but managers of the dominant firm face the problem of dealing with employees who are not familiar with their culture and may have considerably different attitudes.

To understand this better, let's look at what happened when Sports Publishing Co. was acquired by L & L Publishers. Sports was founded twenty years ago by Gerson L., whose purpose was to publish books that dealt with sports topics. Over the years, he expanded from how-to manuals to biographies of sports figures and novels related to sports. Although never a major player in the book world, the company's books sold well and the company expanded into general publishing.

The staff consisted of five senior editors, who dealt with the authors, read manuscripts, and made decisions as to what to accept and reject. Once a book was selected for publication, the senior editors supervised the editorial, art, and production staff in producing the book.

In addition, a team of marketing and public relations specialists, headed by a director of marketing, worked on promoting and marketing the finished product. Although Gerson worked closely with his management team, he gave his senior editors and the director of marketing the authority to make decisions in their areas of expertise.

In 1996, L & L Publishers, a large diversified publishing house, acquired Sports and Martin R., a vice-president of the parent company, was appointed CEO of the new subsidiary. After several weeks of studying the Sports operation, Martin took steps to bring its procedures in line with the parent firm.

Let's look at just one of the changes and how it affected the organizational culture of Sports. Before the acquisition, senior editors had almost absolute power in choosing which books were to be published, dealing with the authors, arranging for the book and jacket design, and determining with the marketing people the number of copies to be printed. They were strong ego-centered men and women who took responsibility for the success or failure of the works they acquired and were proud of their accomplishments.

After the acquisition, this all changed, however. Under the L & L procedures, the senior editors could only recommend acceptances of manuscripts. Their recommendations were then reviewed by several committees: an editorial committee, a marketing committee, and a cost committee—each looking at the prospective book from its viewpoint and making its comments. Final decisions were made by the executive committee.

Naturally, the senior editors felt that they were demeaned by this system. Many had developed close relationships with their authors and were able to discuss a project with the author, give him or her an immediate okay, have a contract drawn up and the book underway in a week or less. Under the new system, it often took a month or more before an author could be given the go-ahead. There was much grumbling among the editors and two of the best left for other publishing firms, taking with them some of Sports' best-selling authors.

Guidelines for Changes Made after an Acquisition

How could L & L have avoided the problems created in this acquisition? Dr. Arthur R. Pell, a consultant who has helped companies integrate newly acquired units into their organizations, sets forth the following guidelines:

1. If the subsidiary is to be operated as an autonomous component, there is no need for it to be run in the exact manner as the parent.
2. Established processes should be thoroughly reviewed by a committee consisting of managers from both the parent and the subsidiary organizations.
3. Suggested changes should be discussed openly with those who are directly affected, and their input should be given serious consideration.

4. When decisions are made to make changes, the reasons for the changes should be made clear to all affected.
5. The manner in which the new methods will be implemented should be worked out in coordination with the people who will actually be doing the work.
6. When committees are involved, as in the L & L Publishers acquisition, if possible, staff members from the acquired company should be on the committees. In this case, the editorial committee should include editors from Sports, as well as L & L editors; the marketing committee should include marketing specialists from both firms, and so on.
7. Meetings (both one-to-one and groups) with vendors and customers who will be affected (e.g., the authors, in this case) should be held to explain the new system and assistance offered to help them through the culture changes.

TACTICAL TIPS

By proper planning and with sensitivity to how the changes will affect those most closely concerned with the new procedures, the transition from old to new will be eased and dissension and disruption will be minimized.

The Family Business

According to the Family Firm Institute, a Boston-based association of consultants specializing in working with family businesses, there are over 20 million companies in the U.S. that are operated or managed by families.

The culture of a family business is often determined by the culture of the family that owns it. Some family businesses are run by domineering entrepreneurs who make every decision without consulting other members of management, but in many others more participative processes are followed—decisions are reached after consulting with managers and employees.

According to Dr. Joseph Astrochan, editor of *Family Business Review,* the cultures of most family businesses tend to be more open, harmonious, and pragmatic than the bureaucratic cultures found in the more impersonal, hierarchical corporations. Because the owner-manager families usually have ties to the community in which the business operates, they are more sensitive to their image in the community than companies that do not have such relationships.

In an article in *Family Business Review,*[1] Astrochan describes the changes in the culture of a company founded by a family, then sold to a conglomerate, and some years later resold to another family.

The company, Quality Commodity Co. of Railtown (the names have been changed to protect privacy), was founded and operated by the Alden family, who had long ties to the community. Under Mr. Alden's management, the company grew slowly but steadily. He was a community-minded businessman who ran the company as "one big family." Group insurance, profit sharing, pensions, and other benefits were provided to employees.

From the very start, Quality was run on a pragmatic basis. Few meetings were held. Mr. Alden and his top managers met informally to discuss problems as they arose. Employee suggestions and comments were solicited and acted on. As the Alden family and most of the employees came from the community and knew each other from childhood, there was a kindred spirit that permeated the organization. The company participated in Railtown's community activities.

When Mr. Alden's son joined the firm, it was assumed that eventually he would take over the business. Nobody resented this since, after all, it was a family business. After his father's death, the son continued his father's policies for another 25 years. The grandson, however, had refused to join the business and had moved away from Railtown.

When the son's health failed, the employees began to worry about their future and formed a union to look after their interests. That same year, the company was sold to Corporal Industries, a large conglomerate.

Corporal Industries and the Aldens had very different styles of management. Corporal imposed its management structure on Quality Commodity. Bureaucracy replaced the informal management style of the Aldens. Frequent meetings replaced one-to-one discussions concerning routine matters. Paperwork had priority over important issues occurring on the shop floor or in the sales field. Too much time was spent on deciding what to do and too little time on doing it. Corporal policy assumed that people were untrustworthy, irresponsible, and self-seeking, and an elaborate system of controls was instituted. Employee's suggestions and ideas were discouraged.

The result: Teamwork and cooperation diminished. Relationships between the employees and management were limited to specific operational problems. Participation was discouraged. The new managers were drawn from other divisions of Corporal—people who had no connection with Railtown and who moved in for a year or two and then were transferred to another division. Productivity fell, morale was low. Eventually Corporal gave up on Quality and sold it to the Newcastle family.

The Newcastles were a husband-and-wife team who shared the management of the company. They studied the situation carefully and determined that major changes in the culture of the company had to be made. Their first action was to hold a company-wide meeting to get acquainted with the staff and explain their way of doing business. They solicited, listened to, and acted upon advice from everyone in the plant.

The Newcastles pointed out that they wanted people to get along with each other and to make it a team effort. They encouraged employees to bring up ideas and allowed them to try things out without having to provide "a hundred pages of justification." This resulted in a plethora of new product and production ideas flowing from the rank-and-file workers. Corporal's cuts in the production process to save money at the expense of quality were eliminated. Emphasis was placed on the participatory nature of all activities.

The team spirit which had disappeared under Corporal soon returned. Under the Newcastle family, Quality's culture stabilized and largely returned to its state before the acquisition by Corporal. The business thrived and continues to grow.

QUOTES & QUIPS

"Ownership is not a vice, not something to be ashamed
of, but rather a commitment, and an instrument
by which the general good can be served."
Vaclav Havel
President, Czech Republic

Of course, all family businesses are not as benevolent as the New-castles. There are undoubtedly domineering patriarchs and matri-archs who run the business like a private fief. The cultures of these firms allow no decisions to be made—even by those in managerial positions—without the okay of the owner.

There are family-owned businesses in which there is constant fric-tion among family members—craeting a tension that permeates the culture of the company. And, of course, there are family businesses in which the family turns over management to professional managers and takes the role of principal stockholders, concerned only with the dividends received.

Let's look at a variety of these types of owners:

The miser. Henry D. prided himself on running a tight ship. His motto: "A penny saved is a penny earned." No purchase could be made without his permission and he insisted on getting several bids on items—always choosing the cheapest, regardless of quality or ser-vice. If an employee needed a new pencil, she had to show Henry the stub of the one that was being used—and it had better be very short. He prided himself on keeping costs of sales down by vetoing lunches with customers and "fancy" sales brochures—never taking into account the lost sales that might have been attained from a more enlightened view. No wonder Henry's company, although always showing a small annual profit, never grew to its potential.

The entrepreneur. Margo was typical of many entrepreneurs. Her favorite saying was, "I created this business; I risked my money in this business. Therefore, I make all the decisions." One of the factors in many family businesses is that the founder may be an inventor—a person with a great concept and the ability to implement it and get the company started. This person may not, however, have the man-agerial skills to operate it after it is underway.

When Margo designed a line of kitchen gadgets, she invested her life's savings, borrowed from friends and family and, within a few years, had a very successful business underway. She hired technical specialists to develop the manufacturing processes and a staff to mar-ket and sell the line.

As the business grew, Margo faced different problems from those she dealt with when the business was started. She frequently over-turned sound decisions made by her subordinates because "it doesn't feel right." Her arbitrary style of management resulted in a heavy turnover of personnel. Business began to decline. Competitors encroached on her market share. Her refusal to recognize that running a business is not the same as starting one resulted in consistent losses and eventual failure of the firm.

The S.O.B. No, this isn't what you think. S.O.B. in this context means "Son of Boss." Friction between the founding father and his presumptive successor—his son, daughter or other relative—has upset the culture of many family businesses, making working there difficult and unpleasant for most everybody. It is not uncommon for the father to want to continue managing a business the way he has done for many years and to resent changes suggested by the younger generation. Corollary to this is the impatience of the younger generation with the "old-fashioned" methods of their parents.

Two such cases came to my attention this past year. When Barry K. graduated with an MBA from a prestigious university, he was offered several jobs with major corporations but chose to return to the family business, which was founded by his grandfather and managed by his father for the past 20 years.

Barry had worked in the business in a variety of capacities after school in his high school days—during summers in his college days, and for three years as a sales representative between his college graduation and his going to graduate school. His first job after returning to the firm was systems manager, enabling him to use his new knowledge in setting up systems and procedures. Several years ago, he was promoted to vice-president administration, and, last year, to executive vice-president.

As the early changes Barry instituted were primarily procedural, his father accepted them readily. But as Barry's authority increased, he and his father had serious disagreements about changes in policy and in major aspects of the company's activities. These arguments became more and more rancorous, leading to dissension within the company—one group of managers siding with Barry; another with his father. After two years of bickering and increased bitterness, Barry left the company leaving a void that will be difficult to fill.

In the other situation, Lara L. had joined her father's company in an administrative job after she graduated from college. Over the next few years, she moved up the ranks and, in 1995, was appointed a vice-president. In this position, she worked closely with her father.

At first, things went smoothly, but as Lara identified problems within the firm of which she had been unaware when she had lower-level positions, she saw indicators of potential problems. When she called this to the attention of her father, he told her she was overly concerned with matters that would go away in time.

Lara persisted that action be taken. Knowing that her father could be persuaded to change his mind when faced with substantial evidence, Lara devoted hours of her free time to document her case and prepare a plan to overcome the problem. When she presented this to her father, he realized that she was right and gave her the authority to implement it.

The nepotist. Many family firms are governed by the "Einstein theory"—relativity. Relatives get first priority in hiring, promotion, and treatment on the job. Bad decisions and even errors made by incompetent family members are often overlooked, forgiven, or blamed on others, resulting in reduced productivity and low morale among other employees, and even in serious problems for the firm.

An example of this recently came to my attention. Andrew G. was the boss's favorite nephew. When Andrew dropped out of college, he was hired as a clerk in the shipping department. Despite his frequent latenesses and absences, the supervisor did her best to train Andrew and, because of his family status, tolerated his slowness and inaccuracies.

When she did complain to his uncle about his work, she was told to be patient as he was "a sensitive young man." After Andrew made a major blunder that required many hours of overtime work to correct, the supervisor gave up on him. She told the boss that unless he removed Andrew from the department, she would have to resign.

Over the next two years, Andrew was assigned to three different positions in the company and failed in each of them. When his uncle discussed this series of failures with Andrew, the young man put the blame on his uncle. "You keep putting me in jobs below my capability," he rationalized. "I'm not cut out for office jobs. With my personality, I should be in sales."

You can guess what happened. Andrew was assigned a sales territory. So far, he has been a dismal failure. He has developed very few new customers, has antagonized some old customers, and has caused the sales support people untold aggravation. When the sales manager brought this to the boss's attention, he was advised: "You must be patient with Andrew. He's a very sensitive young man."

Guidelines for Family-Owned Businesses

Founders of companies need to realize that it takes a different type of mental and emotional set to manage and operate a going concern than it takes to create, develop, and implement a new enterprise. If once the business is underway and your growth appears to be stymied, reexamine your management style. Seek help from mentors or consultants. Listen to your employees and be flexible. A change in your style and the culture of the company may help you move ahead.

Carefully plan the succession of management after you step down. If your heir-apparent is a son, daughter, or other relative, make sure that he or she is capable of handling the job and really wants to become part of the family firm. Discuss the business with your prospective heirs early in their lives. Have them work in the firm after school and during summers.

When they are ready for full-time work, have them start in lower-level positions and test their capability on the job. Don't let your love for them affect an honest evaluation of their assets and liabilities. Train them to reinforce their strengths and build up their weaknesses. Promote them only when they are ready to take on the duties and responsibilities of the higher position.

Build up a team of managers from both family and nonfamily members. Avoid giving preferences to your family. Give the nonfamily members the opportunity to express and implement their ideas. Reward them financially and by recognition. Make them an integral part of management. Your heirs will need their support when their turn comes to take over the firm. By building up a culture of cooperation and collaboration within the management team during your tenure, you will most likely assure its continuation in the future.

For heirs-apparent, you have both a blessing and a curse. Being the son or daughter of the boss puts you in the position of having first crack at promotion and eventually a top-level position in the firm. On the other side of this coin, you are expected to be a superior worker. You are being watched not only by your parent, the boss, but also by the nonfamily managers, other employees, and, perhaps, by customers and vendors. You will have to prove to them that you are capable of managing the firm when your turn comes. Unless you earn their respect, you will not receive the support from them that is essential to your success and the company's survival.

Nonfamily members who work for family firms shouldn't have to assume that because they are not a member of the family they are destined to be restricted in growth. True, they may never be the CEO (although there are many instances where this has occurred), as the company grows, as they prove their worth, but they should be able to grow with the company and move into significant, well-paid, and challenging positions.

SUM AND SUBSTANCE

Diversity

- America is not a "melting pot," but a "salad bowl." Each group in our society maintains specific aspects of their cultural identity. To deal effectively with people of diverse backgrounds, it's essential to understand the differences.
- Diversity training programs by themselves are not enough to assure success. They must be supplemented by action in the work place.
- Companies must take steps to teach the customs and mores of America and/or the locality to employees who are new or not familiar with them. In addition, local employees should be taught to understand and appreciate the perspectives of people from other cultures, or who have different backgrounds.

Mergers and Acquisitions

- When one company takes over another, it's essential that each party understand the corporate culture of the other party.
- Changes will inevitably be made. To assure their successful implementation, they should be preceded by careful study as to how to integrate both cultures.
- Guidelines should be established by the dominant organization to prepare the acquired company to understand and accept the changes and to obtain their willing cooperation in their institution.

Family Businesses

- Many family businesses are the creation of an innovative founder, who dominates the business during his or her lifetime. Often such people are excellent entrepreneurs, but may not be strong managers once the business is established.
- If a family business is to be successful for the long term, a line of succession must be developed, trained, and put into place. These people often consist of other family members (e.g., sons and daughters), or may include nonfamily personnel.
- To assure continuing success, family businesses should avoid nepotism. It's acceptable for relatives to be part of management, but it should not be the prime factor in choosing them. It's essential that the individual(s) chosen have the capability and training to do the job.
- Even in organizations where family members are highly qualified, owners should develop a team of support people who can provide expertise in various aspects of management. To retain and motivate these people, they should be given the power to accomplish their jobs and to be compensated and rewarded for their achievements.

REFERENCE

[1]Astrochan, Joseph H. "Family Firm and Community Culture." *Family Business Review*, Vol. 1, No. 2, Summer 1988, p. 165.

CHAPTER 12

Leading the Organizational Changes

To assure success of any transformation, especially one as significant as a major change in the culture of an organization, it takes more than just good concepts, an effective program, or the best change agents. It requires a cadre of men and women within the organization who have the skills, and the personality, and the dedication to make it work. It takes outstanding leaders.

In recent years, there has been a great deal written about leadership and ways to develop leadership. Much of it, of course, has stemmed from the "Total Quality" movement and other strategies designed to improve organizational performance. While much of the counsel and advice on leadership dispensed by the management "gurus" of the 1980s and 1990s is good, there is a tendency to overstate and overcomplicate this factor.

Although great leaders have faced a multitude of diverse problems, they have followed a common pattern of behavior. They exhibited in their leadership style twelve key traits, which I like to call "The 12 Qualities and Characteristics of Truly Great Leaders."

Here they are:

THE 12 QUALITIES AND CHARACTERISTICS OF TRULY GREAT LEADERS

1. Almost All Truly Outstanding Leaders Have Willing (and Often Enthusiastic) Followers

Often people in positions of authority can compel subordinates to follow orders by virtue of the power of their jobs. Such people are not true leaders, however. Yes, the orders will be followed but that is all that will happen. True leaders develop confidence and trust in their associates. (Note: Leaders think of their coworkers as associates—not subordinates.) This engenders a desire not only to follow the lead of the manager, but to initiate, innovate, and implement ideas of their own that fit into the goals established.

QUOTES AND QUIPS

"Moral leadership emerges from, and always returns to, the fundamental wants and needs, aspirations and values of the followers. I mean the kind of leadership that can produce social change that will satisfy followers' authentic needs. I mean less the Ten Commandments than the Golden Rule. But even the Golden Rule is inadequate, for it measures the wants and needs of others simply by our own."
James McGregor Burns
American historian

In the military, for example, soldiers are trained to obey orders without question. Indeed, if in the midst of combat, subordinates debated decisions made by superior officers, the effect could be disastrous. However, during training, outstanding military leaders take the time, effort, and energy to develop confidence and support among the men and women they will lead in combat. There are countless stories of bravery in battle that can be traced to the inspiring leadership of officers—not just to blind obedience.

Less dramatically, business leaders have built up enthusiastic and loyal followers who put in extra hours, sacrifice personal desires and stretch their thinking powers to help achieve the goals set by a leader to whom they relate, respect, and admire.

When Steve Jobs was asked to return to Apple Computer after the company had suffered a series of major disasters, he agreed to do so with the understanding that he was not looking to take over the company but to just work to bring it back to profitability. He set an example by working day and night to turn the company around. With a leader like that, managers at all levels pitched in and pushed the company forward to achieve its goal—the development and marketing of the highly successful i-Mac computer.

2. Most Outstanding Leaders Take a Constructively Discontented View of the World

Good leaders aren't complacent. They're constantly on the alert for making innovations that will improve the way work is done, assure continuing customer satisfaction, and increase the profitability of the organization. Their minds are open to new ideas and they welcome suggestions. Even after changes and improvements are made, they still look for even better ways to accomplish their goals.

Leaders like this are never fully satisfied. They review practices and procedures on a regular basis to fine tune them. They do not fall in love with their own ideas, but are open to criticism and innovation.

For instance, three years ago, when David D., the owner of the Shasta Dry Cleaners, had computerized his ticketing procedure, he believed that this aspect of his operations was now "state of the art." He concentrated his efforts on other phases of the business.

David, however, was the kind of manager who was never fully satisfied. The ticketing system worked well, but he wondered if he could make even more effective use of the computer. At a dry-cleaner's convention, he learned how some firms used the computer to generate promotional mailings and increase business. He immediately put that idea into operation.

This attitude permeates his entire staff. Sherryl B., the manager of one of his stores, was always seeking new ways to attract customers. Shasta was known for its quality work, but it did charge higher prices than some of the other dry-cleaners in the neighborhood. She looked for ideas from what other quality-based service businesses were doing to attract customers.

When the beauty salon she patronized offered a free manicure to customers who referred new business to them, she adopted the idea. She offered customers a coupon for a free dry-cleaning of a suit or dress for each new customer they referred. Although this program has brought in many new customers, Sherryl is still not satisfied and is still seeking new ways to attract business.

KEY POINT

Never be complacent; never be content. Keep seeking; keep searching for the "One Best Way."

---

3. Outstanding Leaders Almost Always Consider Themselves a Work-in-Progress

Just as effective leaders are constructively discontent about their departments, they are never entirely satisfied with themselves.

They attend seminars and self-improvement programs, purchase and listen to motivational tapes, read books and periodicals to keep up with the state of the art in their fields and to improve their knowledge and understanding in a variety of areas.

Great leaders don't limit their talents to their jobs. They take active roles in professional and trade associations not only to keep in touch with new developments but also to share their ideas with colleagues from other organizations. They attend and participate in conventions and conferences and develop networks of people to whom they can turn to obtain knowledge or ideas over the years.

Another way to improve one's knowledge is to take a sabbatical to go back to school or take on a special assignment. Jonathan R., a young up-and-coming manufacturing executive in the electronics industry, did just this. He had been active as a volunteer at a hospital in his community, and learned that the hospital had been given a donation that would enable them to purchase a much-needed computer. They did not, however, have the funds to hire a computer expert to develop and install the system. Jonathan had only a basic knowledge of computers, but the idea of taking on this challenge intrigued him. He volunteered to do the job.

First, however, he had to learn as much as he could about the computer, how the hospital intended to use it, and all of the ramifications involved. He realized that he could not do this and still deal with his regular work. Fortunately, things were moving along smoothly on the job, so he asked for and was given a six-month sabbatical.

Not only did Jonathan develop, install, and implement the computer system for the hospital, but in doing so became thoroughly knowledgeable about computer systems. This not only increased his own capabilities, but made him far more valuable to his company when he returned to work.

4. Leadership Ability Comes Naturally to Some, But is Inspired in Most

We've all heard the old adage "Leaders are made, not born," and, like most adages, there is a great deal of truth in it. Some people, however, do seem to be born leaders. From early childhood, they take the lead in playing games, and are selected as team captains, as well as elected to student offices. They take charge of everything they are involved in. In some ways (at least according to their proud parents), they always seemed destined for big things in life.

QUOTES AND QUIPS

"Some are born great, some achieve greatness, and some have greatness thrust upon them."
William Shakespeare
Twelfth Night

History is replete with stories of ordinary men and women who rose to great heights when leadership was needed. Lech Walesa is an example of such a man. In 1980 when the workers at the Lenin Shipyard in Gdansk, Poland, went on strike for better working conditions, the Communist government cracked down on them. Walesa was an electrician in the shipyard and one of the leaders of Solidarity, an independent trade union. He had little education and had never considered himself to be anything more than an artisan. When leadership was needed, however, he stepped out to speak up for the workers in defying the authorities. Despite several arrests and imprisonments, his leadership of the strike inspired the Polish people to work to overthrow the Communist regime. In 1983, he was awarded the Nobel Peace Price and, in 1990, was elected president of Poland.

5. Outstanding Leaders Almost Always Demonstrate a Good Understanding of the "Affective Domain"

Great leaders understand people—what causes them to act and react the way they do. They recognize the importance of being a motivating factor for people—appealing to the drives and the feelings of others.

They take a genuine interest in the people with whom they interact. As Dale Carnegie succinctly pointed out: "You can make more friends in two months by becoming genuinely interested in others than you can in two years by trying to get others interested in you."

TACTICAL TIPS

If your goal is upper management, prepare for it now. Tomorrow's leaders won't be specialists. They'll have experience in several management functions and probably in more than one industry. They'll be comfortable working with computers, statistics, financial, and marketing figures. But, most important, they will have superior skills in communications and interpersonal relations.

One of the most effective business leaders who understands human nature is Andrew Grove, one of the founders and, later, CEO of Intel, and *Time* Magazine's Person of the Year in 1997. Grove strongly believes that people really are self motivated and that this motivation comes from the satisfaction we get from our accomplishments. Each triumph generates the confidence to seek greater triumphs; each accomplishment leads to more accomplishments. Here are some of his thoughts on this:[1]

> We spend most of our lives at work. It's certainly easier to sustain a high level of commitment if we enjoy our work. So, I encourage people to do everything they can to enjoy themselves at work. The fun part should support the work part, not detract from it.

Grove identifies the following pointers that help maintain self motivation:

Celebrate achievements. Try to provide as many interim milestones as possible. Supplant the long-term drive toward reaching a major result with a series of shorter steps. Use the occasions when one of these is achieved as an event to celebrate in some small way. Don't let any celebration become a distraction to others who work. Poke gentle fun at each other, including your boss. Keep internal competition light.

Rotate jobs. Even if you stay with one organization, rotate jobs occasionally. Even in the best organizations, any job can become tedious after a while. It's harder to create and sustain energy and drive if you have the same job forever. Rotating jobs and working in different assignments is an excellent way to keep your work interesting. And, it also serves to enrich your skills.

Enjoy the people you work with. Our coworkers are very important to us. Our activities at work are almost always connected with theirs. To do our work well, we are dependent on them, and they on us.

The people we work with are a major factor in determining whether or not our work is pleasant, congenial, and even fun. Often, our feelings toward the people we work with determine if we like going to work each morning. Problems with coworkers, even minor ones, can significantly affect our work and the work of our entire group. Sorting out such problems is important for the benefit of our productivity, as well as for our emotional well-being.

Handle coworker problems directly. It's best to confine the discussion to the specific complaint you have and to avoid generalizations, such as "you always do this . . . and never that."

Enjoy your work. It is impossible to like all of it, of course. Sometimes you will chafe under its unrelenting nature, other times you will be bored, but overall you must enjoy it. I am convinced that you will like your work if you can see that what you do makes a difference, and you approach your work with a bit of zest, maybe even playfulness. Doing so induces a bit of levity when it's most needed and leads to camaraderie.

Be dedicated to your work. Be dedicated to the end result, the output, not how you get to it or whose idea it is or whether you look good or not. Respect the work of all those who respect their own work. Nobody is unimportant. It takes many people to make an organization function.

Be straight with everyone. I hate it when people are not honest with me, and I would hate myself if I weren't straight with them. This isn't an easy principle to stick to. There are always many reasons or excuses to compromise a little here or there. We may reason that people are not ready to hear the truth or the bad news, that the time isn't right, or whatever. Giving in to those tempting rationalizations usually leads to conduct that can be ethically wrong and will backfire every time. When stumped, stop and think your way through your answers.

QUOTES AND QUIPS

"We are what we repeatedly do."
Aristotle, 382–322 BC
Greek philosopher

6. Most Outstanding Leaders Expect More from Themselves than Others

The truth is, the best leaders I know set high standards for themselves and then work hard to achieve their goals. They are also lifelong learners. Like everyone, they make mistakes; and when they do, they view these mistakes as learning experiences and try to turn them into successes. As it has been said: "If you've never made errors, you've never made decisions."

Dave Thomas, founder Wendy's is a good example of a person who leads by example. A high school dropout who worked in every aspect of the restaurant business from childhood on, Thomas got his big break when he met Colonel Sanders, the founder of Kentucky Fried Chicken.

Thomas was working for the owner of a restaurant who had invested in four Kentucky Fried Chicken franchises in Columbus, Ohio, but they weren't successful. The owner offered Thomas a 40% stake in those units if he could turn them around.

Friends and associates tried to persuade Thomas to reject the deal, even the Colonel himself. They said it would kill his career. But Thomas accepted this challenge as his chance to prove himself.

"A lot of people get trapped in their lives and are unwilling to risk what they have," Thomas says, "but that's what an entrepreneur needs to do. I wasn't trapped, because I never made much money."

Thomas put all his time and effort into building up these franchises. He sweated over hot griddles, worked with his staff to clean greasy pots and to sweep floors. He inspired his team to work as hard as he did.

The choice paid off handsomely for Thomas. A few years later, he sold the franchises. He made enough from the deal to launch Wendy's, and build it to the third largest fast food chain in the nation.

Quotes and Quips

"One of the great truths is to do unto others as you would have them do unto you. Learn from your mistakes and correct them immediately. Maintain high values in all your dealings."
W. Clement Stone
Entrepreneur and publisher

7. The Overwhelming Majority of Outstanding Leaders Rely on Some Fixed, Unwavering Set of Convictions or Beliefs that Serves as Their "Guiding Light"

Sir John Templeton, the founder of the Templeton Fund, one of the most profitable mutual funds, has a philosophy of business that the most successful people are often the most ethically motivated. He says that such people are likely to have the keenest understanding of the importance of morality in business, and can be trusted to give full measure and not cheat their customers.

But the most ethical principles, Templeton insists, come from what goes on in the mind. "If you're filling your mind with kind, loving and helpful thoughts," he states, "then your decisions and actions will be ethical."

Hard work combined with honesty and perseverance are key in the Templeton philosophy. "Individuals who have learned to invest themselves in their work are successful," Templeton says. "They have earned what they have. More than simply knowing the value of money, they know their own value."

Using one's talents completely, he adds, also means helping others. He vowed that for every hour he devoted to investments, he would devote an hour to churches and charities. As part of his charitable work, Templeton established the Templeton Progress in Religion prize. The prize, whose past recipients include Mother Teresa and the Reverend Billy Graham, also carries with it the world's largest monetary award.

Businesses that don't apply ethical standards, according to Templeton, ignore the human factor and inevitably fail.

"In general," he says, "people who take advantage in their dealings will get a bad reputation and before long, others won't want to deal with them. Because we've worked hard to be faithful, honest and responsible to our investors, and have put their financial well-being before all else, we have managed to create a superior record. The only success worth having, after all, is success that reaches out and touches others."

Templeton's bottom-line advice to success-oriented men and women: "Try to become useful, work hard, be thrifty, and devote part of your time to your religion, your community, and good causes."

Mary Kay Ash, the founder of Mary Kay Cosmetics, considers her "guiding light" the development of self-confidence and self-esteem in herself and in all the people in her vast organization, which now consists of more than 250,000 independent beauty consultants worldwide.

Mary Kay started her own business in 1963 in a 500-square-foot storefront in Dallas with the help of her family, a life savings of $5,000, and only nine sales-force members. Her sales career had begun twenty-five years earlier when she had joined Stanley Home Products. She often commented that she was not at all successful during her first year and was ready to give up. This attitude changed, however, when she attended her first Stanley sales seminar.

"There I saw this tall, svelte, pretty, successful woman crowned queen as a reward for being the best in a company contest and I determined to be that queen the following year, which seemed impossible," she reported. "However, I decided to go up and talk to the president and tell him that I intended to be queen next year. He didn't laugh at me, but looked me in the eye, held my hand, and said: 'Somehow I think you will.' Those five words drove me and the next year I was queen."

When she opened her own company, she made it a policy to encourage her employees at all levels by helping them affirm their own self-esteem.

For example, despite the fact that Mary Kay has one of the largest cosmetic manufacturing facilities in the southwest, an open-door policy prevails at the company, where everyone can pop in to discuss problems with executives and Mary Kay herself. She prides herself on recognizing and talking to most employees and gives a warm welcome to newcomers.

Her motivational meetings and recognition awards are all geared to build self-esteem and self-confidence in her staff. This has resulted not only in success on the job, but has also had a profound influence on the personal lives of the people in the Mary Kay organization.

QUOTES AND QUIPS

"Success is far more a matter of having good habits than genius. Pick up the right habits and the rest will take care of itself."
Warren Buffet
Financier

8. Many Outstanding Leaders Have Both a "Tough Hide" and an Ability to Laugh at Themselves

Victor Kiam, now owner and CEO of the Remington Shaver Company, tells this story about when he was a salesman selling Playtex girdles. He came up with what he thought was a great marketing gimmick. Knowing that girdles frequently were hard to clean, he offered a special promotion: Women who brought in their old, worn-out girdles could buy a new Playtex model at a discount. The plan worked a little too well. So many dirty girdles were turned in at a New York department store that he was nearly cited for violating health codes.

Kiam looks back with amusement at his early foibles, but even after achieving great success and purchasing the Remington Shaver Co., he still made mistakes that he could laugh at in retrospect. He tells about the buyer for a large retail chain that refused to carry Remington shavers. So Kiam went over the buyer's head and approached the chief executive officer. He might have made the sale, but not after telling the CEO that the buyer was "stupid" and "opinionated." Turned out the buyer was the CEO's brother-in-law.

9. Many, if Not Most, Truly Outstanding Leaders Are Not Deterred by Disappointment, Failure, or Rejection. They Have Strong Views Yet Maintain a "Visceral Equilibrium"

One very successful leader who didn't let failure get him down is Tom Monaghan. Monaghan created and grew Domino Pizzas from a one-store pizza parlor to a chain of several thousand home-delivery outlets over a period of about 30 years, when, in 1989, he decided to sell his hugely successful company to concentrate instead on doing philanthropic work.

His plan, however, did not work out. After two and a half years, the company that purchased the chain failed to maintain the momentum that Monaghan had built and in order to save the company, he was forced to come back.

It took much work and persistence to first rebuild and then expand the organization. The dogged determination that enabled Monaghan to rise from a childhood of deprivation, poverty, and abuse to becoming a great entrepreneur enabled him to not only return Domino to its original prominence, but to expand it to 6,000 stores—of which 1,100 are in countries other than the United States.

But, Monaghan was still to face more troubles. Domino had made as its chief marketing point their policy of fast delivery. They guaranteed the customer would receive their pizza within 30 minutes.

An innovative idea, for sure, but it proved to be a disaster. Domino was sued by a multitude of people who claimed injury from accidents caused by Domino delivery drivers speeding to make the 30-minute deadline. The family of a woman allegedly killed by a Domino driver in Indiana was awarded $3 million and another woman was awarded $78 million in punitive damages. Up to that time it was the largest liability award in history. That was the end of the 30-minute guarantee.

Monaghan, a former marine, carries a can-do attitude into the leadership of his organization. Despite the lawsuits, he forged ahead and inspired his team with the winning spirit that has enabled Domino to recover and resume its position as a leader in its industry.

Fred Smith, the founder of Federal Express, is another entrepreneur who has displayed outstanding courage in his business career. Despite ridicule from "experts," along with opposition from the powerful airline industry, and bureaucratic interference, Smith not only survived, but thrived and created not just a company but also a new industry.

As a child in Memphis, Tennessee, Smith was crippled by a bone disease. Until he was cured at age 10, he was not able to play sports, which made him a target for the school bullies. He refused to be cowed by these taunters, however, and fought back by swinging his crutch. He developed an indomitable spirit that made him a decorated combat leader in Vietnam and that continues to this day.

This strong sense of spirit was evident when Smith was a student in an economics class at Yale University. His professor stated that air freight was the wave of the future and would be the primary source of revenue for the airlines. While most students accepted the professor's opinion, Smith wrote a paper disagreeing. His argument was that the passenger route patterns that were the primary airline routes were wrong for freight. He noted that because costs would not come down with volume, the only way air freight could be profitable was through a whole new system that would reach out to smaller cities as well as big ones and be designed for packages, not people. The professor considered this entirely unfeasible and gave Smith's paper a low grade.

Smith's concept was to start an all-freight airline that would fly primarily at night when the airports weren't congested. It would carry small, high-priority packages when speed of delivery was more important than cost. It would bring all the packages to a central point where, through a specially designed computer program, they would be sorted, dispersed, and loaded on airplanes that were flown to the ultimate destinations. This could be the wave of the future for air cargo and Smith was determined to pioneer it.

Such an enterprise required a great deal of money to start up. Smith believed that venture capitalists would not only be interested but be excited about this innovative idea. To his shock, though, little interest was developed in the financial community.

This did not stop Smith. Through his enthusiasm for the project and his courage to stand for his convictions, he raised an astounding $91 million to finance his untested idea.

Despite opposition from established airlines and overcoming complex legal technicalities, Smith created Federal Express with a fleet of small French-built Falcons. He began construction of his main facility at Memphis and began servicing 75 airports. Federal's planes would pick up packages at airports all over the country and fly them to Memphis, where they were sorted out and processed for immediate reshipment to other cities. Federal trucks then sped them to their destinations. The goal was to get the package to its destination within 24 hours of its pick-up—and this goal was almost always met.

In Federal's first two years, the company kept losing money—losses amounted to almost $30 million. The investors were seriously concerned. Federal was falling far short of Smith's projections. Despite the losses which the investors blamed on Smith, Smith did not lose faith. He hired experts and worked day and night with them to solve operational problems. In the next fiscal year, Federal's revenues reached $75 million, and the company showed a profit of $3.6 million. Seldom in history had a company gone from nothing to that size so swiftly.

Things have not always gone smoothly for Federal Express, as competition from other companies followed rapidly. The tremendous increase in the use of faxes for letters and documents dried up one of Fedex's major markets. The United States Postal Service soon offered overnight service at a much lower price. Other private companies have entered the market, but Smith's continued innovation and dedication to continuous improvement have kept Federal Express the number one carrier in its field.

Smith says that standing up to bullies in his childhood, leading men into battle in Vietnam, and not being intimidated by dogmatic professors in college built up the courage that enabled him to overcome any fear of failure. This also enabled him to create and put into operation an untried type of business, persuade tough capitalists to invest in it, fight the airlines and the Civil Aeronautics Board, overcome the initial losses, and compete to make Federal Express the great company it has become.

10. Great Leaders Are Positive Thinkers

The practice of positive thinking increases one's ability tremendously. It not only brings out the best in a person's abilities, but it also keeps the mind in harmony by killing fear, worry, and anxiety—all the enemies of our success. It puts the mind in a condition to succeed. It sharpens the faculties because it provides a new outlook upon life. Great leaders have a positive attitude to go forward toward their goals—instead of toward doubt, fear, and uncertainty.

Michael Jordan attributes much of his success to positive thinking. In basketball, as in all aspects of life, it is easy to become discouraged when things are not going well. Jordan writes:

"Some people get frozen by *fear of failure*—by thinking about the possibility of a negative result. They might be afraid of looking bad or being embarrassed. I realized that if I was going to achieve anything in life, I had to be aggressive. I had to get out there and go for it. I don't believe you can achieve anything by being passive. I know fear is an obstacle for some people, but to me it's an illusion. Once I'm in the game, I'm not thinking about anything except what I'm trying to accomplish.

"Any fear is an illusion," he continues. "You think something is standing in your way, but nothing is there—only an opportunity to do your best and gain some success."

You should always think positive and find fuel in any failure. Sometimes failure actually gets you closer to where you want to be. The greatest inventions in the world had hundreds of failures before the answers were found. Fear sometimes comes from a lack of focus or concentration. If you know you are doing the right things, just relax and perform. Forget about the outcome. You can't control anything anyway. It's out of your hands. So don't worry about it.

Whether leading a sports team or a business team, the leader who thinks positively will convey that attitude to the entire team. It will pay off with renewed enthusiasm and commitment to achieve the desired goals.

11. They Put the Focus on Getting Things Done

We've all come across people in management positions who appear to have all the attributes of a good leader, but somehow never quite succeed. Somewhere along the line, they have missed the boat. Why does this happen?

A few years ago I had the opportunity to study this first hand. One of my clients had hired a regional sales manager, about whom they were extremely enthusiastic. He had come to them highly recommended. During the selection process, he had impressed the interviewers with his thorough knowledge of their markets, his innovative ideas on how to increase business, and his charming personality.

During the first several months on the job, he developed a creative and comprehensive marketing program. He spent weeks fine-tuning the program, writing materials and creating graphics for it, and making presentations to management and to his sales force. And that's where it ended. He was never able to actually get out and make the program work.

In my investigation of the problem, I learned that in his previous job, he was a staff marketer, who had never had line responsibility. In that capacity he was excellent, but he did not have that key trait of leadership—getting things done.

The best leaders have their eyes focused on accomplishment. Whether it is carrying out their own ideas or those of others, they work to assure that what has been planned is achieved.

QUOTES AND QUIPS

"Knowledge may give weight, but accomplishments give luster, and many more people see than weigh."
Lord Chesterfield, 1694–1773
English statesman and essayist

12. They Understand the Power of the Informal Organization

In Chapter 2, we noted the importance of identifying and cultivating the leaders of the informal organization. Many people have developed a deep distrust of bosses or managers—often due to their experience with current or past managers. They turn to the informal leaders—fellow workers who have gained their respect and whose opinions and actions they admire and emulate. The effective leader recognizes the influence these men and women have in the acceptance of new ideas among their followers.

Barbara W., the supervisor of a department of 15 sewing machine operators, was commended by her boss for running a highly productive unit. At a staff meeting, her boss commented that her department was always the first to accept new ideas, adapt to changes in operation methods and seemed to exhibit the highest morale. He asked Barbara to share with the other supervisors her "secret of success."

Her response was one word: "Rachel." Rachel, she explained was one of her best operators. She'd been with the company for 13 years and was a mother figure to the younger women in the department. They accepted her advice on problems whether the situation was job related or personal.

When Barbara took over the supervisor's job a few years ago, she recognized the important role Rachel played and carefully moved to gain her support. Over the years, she discussed with Rachel problems she had with any of the workers, changes that were to be made in the workplace, and together she and Rachel determined how to deal with them. The result was a long-term, successfully run department.

When Leadership is Lacking in the Culture Change

A good example of how a company may be misled as to the achievements of their culture change goals was called to my attention by a colleague who was the consultant to a national credit card service company.

The company had established several changes that they wanted to accomplish, primarily in the manner in which they serviced the needs of their clients. Due to the enthusiasm and energy brought to meeting these goals, they were very pleased with the results. Something was missing, however. Despite the success of these primary goals, there was still too much stress and tension in the organization. The original

O-MRI had identified a lack of good leadership at the middle and lower levels—often from supervisors who were authoritarian. One of the "secondary goals" was to help supervisors become more participative. The six-month review found that this had not changed at all.

The consultant pointed out that unless this situation was addressed at once, there would be a regression in the progress already made. Initial enthusiasm cannot be sustained without good leadership. Steps had to be taken at once

The DIAS³ Evaluation

He recommended that all supervisors be evaluated by using the DIAS³ (Diagnostic Interview and Assessment cubed) program.[2] This evaluation system was developed by Manchester Consulting to combine some of the better evaluative techniques into a synergistic, comprehensive approach to determine the strengths and weaknesses of current leaders or candidates for leadership positions.

KEY POINT

The three prongs of the DIAS³ Evaluation are:
1. The personal and career history of the individual
2. The objective comparison of the individual against others in comparable kinds of jobs.
3. The perception of the individual within the organization's culture.

To determine this, a set of three instruments is used:

1. The Career Development Interview. This is a structured interview that has been developed by the consultants of Manchester. It consists of 25 questions covering the entire life span of the individual. Particular emphasis is placed on career influences, but it also covers parental family's socio-economic level, birth order, relationship with siblings, and early childhood history. The individual's current family and work situation is explored in great depth.

The purposes of this type assessment include:

- By providing a standardized interview, it reduces the subjectivity of the assessment and makes it easier to compare the individual with others and discuss the individual's profile with other consultants.
- It creates a bonding experience between the consultant and the individual being assessed.
- It helps build a data base of critical events in the person's life story. These critical events will be used to illustrate key points during the feedback.
- It piques the individual's curiosity about himself or herself. The process of recalling significant life events not only elicits submerged emotions but encourages inward reflectiveness in those who are not usually reflective. It engenders a spirit of "collaborative empiricism"—a non-defensive, collaborative examination of the assessment data and its meaning.

2. Psychometrically Based Instruments. The second prong in the evaluation consists of a series of tests, which are used to sample the individual's make-up. The standard battery typically consists of:

- **The Myers-Briggs Type Indicator** provides information about how the individual typically attends to the outside world or reflects about his or her inner world, how the information will be processed, how decisions in life will be made, and how the person prefers to deal with the outside world. It provides the basic perceptual framework for discussion of other data to come.
- **The Edward's Personal Preference Schedule** profiles the needs of an individual. Needs are the forces that organize our perception, judgments, and actions in the attempt to find fulfillment in life.

The **"Management Triad" of Needs** includes *measures of dominance* (the need to control one's environment), *achievement* (the need to do one's best), *affiliation* (the need to belong to a group and work cooperatively with others). This includes:

  ▸ **Boss-Subordinate Needs**
  Autonomy (need for independence)
  Deference (need for respect and get input from others)
  Nurturance (need to help and show affection for others)
  Succorance (need for support from others)

Abasement (the need to take responsibility for things and perhaps feel unduly guilty when things go wrong)
▶ **Interpersonal Modifiers**
Introspection (the need to analyze one's own motives and feelings)
Exhibitionism (the need to be noticed and acknowledged)
Aggression (the need to be critical of others and engage in active disagreements)
▶ **Task Factors**
Change (the need to new and different things)
Order (the need for detailed, precise order in one's environment)
Endurance (the ability and even need to work at a task for long periods of time until one gets a sense of completion)

- **The Life Styles Inventory** is designed to provide insight into a person's thinking style. It provides data on twelve different dimensions related to one's habitual ways of thinking about relations with others, goals, ways of handling stress, ways of gaining cooperation from others and the image one has of oneself.
- **The Thomas-Kilman Conflict Inventory** is designed to predict an individual's typical behavior in situations of conflict. The likelihood that a person will employ a particular kind of conflict resolution style is plotted along several styles—*competing* (the pursuit of one's own concerns at the expense of others), *accommodating* (the neglect of one's own concerns for others), *avoiding* (tendency to withdraw or postpone a possible conflict), *collaborating* (the tendency to seek solutions fully acceptable to both parties), and *compromising* (the tendency to seek a mutually acceptable solution which partially satisfies both parties). The data base for comparison was drawn from a sample of over 500 managers and executives from business and government organizations.
- **The Power Base Inventory** assesses the techniques an individual uses to influence others. The likelihood that an individual will employ a particular kind or influence style is plotted along several types of influence—*use of information* (using facts or reason to convince others), *expertise* (influencing others through superior knowledge in a specific area), *good will* (influencing others by building affection and support from

them), *authority* (influencing others by virtue of one's position), *reward* (influencing others through the ability to reward things that others desire), and *discipline* (influence through the ability to punish). The data base against which an individual can be compared was drawn from over 300 managers from a variety of organizations.

QUOTES AND QUIPS

"DIAS^3 (Diagnostic Interview and Assessment) is a three-dimensional assessment methodology, but each piece of the assessment is integrated with the others, and each separate part has been carefully developed using the best instruments currently available. In some cases it was also necessary to create new instruments."
Raymond P. Harrison
Executive vice-president,
Manchester, Inc.

---

3. Environmental Assessment. The third prong of the DIAS^3 evaluation is a variation of the 360-degree assessment which was developed by Manchester Consulting in collaboration with Columbia University.

You will recall that we used a form of the 360-degree assessment as part of the O-MRI to determine the way managers were viewed by the various people with whom they interacted. Manchester's Survey of Executive Behavior was designed to delve much deeper into these relationships.

It measures executive performance in ten areas:
- **Planning**—Designing managerial tasks such as goal setting and utilization of resources
- **Empowerment**—Providing opportunities for employees to have greater responsibility
- **Team play**—Working cooperatively across groups
- **Communication**—Express ideas clearly

- **Problem solving**—Recognizing problems and responding effectively
- **Developing others**—Fostering opportunities for employees to develop
- **Managing performance**—Fairly evaluating performance of others and providing guidance
- **Strategic ability**—Understanding and putting into operation broad strategies
- **Managing diversity**—Dealing with people of diverse backgrounds
- **Life balance**—Demonstrating an appropriate balance between work and personal life

As a result of the DIAS[3] assessment, the culture change committee was able to identify the causes of the problems that were hindering the managers, and then counsel them to corrective action.

The 360-degree data brought to light the most important activities that had to be changed. The various tests helped pinpoint each individual's strengths and weaknesses compared to comparable reference groups. Other facets of the individual's personality that were brought out were the likelihood of that person to change no matter how motivated, what has worked for that person in the past in terms of learning and developing, and how those strategies could be employed in helping him or her deal with the culture change.

The Leader vs. the Manager

One factor that was identified as a significant contributor to the failure of managers to respond to the culture change was their failure to truly lead. Peter Drucker wrote: "Most of what we call management consists of making it difficult for people to get their work done."

What is it that managers do that instigated Drucker to write that? Too many people in managerial or supervisory positions deal with their people as if they were automatons—expecting them to follow procedures exactly and not to use any of their own initiative, creativity, and brain power when working. They are so concerned with following rules, regulations, procedures, and routines that they overlook the potential that each human being working under their supervision may have.

Managers who truly lead their people, instead of directing their work, not only obtain better results for their organizations, but develop teams of people who are committed to working toward success in every aspect of their jobs and their lives.

QUOTES AND QUIPS

"Most of what we call management consists of making it difficult for people to get their work done."
Peter Drucker
Management consultant and author

Leaders Serve

The true leader serves his or her people—not the other way around. The typical geometric figure we associate with most organizations is the triangle. On the top is the boss who gives orders to his senior managers, who give orders to middle managers, who give orders to supervisors, who in turn give orders to the workers. At the very bottom of the triangle are the customers whom we hope will be satisfied by what is provided (see Figure 12-1).

CEO
Senior Managers
Middle Managers
First Line Supervisors
Rank and File
Customers

Figure 12-1. *Traditional hierarchy.*

The purpose of each layer is to serve the layer above it. In the traditional approach, workers serve their supervisors, supervisors serve their managers, and all eventually serve the big boss. The customer, down at the bottom, is virtually ignored. This should be reversed, as seen in Figure 12-2. Top-level management should serve the middle-level managers, who in turn should serve their first-line supervisors, who are there to serve the workers—and all should serve the customer.

KEY POINT

Managing concentrates efforts on doing things right; leading emphasizes doing the right things.

Be There for Your Team Members

J. Willard Marriott summed it up succinctly: "My job is to motivate my people, teach them, help them and care about them." Good leaders truly care about their staffs. They learn as much as they can about each person's strengths and limitations, what each one likes and dislikes, how each acts and reacts.

Leaders take the time to work with their staffs, to give them the resources, the tools, and the know-how to do their jobs effectively.

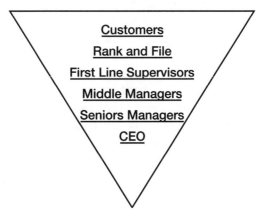

Figure 12-2. *A more meaningful hierarchy.*

They do not get in their way by micromanaging—by worrying more about whether every "i" is dotted and every "t" crossed than whether the individual is contributing and growing.

When surveys are made on what people want from a boss, almost always among the very top items is *"a boss who is there for me."* This is a boss to whom a person can come with a question and not be afraid of being thought of as stupid, a boss on whom one can depend to provide information, training, and suggestions rather than make demands and commands. This is a boss who helps develop the potential of people—and not just uses them merely as a means of getting a job done.

QUOTES AND QUIPS

"You can never *not* lead. Everything you do, and everything you *don't* do, has an effect. You are always leading and influencing. *Effective* leadership is being consciously responsible for your influence."
Kenneth Schatz, author of
Managing by Influence

Empower Your Employees

Real leaders empower the men and women they lead. The word "empower" has become a fad word today, but fad words often concisely express a currently accepted concept. It derives from a legal term meaning to transfer certain legal rights from one person to another. In today's management parlance, however, it's used in a broader sense—to share some of the authority and control a manager has with the men and women he or she manages.

Instead of the manager making every decision as to how a job should be done, the people who will perform the job participate in doing this. When people have some say in these determinations, not only will more varied information as to how a job can be done be obtained but, because they are participators, the workers become committed to its success.

Typically when an automobile manufacturer is about to develop a new car model, a group of designers is assembled to design the body, a group of engineers to design the power train, and a group of manufacturing engineers to put it all together. When all is ready, the process is brought to the factory floor. The Ford Motor Company, however, did something quite different when they designed the Taurus. It brought representatives of each type of factory worker into the earliest stages of design and development. Not only did the development team acquire ideas and tips based on the hands-on experience of the workers, but when the Taurus was brought to the factory floor, it was looked upon by the workers as their car. It became one of the most trouble-free and profitable cars Ford has put out in recent years.

Managing vs. Leading

Managing emphasizes that people follow orders—often unquestioningly. The assumption is: "This is the way it's going to be done, so do it!" Leading encourages creativity in people by soliciting their ideas both informally in day-to-day contact and formally in meetings, suggestion programs, and similar activities.

Managing is more concerned with how the policies are followed, while leading motivates people and teaches them how to get the job done. If it doesn't work out as expected, efforts are made to improve performance by more and better training. Helping people learn is their key tool in obtaining quality performance.

KEY POINT

Managing is telling people what they will be accountable for. Leading empowers people—giving them the tools to make their own decisions within guidelines that are acceptable to all parties concerned.

Managing concentrates efforts on *doing things right;* leading emphasizes *doing the right things.* There are times when it is necessary to manage—when for legal or similar reasons, it is essential that things be done according to the book. Of course, people in managerial positions must assure that things are done right, but this is not their main job. Enforcing rules may be necessary in some circumstances, but it is more important to train and motivate people to be competent and desirous of doing their very best. To achieve this with one's team is the epitome of true leadership.

QUOTES AND QUIPS

"Many corporations are over-managed and under-led."
John Kotter
Management consultant
and author

John Kotter, author of *A Force for Change—How Leadership Differs from Management,* succinctly sums up the difference between management and leadership in Figure 12-3.[3]

Changing from Manager to Leader

It is not always easy to persuade a person who has "managed" a group for many years to change his or her style and become a leader.

	Management	Leadership
Creating the Agenda	Planning and budgeting	Establishing direction
Developing the Human Network	Organizing and staffing	Aligning people
Executing the Plan	Controlling and problem solving	Motivating and inspiring
Outcomes	Predictable results	Useful change

Figure 12-3. *Kotter's Comparison of Leadership and Management.*

Such people just don't have confidence in their subordinates. They say things like:

"My employees won't stretch. They do just enough to keep from getting fired."

"The time wasted by the workers in my department is appalling."

"I just can't trust my employees to do it right. I have to check everything every time or do it myself."

This is not a new complaint. Managers and supervisors have been declaring this for ages. Is this true throughout industry in this country? Of course not. Many companies have overcome employee ineffectiveness by following practices that energize and motivate their performance over and above the call of duty.

Tailor Leadership Style

A good leader takes the trouble to know as much about each member of his team as possible. What works for one person does not necessarily work for another. The leader takes the time to learn the strengths and limitations of each team member and tailors his or her leadership style to their individualities.

For example, before the change was instituted in his company's culture, John was a traditional manager. As a project manager, he supervised six engineers. His thinking was that engineers were all like he was—deep thinkers, sticklers for detail and trained to follow the "blueprints" on whatever they were assigned. Under the old system, if his subordinates did not accept his ideas and order, he gave them poor evaluations and often had to replace them. After a leadership training program, he recognized that even engineers differ one from another.

Although two of his team members did think as he did, the others were quite different. They were more comfortable creating new concepts, developing their own "blueprints" and running with the ball with only limited supervision. He realized that by letting them work their way instead of demanding that they stick rigidly to the rules, they would accomplish more and bring new ideas and energy to their work.

Get Everybody Involved

When people know what is expected of them and how they will be measured, they will be more likely to work to achieve the goals. And if they have participated in setting the goals and determining the standards, they are more likely to be committed to the undertaking.

In an informal survey I once conducted concerning employee involvement, over 70 percent of the companies surveyed reported that both quality and productivity had improved since they instituted a change in their cultures from "managing" to "leading" and more than half experienced increased profitability.

The general consensus was that employees were motivated to help their companies succeed. On the other hand, fewer than half of the companies where no changes were made in the culture and employee involvement was not encouraged, reported that employees were motivated to help the company succeed.

KEY POINT

If goals and standards are established jointly, not only does everybody know what they are, but they are accepted as reasonable and attainable. After all, the people who are working to reach them are the people who set them.

Establishing benchmarks or interim standards will enable the people working on projects to measure their progress and make adjustments when appropriate.

Everybody's a Coach

A good leader is primarily a coach. The coach trains the staff, retrains them when required, gives them pep talks and is there to help. Because team leaders are usually very busy people, they're not always available when needed. One way of dealing with this is to arrange for each team member to take a major role in the training. Team members should be trained and encouraged to help each other. In this way every member is, in a sense, "a coach" enabling the team to become a synergistic, empowered enterprise.

Be Available

A frequent complaint I hear from many supervisors is "I try to be available to my people. After all my job is to answer their questions and provide guidance. But the constant interruptions keep me from getting my other work done. What can I do?"

By careful planning, interruptions can be minimized. A true leader encourages subordinates to make their own decisions. He or she is available at any time to handle critical matters, but routine matters should be dealt with by team members themselves.

A limited number of specific hours to answer questions and deal with nonemergency matters should be established. The team should be made aware that they are not to bring problems to the leader except during those hours unless it is an emergency matter.

This will not only give the supervisor the time needed to deal with the other aspects of the job, but it will engender a major side-effect. Team members, not wishing to wait to bring problems to the manager, will be motivated to solve them themselves.

By helping team members realize their own potential, by getting them involved in decisions that affect their own work, and by encouraging them to help each other, your staff will be energized to accomplish more and obtain more job satisfaction for themselves and more and better productivity for the company.

SUM AND SUBSTANCE

- The twelve factors common to good leaders are:

  1. Almost all truly outstanding leaders have willing (and often enthusiastic) followers.
  2. Most outstanding leaders take a constructively discontented view of the world
  3. Outstanding leaders almost always consider themselves to be a work in progress.
  4. It seems likely that leadership ability comes naturally to some but is inspired in most.
  5. Outstanding leaders almost always demonstrate a good understanding of the affective domain.
  6. Most outstanding leaders expect more from themselves than others.

7. The overwhelming majority of outstanding leaders rely on some fixed, unwavering set of convictions or beliefs that serves as their "guiding light."
8. Many outstanding leaders have both a "tough hide" and an ability to laugh at themselves.
9. Many, if not most, truly outstanding leaders are not deterred by disappointment, failure or rejection. They have strong views yet maintain a "visceral equilibrium."
10. Great leaders are positive thinkers.
11. They put the focus on getting things done.
12. They understand the power of the informal organization.

- An effective tool to assess leaders and potential leaders is the DIAS[3]—a diagnostic process developed by Manchester Consulting. It consists of three phases:

1. The personal and career history of the individual
2. The objective comparison of the individual against others in comparable kinds of jobs
3. The perception of the individual within the organization's culture

- A significant contributor to the failure of managers to respond to the culture change was their failure to truly lead. One must differentiate between being a manager and being a leader.
- Managing concentrates efforts on *doing things right;* leading emphasizes *doing the right things.*
- Empowerment is sharing some of the manager's authority and control with those he or she manages. Instead of being made unilaterally by the manager, decisions as to how a job should be done are made together with the people who will perform the job. When people have some say in these determinations, a wider variety of ideas as to how a job can be done will be obtained. Equally important, because the workers are participators, they become committed to its success.
- Managing is telling people what they will be accountable for. Leading empowers people, giving them the tools to make their own decisions within guidelines that are acceptable to all parties concerned.

- A good leader takes the trouble to know as much about each member of his team as possible. What works for one person does not necessarily work for another. The leader takes the time to learn the strengths and limitations of each team member and tailors his or her leadership style to their individualities.

REFERENCES

[1]Grove, Andrew. "High Leverage." *Executive Excellence,* November 1997. Used with permission of Executive Excellence Publishing (1-800-304-9782).
[2]Harrison, Raymond P. "Dias[3]—A Three Dimensional Method for Assessment and Development Planning." *The Manchester Review,* Vol. 2, No. 1, Spring 1997.
[3]Kotter, John P. *A Force for Change—How Leadership Differs from Management.* New York: Free Press, 1990.

CHAPTER 13

Cementing
the Changes

Now that the major pieces of the culture change effort have been installed, the focus needs to shift to the final stage: the strategy to solidify, reinforce, and continually refine the new culture. Let's never forget that most people will resist change, at least to some extent, and will lean toward reverting to old habits and practices if given the opportunity.

The first step in insulating against any tendency to abandon the new and drift back toward the old is to understand why people react the way they do to change and how best to minimize their resistance to it.

Denis O'Grady, a clinical psychologist, pointed out that there are five fears of change.[1]

1. **Fear of the unknown.** We are most at ease with known things, familiar environments, and secure and safe activities.
2. **Fear of failure.** We fear the consequences of trying something new that may not succeed.
3. **Fear of commitment.** We are afraid to focus on specific goals.
4. **Fear of disapproval.** If you change, some people will likely disapprove. They'll often say, "We always did it this way. Why change?"
5. **Fear of success.** Fear that if you are successful, others will be envious or resent your success.

If we are to work toward improving ourselves, our family, our department, and our company, we must overcome these fears and work toward making the changes that are needed.

QUOTES AND QUIPS

"A competitive world has two possibilities. You can lose.
Or, if you want to win, you can change."
Lester C. Thurow
Dean, Sloan School of
Management, MIT

Manchester Consulting[2] has developed a program to guide people through the process of change by recognizing their fears and doubts and moving along the "transition journey" from the old to the new.

The change process consists of three phases—endings, transitions, and new beginnings.

Endings

Before you can enter into a new situation, you have to end what used to be. It is difficult to give up the habits, practices, and thought patterns that have dominated your life. Too many such changes in their life patterns is synonymous with loss. You are indeed losing a safe and familiar situation and moving into strange and often frightening circumstances. In some cases, it means loss of long-term co-workers, loss of a project in which you have put intensive time and effort, and the possible loss of values that are meaningful to you.

But, as in any loss, it is necessary to let go of the old. It is never easy to detach oneself from the past. It is unsettling and disturbing. It

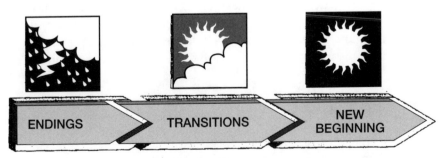

Figure 13-1. *Transition journey.*

can shake up the very core of one's psyche. Some people become angry, others sad, still others confused—many suffer from all of these before they finally let go of the old and embrace the new.

It is the function of the change agent to help people go through the maze of change, deal with it on realistic terms and get to the end more rapidly, more easily, and with minimum emotional drain.

QUOTES AND QUIPS

"You've got to have an atmosphere where people can make mistakes. If we're not making mistakes, we're not going anywhere."
Gordon Forward
President, Chaparrel Steel

Transitions

The transition is not easy. People are caught between the old way and the new way. You often hear gripes and comments decrying the changes and expressing longing to go back to the old safe and familiar ways rather than to push forward into unknown territory.

People are assailed by doubt, fear, and anxiety. They feel uprooted and not quite certain how they will fit into the new order of things. New ways, new methods, and new goals can be frightening even to people who have had past records of success.

The transition period takes people through the process of change, enabling them to resolve their doubts and fears. This is the period when they can redefine their roles, renew their commitments, and re-create their approaches. They can test out new thinking, try new alternatives, and reconfigure their self-concepts. This is an energizing and confusing time because the conflict between past and future is still not completely overcome.

New Beginnings

As the transition stage moves forward, new beginnings replace old ways. People now are open to the change process. Thinking and behavior that were once rejected are now being tried out. Success reinforces the behavior and people begin to feel more confident. They are now ready to move on to more complex applications.

The new thinking and approaches to the work become fully integrated. People see that things they thought were impossible are actually happening. This results in renewed self-confidence, a sense of belonging, and excitement. The new organizational culture is embraced and commitments are made to assure its success.

The new beginnings open the door to total acceptance. What was once alien and frightening is now a way of life. People become acclimated to the new culture and adopt the new ways of operating. They have reshaped their own identity and are proud of having accomplished the transition.

QUOTES & QUIPS

"You have to stop in order to change direction."
Erich Fromm
Psychologist and author

I recently had the opportunity to observe a transition when one of my clients changed a department from a supervisor-directed work group to a self-directed work team. Burt M. had supervised the order processing department for six years. He was an intelligent, creative person, who had run his department efficiently. His staff was well trained and each was proficient in his or her job. Burt planned and assigned the work, solved problems as they arose, and made any decisions that were needed to keep the work flowing.

When Burt left the company last year, management chose not to replace him, but to convert the order-processing group to a self-directed team. This was not a new concept to the company as they already had self-directed teams operating in other aspects of the business. My job was to aid in making the transition.

Endings: A meeting was held at which the General Manager and I explained the concept to the seven people in the department. The reaction was predictable. Although their overt reaction was positive, their uneasiness and concern was apparent. Interviews with individuals brought out such comments as:

"Why change? I know my job—and do it well, but I don't feel competent to make decisions on other aspects of the work. I'd rather have a boss make those decisions."

"Not a good idea. I'm good and I know I could do it. In fact, I had hoped to get Burt's job. The others are okay, but don't have what it takes to make decisions."

"I wasn't hired to make decisions. Let someone else do it."

"I think I'd like to work as a team—but I'm afraid of the responsibilities."

"You said we'd make more money with the new compensation plan for teams, but suppose we mess up?"

Transitions: By individual counseling and a series of group activities, we worked out approaches to help each person deal with his or her own concerns. To put some semblance of order into the chaos of the transition, we quickly identified the routine day-to-day activities and agreed to keep working on them the same way as in the past. This alleviated concern about filling current orders.

Team meetings were held every morning to plan the day's work and to deal with new problems. At the first few meetings, a member of senior management sat in to provide information or suggestions if needed. Team members were encouraged to contribute their own ideas. It became apparent from the beginning that some members were reluctant to say anything, while one or two dominated the meetings. As change agent, I worked to correct this situation by special training and coaching.

The first new projects given to the team were variations on the routine. As they were relatively easy to solve, it gave team members confidence in their abilities to deal with them. Over a six-week period, the work of the department was phased into the new system.

New beginnings: The self-directed team began to function effectively without supervision once the fears and concerns were overcome. Of the seven team members, only one asked for a transfer to another department because she did not feel comfortable in the team environment. One of the others is still coping with his fears, but other team members are encouraging him and providing support.

KEY POINT

Managers must not assume that because the change will benefit the organization, it will be accepted by the staff. It is normal to resist change. The challenge is to overcome this resistance.

GUIDELINES FOR PEOPLE FACING CHANGE

Here are some additional, even more specific suggestions from the consulting division of Manchester, Inc. to help initiate and then solidify necessary change:[3]

Endings

- Keep a balanced perspective. Changes that appear to take an eternity to accomplish now will seem like a "flash" in the years ahead.
- Confide in a trusted friend about the losses you feel and the difficulties of "letting go" of the way things used to be.
- Recall other endings in your life that led to new friendships, more gratifying jobs, and wonderful opportunities.
- Take just one day at a time and trust that you'll have everything you truly need.
- Give yourself permission to feel your pain and grieve your loss.
- Share your story with others.
- Stop fighting the circumstances that are changing. Instead, accept their passing as an opportunity.
- Be willing to face what is happening. Test out the "new realities" with a friend who knows you and can support you.

Transitions

- Look upon the time in between as necessary and valuable. A redefinition is taking place, your new identity is emerging and you are bringing completion to the past.
- Practice letting go of the old, so the new can emerge.
- Spend time learning about the change.

- Look for the opportunity. The "what's in it for me" is not always obvious. Keep looking.
- Stay in charge of your attitude. You can make the day as bright as you choose.
- Let go of the need to control. When you do, breakthrough happens.
- Prepare yourself for something new. No door is ever closed without another one being opened.
- Feel your fears and do it anyway. Think of fear as energy in disguise.
- Reframe your perspective. Change negative thinking into positive. Practice optimism.
- Be open to new experiences. They will be the right ones for your growth.
- Seek and listen to all the career advice you can get. Move ahead on what feels right for you.
- Trust the process. The path will open. The answers will come.

New Beginnings

- Decide it is up to you to make the change work. Take personal ownership.
- Dive into the new situation with your full energy.
- Adopt new thinking, new tools.
- Go for the new and untested; drop the old tried-and-true.
- Take time to build relationships on the new team. Do what you need to do to feel like you belong.
- See problems as the price of progress. Tackle them with high spirits.
- Make a decision to commit to the new goals and don't look back.
- Live from a place of gratitude. It will bring forth abundant fruit.
- See the positive changes in your coworkers. This will help you see that you are changing, too.
- Celebrate the small wins and early successes.

Tracking Results

You've instituted a variety of changes in your organization's culture. You've worked hard to help those involved accept change, to accept endings, and to endure transitions and endorse new beginnings, but how long should it take before these changes begin to show results?

Obviously, the more radical the changes, the longer it will be before you see significant change, but to assure that the process is progressing, reality checks should be made periodically to determine just what is being accomplished.

The first such check might be an informal review 30 days after the program is underway. If you find that the process is veering off course, this will enable you to make adjustments to bring it back to where it should be.

The change leaders should establish benchmarks which should have been reached by that time. For example, the major organizational change instituted by one of my clients was to move from traditional supervisor-subordinate groups to collaborative teams. They planned to try out the team concept in two locations to determine what problems might arise and how the employees would react.

In addition to ongoing support to the new teams, the Change Committee set up the following checklist to use as a guide during their evaluation:

For the team leader

- Does the team leader give team members the opportunity to participate in planning?
- Does the team leader encourage team members to suggest new ideas, methods, and procedures?
- In what manner has the team leader changed his/her style of management to fit the team concept?
- In what ways can we help the team leader become more effective in leading the team?

For team members

- How have team members as a group reacted to the team concept?
- Which team members have been most participative; which least?
- What problems have individual members had in adapting to the team concept?

Regarding team performance

- How has the team performed in accomplishing the team's activities and productivity?
- What changes have occurred in absenteeism, tardiness, turnover, and morale?
- What other problems have arisen?

The evaluators observed the team in action, interviewed the team
leaders and each member of the teams, and obtained specific examples to back each of the responses. They learned that although
progress was being made, it was too slow. Team leaders were reluctant to give up power or were afraid that if productivity fell, they
would be held responsible. This resulted in their overriding team decisions with which they did not agree.

Despite the added training in collaborative techniques, some team
members participated only minimally and others dominated the
group. Productivity and morale factors also had not changed significantly. The evaluators learned from this feedback that much more
training was needed if the team concept was to bring the results
hoped for.

KEY POINT

A systematic review of the change process may require conducting another Organizational M.R.I.

The 90-Day Review

Where the 30-day review is informal, a 90-day review is a well-
structured systematic review of the entire process. It may be conducted by the Change Committee or by an outside consultant—usually,
but not always, the consultant that instituted the program.

It starts with a meeting of the organization's leaders. It is important that the CEO and other senior managers participate. The first step is to review what they had hoped to accomplish during the first 90 days of the program and to set up a procedure to check this.

This may be done by conducting another complete O-MRI (see Chapter 2). From this, the current "as-is" situation can be determined in a systematic manner—not just on the basis of cursory observations.

A list of goals that were expected to be achieved should be developed and listed on a control sheet. The O-MRI will indicate how closely these goals have been met (see Figure 13-2). If goals are not being met, corrective measures must be instituted immediately to move the culture change along.

Dept. _____

Supervisor: _____

Goals	Achievements	To Be Done

Figure 13-2. *Control sheet.*

Follow-Up

A study of the control sheet will pinpoint areas where the process must be reinforced and in some cases redeveloped. Digressions must be caught before they metastasize into major problems.

In the follow-up O-MRI at one company, one area that was identified as needing reinforcement was cross training. The goal that had been established was that all team members should be trained to assist all other team members in their assigned tasks. By the end of three months, each person should be competent in the skills needed for at least one function performed by another member; by the end of six months, each person should be competent in the functions performed by at least two other team members; and, by the end of the year, all team members should be able to do all the functions of the team.

The 90-day review showed that very little cross training had been done. This aspect of the process had been virtually ignored. The team leader pointed out that because other phases of the change took more time than expected, the cross training had been put aside.

As cross training was a key point in the long-term process, steps were instituted immediately to set up a training timetable to get this phase under way.

This, of course, is not the end of the review process. To assure that continuing progress is made in the culture change, additional reviews should be scheduled on a regular basis. They may take the form of informal 30-day or detailed 90-day evaluations as determined by the needs of the organization.

Bolstering the Excitement

It's human nature to lose enthusiasm about any project as it drags on over time. The initial excitement fades as the changes are accepted and become routine. As each part of the process is phased in, enthusiasm must be renewed. One way of accomplishing this is to hold periodic meetings in which the progress made is celebrated and commitment to the balance of the program is reinforced.

When the Supreme Fabrics Co., a medium-sized textile converter, completed the first phase of their culture change, they had a party at their plant. The change committee prepared a slide presentation showing the changes that had been made and how they had already paid off in increased productivity. Representatives from several departments volunteered to tell how their jobs had changed and how much they gained from the changes. The CEO congratulated the employees for their accomplishments and described the next phase of the process and how it would continue to benefit all. Each person was given a gift to commemorate the occasion.

The End of the Process

Does the change process ever end? There is no question that change is ongoing. However, to make the culture change process meaningful, some form of closure must be established. At the onset of the process, it should be determined how long it should take to reach the goals established. Depending on the complexity of the situation, this may range from short-term goals of less than one year to long-term goals of several years.

In my experience, if the time set is too short, critical problems may be addressed and corrections started, but lasting changes that truly transform culture will not be accomplished. If the time set is too long, the enthusiasm and commitment to the process may wane.

Although there is no ideal time frame, I have found that a one- to two-year period gets the best results. It generally takes three to six months to evaluate and plan the process; another three to six months to get it underway; and the balance of the time to implement, check and revise, and finally complete all phases.

When the project is completed, celebrate the accomplishment in a lavish way. For example, Supreme Fabrics held a banquet at a nearby catering hall for all employees and their guests. The CEO greeted each couple on a receiving line. He thanked them for their cooperation and commitment and announced that as a result of the increased productivity and cost reduction, the profits of the firm had increased and as the company had a profit-sharing program, this year's bonus check would be substantially higher than the previous year's.

Change Never Ceases

As previously indicated, part of any transformation of a corporate culture should be the development of a spirit of constructive discontent. Managers and employees alike should be indoctrinated with the attitude that things are never perfect and that each should be alert to making the job even more effective. Not only should each individual become a source of new ideas and improved methods, but the company itself should establish a procedure to encourage these ideas and to process them so they reach the levels of management where decisions can be made.

No matter how successful the culture change has been, it is not a static situation. This is not the time to become complacent. Yes, you have accomplished the goals you set when the process started, but just as changes in technology, changes in marketing, changes in interpersonal relations will continue to be made, so must you be prepared to keep updating and revising your corporate culture to remain at the peak of effectiveness.

Future Trends

One thing we know with certainty is that whatever a given organizational culture is today, it will not be the same tomorrow. Just as we have seen major changes in technology and management over the past ten years, we can expect changes at least as great over the next ten years.

Based on what's already in the works, let's explore a few of the changes we can expect in the nature of organizational cultures in the relatively near future.

Older People Will Delay Retiring

Much has been written about the impending flood of retirees as the baby boom generation reaches the traditional retirement age of 65 or opts for early retirement in the first and second decades of the 21st century. Not only is there great concern about how this will impact the social security system, but companies have worried about losing highly skilled and technically trained personnel at a time when their talents are direly needed.

However, there are increasing indications that older people are opting to remain in the work force—even into their late 70s or beyond. According to 1997 data compiled by the U.S. Bureau of Labor Statistics, one in eight seniors between 70 and 74 works full or part time—and this does not include volunteers.

Employers report that older men and women are in demand because of their work ethic, dependability, and productivity. They're encouraged to work because studies have shown that those who continue working or come out of retirement live longer and healthier lives.

QUOTES AND QUIPS

"If you take all the experience and judgment of people over fifty out of the world, there wouldn't be enough left to run it."
Henry Ford, 1863–1947
Founder, Ford Motor Co.

Some companies that have offered early-retirement deals in their endeavors to downsize have suffered from the loss of critically needed people and have called them back as consultants or have out-sourced work to them.

Human resource professionals are confident that older workers are at least as flexible, easy to train and dependable as their younger colleagues, but so far, relatively few HR departments are taking steps to recruit and retrain employees 50 years of age or older, a survey has found.

The Society for Human Resource Management in conjunction with the American Association of Retired People conducted a poll in February 1998, of 2,717 randomly selected SHRM members.[4]

The SHRM/AARP Older Workers Survey confirmed that HR professionals indicated that half of the 392 respondents said their organizations find older worker issues somewhat important, and 32 percent said the issues were regarded as very important. However, 65 percent of the respondents said their organizations do not actively recruit older workers to fill open positions, and 55 percent said their organizations do not actively seek to retain workers who are 50 years old or older.

However, the survey brought out that respondents were rethinking this policy and were working on plans designed to recruit and retain older workers before the retirement of baby boomers—those born from 1946 through 1964—hit with full force.

Eighty-nine percent of the human resource professionals surveyed agreed that older workers do not have higher rates of absenteeism than younger workers. Seventy-seven percent agreed that older workers tend to be more reliable and have higher levels of commitment to the organization than younger workers. Forty percent said they agreed that older workers tend to be more motivated to do their work than younger workers.

The most notable challenge for older workers, according to human resource professionals, is overcoming a fear of technology. Sixty-six percent of the respondents agreed that older workers tend to be more fearful of technology than younger workers.

Of the strategies currently used to encourage older employees to work past retirement age:

- 62 percent said they hire retired employees as consultants or independent contractors.
- 47 percent provide training to upgrade older workers' skills.
- 29 percent provide opportunities for workers to transfer to jobs with reduced pay and responsibilities.
- 19 percent have a phased retirement program that gradually reduces work schedules.
- 10 percent provide alternative career tracks for older workers.

QUOTES AND QUIPS

"As I approve of a youth that has something of the old man in him, so am I no less pleased with an old man who has something of the youth. He that follows this rule may be old in body, but can never be so in mind."
Cicero, 106–43 B.C.
Roman statesman

Impact on the Organizational Culture

Retaining older workers adds a new dimension to the culture of an organization. Let's examine three ramifications of this.

Continuing effective performance by older workers. Under the Age Discrimination in Employment law, it is illegal to terminate an employee because of age—no matter how old he or she may be. Does this mean that if an employee is no longer competent to perform a job due to decline in physical or mental abilities, he or she must be retained? Not at all. What it does mean is that performance standards must be clearly defined and performance reviews must be structured so that measurements will be based on concrete factors not perceptions that may be biased.

Every effort should be made to work with employees whose performance begins to slide to keep them at satisfactory levels. This presents a challenge to team leaders and managers to seek new approaches to training, new thinking about motivation, and more patience in dealing with this type situation. Companies should establish policies and procedures to deal with this issue, including options of transfers to other positions which the employee is capable of performing or working part-time as a transition to full retirement.

Older people tend to be more fearful of technology than younger workers. Fear of learning is easier to overcome, however, than the incapacity to learn. People who are familiar with the old processes may resist change in the familiar, comfortable old ways, but *do* have the capacity to learn new ways—once motivated to do so.

There are sure to be some workers who are "computer-shy" or technologically blind-sided, but most people—no matter what their age—can be motivated to want to learn. This is the challenge team leaders and supervisors have to meet.

An organization culture that encourages learning, rewards new ideas, and stimulates creativity will help leaders help their teams develop the desire to keep learning and even look forward to acquiring new skills.

If older employees continue working—often for years after the time when they are eligible for retirement, how will this affect the careers of the younger men and women?

Ambitious young employees want to move up in their organizations. Indeed, opportunity for advancement is a major motivator. If the higher-level positions are all filled with older employees who have no plans to retire, how can the organization satisfy the need for its young people to get the experience, meet the challenges, and reap the rewards that come with promotion to positions of responsibility and authority?

This problem has been compounded by the leveling of many organizations—eliminating many middle-management positions as part of the re-engineering process that many firms underwent in the 1980s and 1990s. There is no easy solution—and, as we will discuss in the next section, the loss of good younger people has been felt by many companies because of this.

One approach which has been of some value is the increased use of teams. Team leadership provides at least the opportunities for younger men and women to acquire the skills of decision making, planning, and dealing with day-to-day personnel problems and with group dynamics.

The challenge for the organization of the 21st century is to create other ways to provide opportunity to all employees. Some companies are planning greater decentralization, in which individuals will have more personal responsibility in managing autonomous units; others are encouraging bright high-potential people to set up independent businesses and become subcontractors. Most are still seeking new ways within their organizational structure to meet the needs of the next generation so as to ensure their continuity and increase their success.

Decline of Company Loyalty

The days when a young person joined a company after graduating from high school or college and remained there until retirement are long gone. One reason for this has been the great number of organizations that have reduced staff during the past decade or because mergers or acquisitions have eliminated many positions.

One of the major challenges managers will face over the next decade is to engender a new feeling of loyalty in employees, to recognize what employees want from their jobs and to adapt their cultures to accommodate this.

QUOTES AND QUIPS

"He who is not loyal to others will not find others loyal to him."
Old Chinese Proverb

In the 1990s, we have already seen signs of how the younger generation views their work and their lives. More and more men and women have opted for lifestyles which give priority to their families, their personal interests, and other non-job related factors over their careers. Opportunities for promotion have been declined if the new position will require being away from home for long periods of time or relocating to a different community.

Executives have also taken leaves of absence to participate in activities in which they are interested or to perform community service. Fathers, as well as mothers, have requested time off so they could spend more time with their children or care for elderly relatives. Organizational cultures will have to accommodate for demands on employees' personal lives if they wish to attract and keep high-potential people.

These concepts are already underway in progressive organizations. The 1998 Business Work-Life Study by the nonprofit Family and Work Institute of New York[5] reviewed more than 1,000 companies with 100 or more employees. The No. 1 business reason that employers gave for striving to improve their work-family programs is that they are finding it harder to retain employees, and they believe this will make a difference.

A 1997 institute survey of workers showed that more supportive employers and better jobs were more likely to yield satisfied, loyal workers—an important finding in today's tight labor market and a portend for the future.

The report highlights 30 companies that have recognized the importance of addressing the personal needs of employees as a means of retaining, motivating, and ensuring their loyalty. The report also pointed out that the needs of employees differ and the solution is not "one-size-fits-all." It is important to identify these needs and to tailor programs to fit them.

One example was J.C. Penney Co., which held focus groups to discover how its staff wanted to care for their own children rather than to rely on institutionalized care. As a result, the company began a program allowing workers to determine their own schedules on a daily basis.

Another approach is to use flexible work arrangements. This allows time off for parenting duties, and arranges return-to-work schedules on a gradual basis following childbirth and adoption. One major policy allows workers to stay home to care for sick children or elderly parents without using their vacation time or losing vacation pay.

About two-thirds of the companies studied allow employees to periodically change starting and quitting times. Nearly half perceive their flexible scheduling programs as a positive return on investment.

Job sharing and allowing workers to work at home or off-site on a regular basis is less common, but is expected to grow in coming years.

More than half of the surveyed firms offered employee assistance programs designed to help employees deal with problems that may affect their work or personal life. Another 25 percent offer workshops or seminars on parenting, child development, care of the elderly, or work-family problems.

Merck & Co. instituted a program to hold managers accountable for how well they manage their staff's work-life needs. Starting in 1997, Merck began to rate managers on their leadership capabilities—and part of the evaluation is whether they treat employees with respect and sensitivity when personal issues arise.

The survey concluded that when companies seriously take into consideration the personal needs and desires of their employees, turnover will be reduced, morale will be improved, and both employees and the organization benefit.

Encouraging Self-Employment

Many top-level people leave a company when advancement has been stymied. They realize that there is no way they can move into the type of position in which they can exercise their talents within the organization. One way to retain these employees is to offer them the chance to go into their own businesses and provide services needed by the organization.

For example, it was becoming obvious to Sam D., the president of Paper Products, Inc., that his best salesperson, Nancy S., was getting restless. She was earning high commissions, but her real goal was to be a sales manager. As his sales managers were all doing well and were not planning to retire in the near future, there was no way he could promote Nancy.

Rather than lose Nancy to a competitor, he offered her the opportunity to become an independent sales representative. She could start by having exclusive rights to selling Paper Products' line in her current territory. This would assure an immediate source of income and she could seek other non-competing lines that were sold to the same market.

Nancy accepted this great opportunity and went on to build her own successful organization. By helping her start the business, Sam not only gave Nancy the chance to meet her personal goals, but protected his company from losing her accounts to a competitor and set a precedent he could follow in the future.

As companies become leaner and meaner, there will be less opportunity for high-potential men and women to move ahead in the traditional hierarchy. Managers will have to use their creativity to find ways to satisfy the desires of these people without losing their contributions.

Decentralization

As the technology for instant and continuous communication evolves, the need for people who work together to be at the same physical location becomes less important. One major innovation is the use of global calling, which has enabled managers in several locations to discuss a problem with other stakeholders without leaving their desks. When graphics, charts, tables, and other printed data are needed for the discussion, they can be faxed instantly to the participants.

Already in place in some organizations to augment or totally replace the conference telephone call is teleconferencing, in which participants at several locations—anywhere in the world—can see each other via closed-circuit television. Conferences and meetings become almost as personal as if all the participants were in one room.

Add to this the increasing use of computers in every aspect of organizational activity. We have progressed in a very few years from concentrating all computer use to a large mainframe unit in a central location to the personal computers that we find on almost every desk, to the lap-top and pocket-sized units that can be carried anywhere.

As this technology improves and becomes less expensive, the need for large central offices will decline. People will be able to work in smaller groups at a variety of locations and in many instances at home with the same or even higher level of effectiveness.

Training and Development

Where there is change, there must be training to allow employees to adapt to the new methods and techniques. Training will become even more important in the next decade than it has in the past. Companies will be investing more and will expect more from it. New approaches, especially the utilizing of new technologies such as CD-

ROM, interactive computer programs, and teleconferencing will replace or be added to traditional training programs.

The future can often be predicted from what leading edge companies are doing today. In mid-1998, the American Society for Training and Development (ASTD), in conjunction with the Times Mirror Training Group, the Forum Corporation, and the U.S. Department of Labor, conducted a survey of 540 randomly selected firms with 50 or more employees.[6]

QUOTES AND QUIPS

"Though the $55.3 billion spent by employers on formal training in the United States seems like a substantial amount, it is paltry compared to the need so many companies express for a work force that can compete on the strength of its brain power."
Curtis Plott
President and CEO, ASTD

According to the survey, leading-edge companies typically invest higher than average amounts on training. They also train a larger percentage of employees and maintain a lower employee-to-trainer ratio. They tend to be technology leaders, taking advantage of learning technologies such as interactive video, multimedia, intranets, and electronic performance support systems, and they tend to combine innovative training methods with innovative work and compensation practices.

Industry-by-industry highlights from the survey include:

- **High technology**—Companies in this industry have large internal training staffs and invest the most per employee of any industry group. They also use learning technologies to deliver training more than other companies in other industry groups.
- **Finance, insurance, and real estate**—These firms typically invest a great deal in training and have large staffs of in-house trainers. They engage in much computer, sales, and product training and are heavy users of computer-based training.

- **Business services**—Possibly due to their diversity, business services employers don't have consistent or exceptional practices, except for a larger-than-average use of computer-based training and computer training.
- **Heavy manufacturing**—Workplaces in this industry are complex with heavy use of high performance work practices, quality initiatives, and apprenticeships. A large portion of the total training expenditure goes to external providers, including educational institutions. Heavy users of computer-based training, these companies predict the largest increase in total and outside training expenditures.
- **Light manufacturing**—These companies are most dependent on outsourcing, with the largest percentage of total training expenditures going outside and the second largest percentage of outside dollars per employee. Their use of delivery technologies isn't heavy, though they predict more use of computer-based training, internets, and intranets in the future.
- **Transportation, communications, and public utilities**—With a lot of safety, technical, and customer-service training, these companies have higher-than-average expenditures. They are characterized by leading-edge training practices and a high use of computer-based training and other technologies.

According to the survey, other groups such as health care, hospitality, retail, and business services have not increased emphasis on training and have not taken advantage of technological improvements in training methods. However, within these groups, there are a good many individual companies that are ahead of the competition and have instituted excellent training programs.

The experience of most organizations over the past ten years has demonstrated the importance of creating and maintaining an organizational culture that enables the company to adjust rapidly to changing times. We have faced and mastered tough problems and have learned much from this experience.

The leaders of tomorrow are aware that they will face even more complex problems as we enter the 21st century. However, I'm confident they have the background, the training, the flexibility, the innovative ideas, and the access to resources that are needed to adapt their organizational cultures to meet these challenges. We're in for an exciting and rewarding time.

SUM AND SUBSTANCE

- There are five fears of change:
  Fear of the unknown
  Fear of failure
  Fear of commitment
  Fear of disapproval
  Fear of success
- The change process consists of three phases—endings, transitions, and new beginnings.
- It is never easy to detach oneself from the past. It is unsettling and disturbing. It can shake up the very core of one's psyche.
- Transitions are loaded with frustrations due to the uncertainties and ambiguities that are incumbent to such changes.
- As the transition stage moves forward, new beginnings replace the old ways. People now are open to the change process.
- You and your staff can deal with change. Review the guidelines for dealing with endings, transitions, and new beginnings outlined in this chapter.
- To assure that the process is progressing, reality checks should be made periodically to determine just what is being accomplished.
- Conduct a detailed 90-day review of the entire process. One effective way is to conduct another complete O-MRI.
- Pinpoint areas where the process must be reinforced and in some cases redeveloped. Take immediate action. Digressions must be caught before they metastasize into major problems.
- To maintain a spirit of enthusiasm, hold periodic meetings in which the progress made is celebrated and commitment to the balance of the program is reinforced.
- When the project is completed, celebrate the accomplishment in a lavish way.
- Part of any transformation of a corporate culture should be the development of a spirit of constructive discontent. No matter how successful the culture change has been, it is not a static situation. This is not the time to become complacent.
- Just as we have seen major changes in technology and management over the past ten years, we can expect changes at least as great over the next ten years.

- Among the changes we can expect in the organizational culture in the near future are that more older people will delay retiring, remain in the work force and require retraining in the new technologies in their industries.
- To maintain a motivated work force, companies will develop new and exciting programs to attract and retain top-level employees.
- Organization venues will change from large centralized office complexes to smaller, compact, interactive, diverse segments interacting through internets, intranets, and teleconferencing.
- To keep up with the rapidly changing organizational cultures, companies will put more emphasis on employee training and development.
- The leaders of tomorrow are aware that they will face even more complex problems as we enter the 21st century. I'm confident, however, that they will have the background, the training, the flexibility, the innovative ideas, and the access to resources that are needed to adapt their organizational cultures to meet these challenges. We're in for an exciting and rewarding time.

REFERENCES

[1] Interview in *Bottom Line*, July 15, 1994.
[2] Adapted from *Mastering Change—Leader's Guide*. Manchester Consulting, August 27, 1997.
[3] *Mastering Change—Leader's Guide*. Manchester Consulting, August 27, 1997, pp. 13–14.
[4] Society for Human Resources Management, 50th Anniversary Conference, 1998.
[5] *The 1998 Business Work-Life Study, A Source Book,* Family and Work Institute of New York, 330 Seventh Avenue, New York, NY 10001.
[6] *1998 ASTD State of Industry Report*, ASTD, Alexandria, Virginia, 1998.

Index